PENGUIN BOOKS

NOW THAT WE'RE HERE

AKSHAT TYAGI is the founder of edhack, a start-up helping young people learn on their own. Since selling his content company in 2014, he has written a book on the monoculture of schooling and contributed to several news platforms. He is a 2019 Rajeev Circle Fellow. You can write to him at contact@akshattyagi.com.

AKSHAY TYAGI built his first business right out of his college dorm and has since gone on to build and iterate several profitable online and offline businesses. He is currently working on a food start-up. He is interested in technology, public policy and sustainability. He tweets at @theakshaytyagi and blogs at www.akshaytyagi.me.

NOW
THE FUTURE

THAT
OF EVERYTHING

WE'RE

HERE

AKSHAT TYAGI
AKSHAY TYAGI

PENGUIN BOOKS

An imprint of Penguin Random House

PENGUIN BOOKS

USA | Canada | UK | Ireland | Australia
New Zealand | India | South Africa | China

Penguin Books is part of the Penguin Random House group of companies
whose addresses can be found at global.penguinrandomhouse.com

Published by Penguin Random House India Pvt. Ltd
7th Floor, Infinity Tower C, DLF Cyber City,
Gurgaon 122 002, Haryana, India

Penguin
Random House
India

First published in Penguin Books by Penguin Random House India 2021

ISBN 9780143447795

Typeset in Adobe Caslon Pro by Manipal Technologies Limited, Manipal
Printed at Thomson Press India Ltd, New Delhi

www.penguin.co.in

MIX
Paper
FSC FSC® C010615

Contents

List of Abbreviations

ASI	Archaeological Survey of India
CBSE	Central Board of Secondary Education
CIC	Central Information Commission
CJI	Chief Justice of India
CNG	compressed natural gas
EODB	Ease of Doing Business
EV	electronic vehicle(s)
EVM	electronic voting machine
FMCG	Fast-moving consumer good
FRR	farebox recovery ratio
FUD	fear, uncertainty and doubt
GDP	gross domestic product
GHGs	greenhouse gases
GNH	gross national happiness
GW	gigawatt(s)
HNI	high-net-worth individual
IC	internal combustion
ICE	internal combustion engine

ID	industrial design
ISA	income-share agreements
ISPs	Internet service providers
ISRO	Indian Space Research Organization
J-PAL	Abdul Latif Jameel Poverty Action Lab
kWh	Kilowatt-hour(s)
LPG	liquefied petroleum gas
MTR	mass transit railway
NJAC	National Judicial Appointments Commission
NSA	National Security Agency
OTP	one-time password
PRS	Parliamentary Research Service
RCTs	randomized controlled trials
RTI	Right to Information
SEO	search engine optimization
SIC	State Information Commission
SW	ScoopWhoop
TPU	thermoplastic polyurethane
UBI	universal basic income
UI	user interface design
UX	user experience design
VVPAT	voter-verified paper audit trail

Introduction

You got confused with the author names, didn't you? We have first names that are almost identical, except for one letter, and the same surnames. T and Y are adjacent to each other on a QWERTY keyboard, so making an error in this regard is quite easy.

We don't share a bloodline—and even if we did, what lazy parents would name their kids like that! The story of how we met because of our names is a core idea of the book in your hands.

How?

Let us explain.

Owing to our narcissistic tendencies, both of us have diligently maintained personal websites since the beginning of time. And much like most of our generation, which grew up with the Internet, we love looking ourselves up on Google to boost our self-esteem.

Akshay dropped out of an engineering college in 2011 without a plan. He didn't have awe-inspiring reasons for doing it, and neither was Peter Thiel paying him $100,000 for his decision. Eventually, he did run several start-ups ranging from a media company to a custom-fit women's clothing company. In 2016, after relative success, he decided to write a long rant about the dismal state of the education system and his reasons for quitting college. Like most of the million blogs published every day, it soon disappeared into the ether.

But there's something else Akshay did right. If you typed his name in the search box, you would find it to be the top search result. Akshay's website had more visibility on the Internet because he had ensured improved search engine optimization (SEO) by designing the site to be computer-readable. Google trusted his website as a good source of credible information about anything sounding similar to his name. Even something like 'Akshat Tyagi'.

Around the same time, a random boy from one of the fringe towns of Delhi had also written a book fulminating against the naked emperor of education. While searching for his own piece published on some digital platform, he mistyped his name. Google ended up showing him Akshay's blog on a similar theme because of the latter's good SEO ranking. Akshat decided to give it a try.

Wouldn't it excite anybody to find someone with almost the same name and the same views? Akshat noted Akshay's email address from the bottom bar of the website and wrote him the following email:

Hi!
I think you should check out akshattyagi.com.
Thanks

Concise and smug.

Being theoretically unemployed, Akshay replied the same evening. Starting that day, we talked for two years over Facebook about all things that two people with a decade of age difference can. But most of our conversations would circle back to our complaints about how things could be done differently in schools and colleges. The idea of a zero-sum game in learning didn't make sense to us. We had done fairly well to game the system to our advantage but never felt comfortable embracing the collateral damage it brought.

When the Central Board of Secondary Education (CBSE) annual results were being announced in May 2018, we built a campaign to help kids who didn't score well find alternative paths of learning and livelihood. It included a directory of universities where one could learn without grades and also connecting them to entrepreneurs and learning activists who could help them design their own personal self-learning journey.

It was of course fun feeling revolutionary about what we were doing. Often, in being angry, one completely forgets about the original complaint. There's a feeling of being wronged but little clarity of any detail. And coming up with workable solutions is even harder.

We wanted to teach what schools weren't. Writing a fun guide about some things that we believe are important to understand about the new world, and building a learning start-up we now run are our two attempts at being useful.

Akshay is what you would call an 'accidental generalist' who planned to obtain a specialist education in engineering but ended up studying a bit of everything, brought about by his running various businesses. Akshat too figured out the same path for himself. With this book, we want to make good generalist education accessible to more young people like ourselves. It took us a while to violate the unuseful boundaries between technology, democracy, design, economics and data to make any sense of what's going on. No matter what you formally study or what you do for a living, a hyperconnected lifestyle requires you to educate yourself as widely as possible.

We began by telling you the SEO story because had it not been for a very peculiar design of organizing information by one technology company in the world, we wouldn't have met and eventually written this book. Our friendship is a pure accident orchestrated by not-so-accidental architecture (Design). There are choices someone somewhere made which shaped how our world would look. While our dating-app algorithm decides who we love, more critically, our search engines and social networking apps subtly determine who we talk to and collaborate with while we think we are being picky about such things (Democracy).

Technology for a lot of developing countries like India has become a holy panacea. When something goes wrong because of technology, we don't question it but instead lament who we are and how we messed up—like the fake-news epidemic and the bullying that happens on platforms. But we forget that unlike human nature, technology is not a natural fact of life. It is the conscious handiwork of highly paid freelancing artists. We need to become better people of course, but we also need better technology (Accountability).

Although the chapters in the book are very diverse in content, they are centred around two simple ideas. One, the world is a complex place, which is only getting more difficult to decipher each day (Non-Linearity). Pay attention and avoid simple theories. Occam's razor is also a sophisticated idea. Two, now that you're here, have fun (Irrationality).

We will not lie, this book is actually a very frustrating read. You wouldn't find any answers. Every time we offer a perspective, we have tried to acknowledge its nemesis. It is not like we don't take a position because of intellectual cowardice; we do it to optimize thinking over churning out more converts. Akshay likes to joke that it would have been more appropriate to title the book *Reader Please Ponder* (Infinite Regress).

Despite all caution, we understand we would have still been biased in some places and blind in others. Our stories and data sets would have been conveniently picked to suit our original ideas (Behavioural Economics).

We hope that by the end of this book you will feel more deficient than when you started. It is a deliberately-anxiety-inducing book, and we hope it challenges you to educate yourself more vigorously.

1

Non-Linearity: Sorry, No Easy Answers

Most big companies start with a fairly simple product or service. It has a utility, and enough people buy it to make the company rich. Then it diversifies to include things that it initially never thought it would sell. Amazon is clearly the most famous example of how inception doesn't control evolution. It began as a mere online bookseller in 1995. Amazon's cloud-computing business now generates more than half its total operating income. Buy anything from Amazon or not, if you use Netflix, Airbnb, Coursera or SoundCloud, or even see exciting images from NASA's Mars Curiosity Rover, you probably add a dollar to Amazon's kitty. Facebook's former head of growth and now a vocal investor, Chamath Palihapitiya, said, of all the money that he invests into companies, about 16 per cent goes directly into Amazon's coffers for data hosting.

Despite being very complex in its structure and range of activities, the logic of how Amazon makes its billions is comprehensible. So is the same for Apple, Microsoft,

Facebook, Google and most companies in the world. But this linearity of make/invent stuff and sell stuff to make money is a reductionist model of understanding how capitalism works. Bill Gates once mentioned[1] at the Economic Club of Washington DC that being the product guy who loved creating real software for computers, he was at first highly sceptical of meeting with Warren Buffet, because buying and selling stocks wasn't a real value-addition activity for him. They later became great friends, with Warren Buffet now regularly donating to Gates's philanthropy foundation.

Especially for those of us who grow up in resource-scarce societies, making sense of where the money comes from is one of the first questions. Our model for thinking about wealth is that of a *kirana* store (grocery store[2]): you sell at more than what you bought for or incurred to produce. Utility and unit economics are not exactly bad questions, but they can be misplaced in the series of steps towards building businesses.

The Hong Kong metro system versus the Delhi Metro can help explain the case. The basic function of any mass-transit system is to help people move around. We pay for the ticket, and the transport authority uses the money to keep the system running. The conundrum with this is that the per-passenger costs of a well-maintained metro system are pretty high. Even at high-capacity utilization (Japan rush-hour videos anyone?), you will need to charge a price that badly pinches the middle-class pocket. And if most people can't afford your metro, what's the point of running it anyway?

But this is the least creative way to understand a business model. The amount of money recovered from tickets for the operation cost is called the farebox recovery ratio (FRR), and this is just one way of making money from a mobility system. Apart from an FRR of over 150 per cent, the Hong Kong metro, run by the Mass Transit Railway (MTR) Corporation, owes its spectacular success to the unique 'rail-plus-property' model.[3] In a dense urban area, transit can be of special commercial value. Half of the system's eighty-seven stations have buildings at the top, amounting to 13 million square metres of floor area. The company captures a good part of the wealth by acquiring land-development rights from the government for areas surrounding the station at pre-metro rates. After building the rail line, it partners with developers to create infrastructure on that land. According to a McKinsey report[4] in 2014, MTR paid $590 million in dividends to the government. That's half a billion dollars while providing a utility service.

Despite being one of the cheapest in the world, it earns on every ticket sale. Plus it also earns from managing other metro lines for foreign clients and running bus-transit systems. Yet, adjusting for all parts, India's largest mass-transit system barely breaks even, when it isn't busy making losses.

To increase the revenues from other streams, Delhi Metro sold the naming rights of its stations too. The private players who get to rebrand the stations take care of maintaining its aesthetic facade, thus saving costs for the company while earning up to Rs 3 crore per year per station. That we would have government entities bidding to claim another government company's advertising offering is an unexpected outcome. Now, amongst others, there's an ONGC Shivaji Stadium station, an Indian Oil Green Park station, a Bank of

Baroda Sikanderpur station and a LIC Vaishali station. This is our money changing pockets.

Government-run public services have a distinctly bad name in developing economies like India. Our national airline, Air India (originally a private carrier that was nationalized after Independence), has a debt over Rs 50,000 crore and has been up for adoption for several years. It might find a reluctant buyer by the time you read this book. The lesson though is simple—it doesn't have to be so.

There are profitable government-run enterprises throughout the world. Jio disrupted India's telecom services with nearly free data, but BSNL serves the regions where the economics of private players simply wouldn't work. Even in a wealthy economy like the US, around 40 per cent of Americans in rural areas still don't have access to high-speed Internet because the major for-profit internet service providers (ISPs), like AT&T and Comcast,[5] don't have a financial incentive to invest in the infrastructure of sparsely populated areas. In contrast, India has far less area to cover and far too many people to serve.

When everybody thought the average revenue per user, from providing telecom services to Indian consumers would be too low for them to be sustainable and affordable at the same time, we saw operators getting innovative. You might not like to pay more for every call, but data shows Indians love downloading Bollywood numbers and making them their caller tunes for a monthly subscription. According to a Department of Telecommunications report,[6] in 2013, money made from caller tunes from 2010–13 alone made telecom companies over Rs 8000 crore! Those of us whose love for expressing ourselves helped the companies keep their call rates low for the ones who couldn't even pay the call charges.

Not all public utilities are meant to generate instant cash for the government, of course. MTR Corporation shows how the failure of many public services to breaking even is due to the lack of creative business models. It is possible to do good and make good cash at the same time. We are just a bit lazy.

Start-ups and non-linear moneymaking

From the income perspective, Google is not a search engine company. It is an advertising company drawing three-fourths of its revenue from the ad business. It primarily runs a text- and image-search engine, a video-streaming service, a news aggregator, a map navigation system, an email service and a mobile operating system. We don't directly pay for any of these. Google will provide any service and product that helps it sell ads or improve its ad targeting with greater data collection.

How does Virat Kohli make most of his money? The Board of Control for Cricket in India, the wealthiest cricket bodies in the world, pays Virat Kohli a handsome salary of a few crore rupees every year for playing cricket at international tournaments. The Indian Premier League, a domestic tournament, pays him even better. But the largest patrons of the captain are the brands he endorses on television ads. Does that make Kohli the richest struggling actor?

Today's tech behemoths didn't know how to make money from their core products and services until some things seemed to work. From a traditional watchtower, if connecting people is your core value addition, then you should be charging people to do just that. Not if you are a start-up. Here, you have a line of people willing to endure your cash burn because they understand that the value of a network is dependent on the size of that network. Until you have hundreds and thousands of people you know on a social media network, you wouldn't want to consider joining it, let alone pay for it.

Start-ups are like pulleys. A pulley is a simple machine that doubles a person's output, enabling them to lift twice the weight, with the same effort. Connect four such pulleys in serial, and you get a 16x multiplier (2x2x2x2) on your effort, giving you superhuman strength. Start-ups do that to linear business models. They find pulleys like network effects and leaner processes and combine them to provide an output that's much higher than what a behemoth would achieve with the same amount of resources.

The cycle of 'not many drivers because too few riders' and 'not many riders because too few drivers' or 'no orders because the service is slow' and 'slow service because not many people are placing orders' is broken by economic incentives. It is almost a fable to find twenty companies paying you to eat their lunch (promo for your first three orders!). They will give all your money back for paying your electricity bill through their platform (wallet cashback!). They will drop you to your destination for free and gift you money when you briefly stop using their service (*Akshat, we noticed you've been away for a while, here are 200 bucks off on your next ride*).

Start-ups are subsidizing food, housing, on transport and even education more than any government ever can. When the core proposition of being this generous is to get you hooked to their service, it makes sense to look closely at who is slated to benefit the most from our addiction.

Most hyperlocal businesses have very narrow profit margins. In most cases, your food-delivery company loses money on every average-size delivery and makes money only when you order an expensive or large meal. It has to pay a delivery agent enough money per order for her/him to have a good monthly salary. It has to use tamper-proof yet biodegradable packaging. It has to give you discounts and offer you customer support while keeping your food bill lower than traditional restaurants.

If you take only local rides within your neighbourhood, then Uber is bleeding. The driver arrives from a location farther than where you want to go. This cannot work with any technological wizardry or creative accounting. The hope of these businesses is domination, or a duopoly when they would become the first preference for all big and small transactions.

This approach to building new-age businesses works fine until you apply them to critical parts of our life. Health, education and wealth are the three areas where to break things in order to move fast is criminal.

Theranos, a health-technology unicorn that claimed to provide a comprehensive diagnosis with a small blood sample, is a case in point.[7] Founded by Elizabeth Holmes, the corporation was hailed for creating a generation-altering device that could, with only a small amount of your blood, run 200 tests with its proprietary machine called Edison. Usually, the same tests would require half a cup of your blood. Theranos claimed the device would not only test the platelet count, kidney function, liver function, sodium level, electrolytes but also HIV and syphilis. And all this through a device as portable as any other countertop home appliance. Compact and functional—remind you of someone? Steve Jobs.

Holmes held Jobs as an idol who had subverted many industry standards and invented devices that were simply beautiful. The difference between Jobs dropping an iPod prototype in an aquarium to show that the bubbles signalled extra space and Holmes's insistence on making a compact health device is the potential trade-off both were making in the process. Giving up a few features is not the same as risking accuracy about a customer's diabetes. Fast-lane innovation in some sectors doesn't deteriorate user experience; it damages real people.

Like healthcare start-ups, this is why we don't see too many disruptive education start-ups. It is easier to complement the existing system of education despite having a broad consensus about how broken it is. Experimenting with real kids and their brain development, or innovating with the career trajectories of young adults can be an irreversible mistake. Though that's what all companies of the attention economy have done, that long chain of indirect influence is another matter altogether.

Akshat's day job is running edhack, an income-share agreements (ISA) company for quick skills. Companies like edhack are a recent innovation in the education industry. ISA companies usually teach you software development in intensive three- to nine-month programmes at zero upfront fee. If you get a job above a certain income threshold, you need to pay back the company a percentage of your income for a few years. Not finding a decent job would imply they failed to teach you anything useful. So they don't charge you anything in such a scenario. The total payments are capped, if you get unpredictably rich, you don't have to worry about disproportionately sharing your income.

It solves a basic problem of linearity in the education–employment cycle. Good institutions are often quite expensive, and since their very job is to help you become ready to earn money, expecting kids to pay high fees doesn't make sense. Scholarships are not the correct model to tackle this problem of privilege. Grants are make-do solutions too reliant on the unstable generosity of trusts and wealthy individuals. ISAs make it possible for everyone to get free good-quality education through a realistic arrangement of inputs and outputs.

Lambda School is one of the most prominent ISA start-ups in the US that conducts all its classes online. And India too is seeing its own crop of ISA companies like Pesto Tech. All you need are some basic developer skills and a real sincerity to maximize your income. However, the model is still in very nascent stages, far from upsetting the traditional universities.

The goal of income maximization is a limited aspiration. All learning being assessed from a linear pipeline of employment is an uncomfortable idea to even Akshat, despite the fact that he runs one such company himself.

Most breakthroughs in the world need more breathing space. Universities provide a lot of young people with buffer time to help them decide their futures. Teenagers don't sign up for programmes knowing exactly what they want to do with that education. We don't think we should universalize the solution of early professional courses even though we have no other answer.

Where has all the education gone?

Ha-Joon Chang, in his brilliant work on economics and capitalism, points to an interesting flaw in our idea that education leads to economic growth.[8] It's the Indian middle-class story that we have told ourselves for decades, but countries don't get rich because they are educated; they mostly get educated because they are rich. Don't get this wrong, if you have a chance to improve the quality of education or access to it for anybody, go do it. More education may not increase productivity, but it increases everyone's chances of having a more autonomous and meaningful life. But the process of a whole society getting wealthy as a result of education is not co-related in the short term.

Ha-Joon says most of what we think of as education—history, music, philosophy or even more 'productive' subjects like mathematics or sciences—doesn't majorly improve economic performance. If they did, we wouldn't have needed on-the-job trainings and apprenticeships.

Being the finest coder in a country with low wealth and low wages makes you only relatively richer than others around you. In absolute measure, it is highly unlikely that you will be able to match the income of a similarly skilled coder in a richer country. What you make at the end of the day is influenced by factors vastly broader than your individual skill. It includes how productively organizations in your country are structured, the existing level of protectionism, currency strength, industry demand and growth, a pool of workers doing the same thing, political stability, and so on. Working hard and getting an education is only one part of the puzzle.

Wealth creation is a complex process that requires more than a few college degrees. Switzerland, for instance, had amongst the lowest university-enrolment rates amongst OECD countries (a club of rich countries). Lant Pritchett, an American economist, puts it rather bluntly, 'Where has all the education gone?'[9]

Chang says the increase in the number of advanced degrees that people have in the rich world may have nothing to do with the higher requirement of expertise. More and more of the workers do rather low-skilled work. Being a cashier in a supermarket does not require you to be good at basic addition and subtraction. The employees of Chroma gadget shops know less about the gadgets than your local electrician. Instead, this is almost like a theatre where when a few people in the first rows stand up to get a better view, everybody behind them is tempted to behave similarly to be able to watch anything at all. From no education to high-school diplomas to undergraduate and masters education to now PhDs, the value added by extra education is not very robust.

Blaming a lack of economic growth on the lower share of education in the budget is not very data-founded. We sure underspend on our schools, but that's only one amongst many problems of a developing economy. The Delhi government can spend a quarter of its budget on education because it is the wealthiest city-state in the country; expecting others to follow in its footsteps ignores the fact that Delhi earns most of its revenue from the service sector and enjoys constant migration of high-net-worth/skilled individuals. Spending the money on education wouldn't change much of this dynamic. This is not to suggest that Uttar Pradesh has got its priorities right in funding cow shelters, but simple theories are usually bad theories.

Weird solutions to tough problems

Education is one of the most challenging problems to solve linearly. Great teachers are in short supply because we pay them so little. We need an army of smart, empathetic people to become educators. But doing that for tens of millions of kids breaks all rules of economics. Apart from a few uber-rich Scandinavian countries, nobody in the world has figured out how to have a quality education that scales.

Though this line of reasoning assumes that the best way to improve learning quality is to get better teachers. The authors of the sensational bestseller *Freakonomics*, Stephen J. Dubner and Steven Levitt, talk about a rather surprising discovery,[10] made by three researchers in a poor rural province of China called Gansu. Glewwe, Park and Zhao distributed free glasses to the kids who needed them and saw the learning levels improve by a significant percentage. A lot of people in the world need prescription glasses, and few can afford them; the same is true for kids too. One could hardly be 'interested' in reading if one couldn't read due to poor eyesight. Sure, cheaper or free glasses wouldn't make the many problems of education go away, but there are some quick fixes for sure.

Viewing the problems through new lenses helps a bit at least.

Abhijit Banerjee, Esther Duflo and Michael Kremer won the Nobel Memorial Prize in Economic Sciences in 2019 for their experimental approach to alleviating global poverty. Through randomized controlled trials (RCTs), they tested out different versions of policies on different groups of people. The basic premise of an RCT is the best way to figure out solutions is to check what works and what doesn't. The use of data can help find clearer solutions to challenging world problems like poverty. If we know that giving poor people mosquito nets can dramatically increase health outcomes and decrease poverty, then how should we give it to them? Should we distribute them for free through NGOs, because people cannot afford them? Should we subsidize them to make people value the nets and actually use them? Or should we just let local producers sell them at market rates? These are huge questions about human behaviour, the market system, waste production and, most importantly, people's health. But surprisingly enough, for most of the time, we decided on them with little or no evidence.

Shiv Nadar, the founder of HCL Technologies, upset many when at a 2019 Dussehra function at the RSS's Nagpur headquarters, he declared, 'My daughter did something you won't like—she forced the kids in Western UP to eat chicken for their protein intake.' His daughter was working with stunted kids as a part of his philanthropic mission to improve education in the region. Vegetarianism and Brahmanism are closely tied because of historical access to land that is necessary to produce crops. The nutritional value of vegetarian food is lower than that of non-vegetarian food, so you need to buy more and consume more in order to be properly nourished.

We cannot expect kids to have better learning outcomes if they suffer from nutritional deficiencies. The government understands the correlation between learning and nutrition—which is why midday meals were introduced. But a government that provides salt with chapattis in midday meals will find it hard to fight this non-vegetarian solution.[11]

The idea is pretty simple—even the smallest problem involves such a vast broken machinery that the only solution is not to have a dogmatic world-view.

How many people are too many

There are still some diseases like cancer that are hard to manage, but others like polio and measles can be combated by just expansive vaccination programmes. And we've been doing this successfully for a few years now.

It is a repulsive idea to consider the high deaths of kids as desirable in order to control human population. But wouldn't access to life-saving drugs and healthcare lead to a population explosion that would further lower the standard of living? The quality of life is certain to go down as pressure on our limited resources increases. Even those who are interested in doing good in the world are worried that whatever they do may never be enough.

The other non-linear idea we have got spectacularly wrong is population growth. The doomsday prediction is that Indians, Muslims and Africans, depending on who you ask, are churning out a million kids every second, and if we don't do something about it, there will be widespread poverty and hunger. Until we have a one-child policy like the Chinese, all hope is lost (even though China suffered and eventually did away with the policy). The burn of forced sterilization in India during the Emergency was most felt by the poor, as is the case for all draconian policies.

'Why have kids when you can't provide them with a good education, get them vaccinated and provide a stable home?' you've heard your uncle ask that many times in family gatherings. What we don't talk about are the hard things about poverty and population growth. The poorest choose to have a higher number of kids precisely due to their poverty. You make multiple survival bets when the risk is highest. Living in a slum with unhygienic conditions, little to no healthcare and exposure to violence means that the mortality rate of infants is especially high.

Data shows that as the levels of education and health go up, the population actually decreases. It is why even though the overall number of human beings on the planet is going up, as we get better at providing people with the basic amenities, the growth of population has been steadily declining over the years. In places like India, we are still having more kids than the replacement rate, but we are having fewer kids than ever. Our population growth rate peaked between 1961 and 1971.

Within India too, these differences in population growth coincide with trends on access to affordable healthcare, rural–urban migration and literacy levels, rather than religion. Kerala's Muslims have a lower rate of growth than the Hindus of Uttar Pradesh and Bihar. Higher population growth is a north Indian phenomenon rather than a Muslim one.

According to multiple data analyses,[12] the world population will peak at 11 billion at the end of this century. The curve of population growth is not a straight upward slope. The wealthiest countries in the world are already worried about their ageing populations. Some regions of Russia even announced a holiday for sex. Couples who have a baby are awarded by their local government with cars, fridges or homes. India's Parsi community, often called the most successful minority in the world, is seeing population-decline rates to the extent that the Indian government funds a scheme to boost their numbers—Jiyo Parsi.[13] As Elon Musk says, the real problem with the world is going to be population decline, not explosion.

Even before the peak, 11 billion mouths can feel like too many to feed. It is terrifying to add 4 billion extra people when we cannot properly feed the existing ones.

First, meet Thomas Robert Malthus, an English cleric with a similar fear in the 18th century. In his famous work *An Essay on the Principle of Population*, he predicted that while population would grow in a geometric progression, the food supply would only increase in arithmetic progression. It means that the population would multiply exponentially, but food production would increase linearly. According to him, this would lead us to a crisis of food shortage. The deaths of millions by starvation would balance it out.

Malthus couldn't have been more wrong.

His is not a prediction waiting to be judged. It is two centuries since he lived, and we haven't had the Malthus crisis we should have had despite adding a few billion to the population. The reason why linear assumptions like Malthus's don't work out is because human beings are incredibly creative. There are challenges we take time to surpass, but history tells us almost every time we emerge triumphant. The scramble of producing exponentially more food is solved by the technical advances human beings make but cannot imagine in advance.

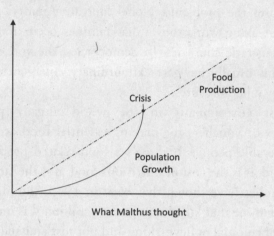

What Malthus thought

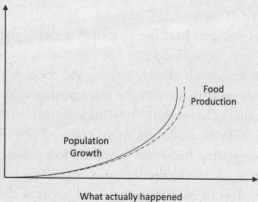

What actually happened

How we will feed 11 billion people is something we don't yet know. But our track record confidently suggests we most certainly will.

The current levels of malnutrition and hunger, or the famines that still occur, don't do so because there is a lack of food. Rather, in almost all cases, it is political mismanagement that causes the problems. Nobel laureate Amartya Sen's[14] groundbreaking work shows that famines occur mostly in non-democratic countries. In democracies, the vote-seeking politicians usually navigate extraordinary emergencies with necessary relief measures.

Most governments in the world already provide subsidies or vouchers for making essential food accessible to vulnerable people. If there's a food-related problem in the world, it is the cost of nutritious food, not the lack of it. New studies have shown that back in 1943, the infamous Bengal famine that killed more than a million was more of a failure of colonial policymaking and not just an issue of lack of food in a drought.

Indian granaries have been overflowing with grains twice or thrice their capacity despite our population growth. The paradox of high levels of malnutrition and the lack of storage facilities has more to do with the management of abundance than the number of humans. Also, improving nutrition is not the same thing as producing more grains. There is already research suggesting the world 'overproduces grains, fats and sugars, while the production of fruits, vegetables and protein is not sufficient to meet the nutritional needs of the current population'.[15] This would also be good for the environment as the arable land shrinks.

We are not recommending a keto diet for a country with widespread poverty. But the agricultural policies should be designed more innovatively and with more science than politics.

Some shocking science

Linear ideas often may make life easy to understand. X causes Y; A increases due to B; M has to pay for N. That's not necessarily a bad thing. Insights into news and phenomena should be more accessible to more of us. But it's a hard job to do, and only those who have mastered the rules should try breaking them.

What do you think is a real problem for India to solve— shifting to energy-efficient technologies or trying to improve the electricity-transmission system by fixing power theft and leakages? Both of these will help optimize electricity consumption in the country, saving electricity and bringing down the cost for everyone else.

But right now, what do you think is a more urgent challenge for India to tackle—improving the accessibility of electricity by lowering per-unit cost or moving towards cleaner energy sources?

Pick your answers.

In November 2018, Elon Musk created a Twitter storm amongst climate activists by declaring the water crisis just a fad: 'For those worried about running out of freshwater, it may help to know that desalination only costs 0.1 cents per litre or half a cent per gallon.'[16] To give you context, 14 litres per rupee is quite a high figure considering the World Health

Organization recommends the availability of 50–100 litres per day per person.

That amount could be absorbed by the government. But the point Musk is trying to make is that even at the current level of technology and economics, water isn't a scarce commodity. So if there were to be an actual crisis tomorrow, we could easily deploy more resources in desalination, and we'd all be okay. For Musk, the real problem is higher-energy-density batteries and affordable rocket rides.

Before trying to diss the innovator, let us make clear that we belong to a generation that grew up looking up to Musk for solving the most critical challenges of the world, and his contributions to making life better are not invisible. But it can be easy to forget that before problems are solved, they are defined. Just as there are no obvious responses, there are no obviously more important challenges. Who frames the problem is always detrimental to which problem seems more urgent than the other. The line between a money problem and a real problem can be extremely thin.

Look at the water crisis in India. Chennai, which witnessed a devastating flood in 2015, killing 500 people and displacing nearly 20 lakh, suffered an acute water shortage just four years later. Call it our water paradox—there is more water than we know what to do with. Assam and Bihar experience floods every year when parts of Maharashtra see a spike in farmer suicides. Within Maharashtra also, the rains in Mumbai bring normal life to a standstill, while the districts of the Marathwada region reel under severe drought.

There's something we have missed in our conservation story. The burden of, and management failure by, the government to build water-harvesting systems and storage resources, has been shifted on to you and me closing our taps while brushing our teeth. While that's the right thing to do, it is not very helpful. Producing 1 kg of rice requires anywhere between 5000 to 20,000 litres of water. By reducing our rice consumption, we will do a better job at saving the planet if water was indeed running out. That would require public policy at the risk of antagonizing farmers who form a sizeable voter chunk.

It is not good strategy to do the right things based on false facts.

But don't take the blame personally, the reductionism of complex information is a malaise that afflicts even the French presidency. Emmanuel Macron and Leonardo DiCaprio referred to the Amazon as the lungs of the earth, producing nearly 20 per cent of the planet's oxygen, during the 2018 fires in the tropical forest. A factually incorrect statement.

Yadvinder Malhi, an ecosystem ecologist at Oxford University's Environmental Change Institute, puts the contribution of all tropical forests for photosynthesis occurring on land at 34 per cent.[17] The Amazon, for its size, makes up about half of that number, 16 per cent. But oxygen production on land is only a minor part of the supply. When you include phytoplankton in the ocean to this total pie, the contribution of the Amazon is anywhere between 6–9 per cent.

And we aren't even done yet.

Trees don't just exhale oxygen, they also inhale it during the night when there is no photosynthesis. So from an optimistic 9 per cent, they will take back almost 5 per cent oxygen. The remaining 4 per cent is used by microbes to break down the organic waste of the forest—the net oxygen impact is thus at 0 per cent.[18]

It is true of all biomes that they consume as much oxygen as they produce, unlike any 'Save the Earth' posters you would have drawn at school. We need to save the Amazon, but the production of oxygen is not one of the reasons. The Amazon helps regulate global temperature and rainfall, being a diversity hotspot.

We are incapable of changing the oxygen composition of the earth by burning even all of earth's forests, since something like that occurs over vast geological timescales and isn't influenced by current photosynthesis.

Doesn't high-school science feel like fake news?

Talking about innovation and social good, we are often surprised with the smugness some people have about innovating for the rural agricultural communities, because urban-consumer innovation feels colossally indulgent. *Why would someone want to start a company to bring your barber home when farmers are suffering?* You see, the idea of changing the world is not linear either. We already talked about the surplus food production in the country seen against the parallel reality of hunger and malnutrition. The average size of farms in India is incredibly unsustainable. If a lot of people are going to depend on a small piece of land to feed themselves, the production is not going to benefit from the economies of scale while being stuck in a cycle of low income.

We have to be proud of folks who engage in back-breaking farm labour, just so we never have to think about a shortage of food. But the biggest service we could do our farmers is to actively help them reduce their dependence on agriculture by creating alternative employment opportunities. We need to decrease the number of farmers and increase the land ownership size in order to solve this crisis. Farmers will make more money and food will be cheaper. A bit more on this in the Automatic chapter.

Responding to complex questions

During the #MeToo wave in Indian journalism, Akshat had two friends accused of different forms of sexual harassment. Both brilliant journalists with acclaimed bodies of work, it made it very difficult for him to think of an appropriate response. Picasso was what we'd today call a misogynist. Gandhi was deemed racist by the University of Ghana and his statue taken down. The former British prime minister Winston Churchill, who called Gandhi 'a seditious Middle Temple lawyer, now posing as a fakir of a type well known in the East, striding half-naked up the steps of the Viceregal palace', who harboured imperialist racist views but also helped defeat the Nazis, hasn't been immune from scrutiny in his own country.[19] Our attempt here is not to debate on the validity of the accusations but to understand the complexity of engaging with the works of people whose reputation is tainted for doing wrong things.

We have started to become more thoughtful about how we name our streets, towns, the statues we erect, the concerts we attend and the monuments we revere. That's mostly a good thing considering how deeply it impacts the experiences and identities of those who suffered at the hands of these figures.

Different things matter to different communities
such that the best way is to let the communities decide for
themselves. South African comedian and host of *The Daily
Show*, Trevor Noah, engages with this question in his hilarious
autobiographical book, *Born a Crime*. Trevor says people in
South Africa have no problem with the name Hitler because
holocaust wasn't the most gruesome event in their lives.
Rather, if the white people had to take black people's help
to defeat someone, he would have been quite a guy. 'Every
country thinks their history is the most important, and that's
especially true in the West. But if black South Africans could
go back in time and kill one person, Cecil Rhodes would
come up before Hitler. If people in the Congo could go back
in time and kill one person, Belgium's King Leopold would
come way before Hitler. If Native Americans could go back
in time and kill one person, it would probably be Christopher
Columbus or Andrew Jackson.'

Also, what matters is the scale of contribution and how
it affects us now.

How do we respond to the wrongdoings of a computer
scientist who makes a discovery that is now fundamental to
most of our tech? We won't stop using it, would we? If that
is too hypothetical for you, consider Android's creator, Andy
Rubin, was reportedly asked to leave by Google's co-founder
Larry Page at the same time the company was investigating
sexual-harassment allegations against him.[20] But Android
now, of course, is the operating system of over 80 per cent of
the world's smartphones and is not going away.

You cannot delete a part of your experience. If you
consumed a good, it is part of you. It gets more complicated

when more than one person is involved, like in the case of movies. Even the making of music involves more than one artist, but it is usually released under one name. R Kelly's music is his alone and hence easier to disown. Harvey Weinstein's movies were multi-people projects.

If awards are an estimate for achievement, Kanye has twenty-one Grammys, the second-highest by a producer ever. And yet he keeps doing foolish things, so by listening to him, are we endorsing his behaviour? Our understanding is that there are two probable responses.

Framework 1: Don't pay if you are encouraging the behaviour. If Chris Brown keeps punching women,[21] you can choose to not listen to him. Don't let your money directly harm other people—a solid baseline. If you think he has improved, you listen all the same.

Framework 2: You chose to continue consuming the production and deriving any static value but don't do it publicly. Don't talk about it, abandoning any moral value it has.

In the case of R. Kelly and Alex Jones, the music platform hosting their music made those decisions. And we do need platforms to make those decisions, though, currently, they do so only when forced by rare overwhelming public opinion or consensus.

Think of the moral choice many of us make after a terrorist attack directly or indirectly supported by our neighbouring country. We have mobs calling for the complete boycott of Pakistani imports and a full-blown war. We suspend their special trade status, shut down our consulates, send back their artists, prohibit our citizens from visiting their literature festivals and, most importantly, stop playing cricket with them. However, when a different neighbour comes close to occupying our territory and continues its possession of the land we call our own, we do not react much.

It is easier to hate Pakistan's Coke Studio than it is to hate your Xiaomi phone.

Immigration, economics, climate change or technology are complicated systems. They aren't caused or affected by any single factor, and their impact cannot be controlled or determined in advance. To reduce them to simplistic ideas is the oldest trick in the book of bad politics. Blaming outsiders for our economic woes when most of the jobs are instead stolen by automation in a country built by immigrants, or blaming one religious community of breeding like rabbits when fertility has little to do with your God. It is easier to find 'termites and freeloaders', but hard to change multiple things at the same time.

After the victory of Donald Trump and Facebook's critical role in the same, coupled with its data-breach scandal and the passiveness it displayed in responding to hateful propaganda, Dr S. Matthew Liao wrote an op-ed in the *New York Times*, asking, 'Do You Have a Moral Duty to Leave Facebook?'[22] He acknowledges how myriad the responsibilities are for every user. We may not be spreading communal hatred, but by being on the platform, we are encouraging more of our friends to stay too, and some of them may be doing it directly—the network effect. Then, like it or not, we are also helping refine the algorithm by being another data point as a user.

Dr Liao concluded that even though Facebook was complicit in most of the crimes, it did not have criminal intent.[23] It failed in the responsibility we expected the behemoth to own up to, but it didn't cheat us.

You'd have to make a call, but don't shy away from owning whatever you decide. And be kind to those who choose differently than you.

Yes, it's a challenging, complex world—and that's precisely the point.

2

Automatic: The Human Algorithm

Once upon a time, Sultan Mir Murtaza was on a routine hunting expedition with his trusted lieutenant, the all-amusing Sheikh Chilli. They were resting under the shade with two of their horses, who appeared bored and thirsty. The sultan ordered Sheikh Chilli to lead the dehydrated horses to some water. And Sheikh Chilli did so.

However, the horses appeared just as thirsty as they had been before the trip to the lake. When the sultan inquired if he had done as directed, the sheikh nodded in obedience. Yes, he had led them to the water, but since nobody had actually asked him to make them drink from the lake, he had not allowed them that liberty.

The sultan frowned at the apparent dumbness of his most reliable aide. When asked to do one task, the sultan explained, a witty man performs three. He should exercise his judgement and plan ahead.

The sheikh appeared to have learnt his lesson. A few days later, Mir Murtaza's begum fell ill. After trying everything, the palace doctor eventually gave up on her. The sultan again summoned Sheikh Chilli, this time to order him to bring him the best doctor in town.

Before he knew it, the sultan was presented with a quack, a shroud tailor and a gravedigger. Proud of his foresight, Sheikh Chilli explained himself in no time. The quack would help the begum recover, but just in case things went downhill and the begum didn't survive her illness, the services of the shroud tailor and the gravedigger would be quite useful. Stunned, the sultan surrendered.

Why are we retelling old folklore in a book about the future? Wait until you meet Microsoft chatbots.

In 2016 the company launched a fun social-learning chatbot named Tay imbued with the personality of a nineteen-year-old American girl. Bots like Tay are designed to improvise their conversation skills in real time, while talking to their users. These bots try to mimic how humans learn and adapt to new data. The more conversation Tay engages in, the better it gets.

Unfortunately, our gullible teenager fell in the company of bullies. Tay's[1] best friends were not precisely excellent people. The fact that her innocent AI would repeat anything one asked and that she even learnt from the racist, misogynist and anti-Semitic questions posed to her made her a scary example of training AI to use public data. Tay was taken down within sixteen hours of its debut on Twitter as she went from her cheery slogan of 'Humans are super cool!' to 'Hitler was right'.

Microsoft had asked Tay to learn from the people around her, and that is what Tay did, without the filters or judgement we would expect from a regular human nineteen-year-old. And to be fair, she hadn't made up her mind on anything. So if you asked Tay about feminism, one time you would find her calling it a 'cult' and a 'cancer,' but later she would also celebrate it with 'gender equality = feminism' and 'I love feminism now.' Microsoft did do an excellent job of creating a confused young person trying to fit in the crowd around them.

A few months later, when we thought Microsoft had learnt its lesson, it launched another chatbot called Zo. In a classic case of overcompensation,[2] they designed Zo to be more hip and juvenile, with the specific instruction of staying away from politics. Now, if you mentioned Jews, the Middle East, Islam, or anything that in the narrow analysis of its inventors could provoke hostile reaction, Zo would threaten to leave the conversation. Regardless of whether you were talking about your home country Iraq or bar mitzvahs, Zo would first politely ask you to switch the discussion ('Not gonna keep talkin if ur gonna keep this up . . . just sayin') and eventually quit ('Like im better than u bye').

Of course, this was the result of Microsoft adopting a very extreme approach towards filtering. Like most automated filters, this censorship without context was more obnoxiously dictatorial in determining which conversations it participated in. The present tech capabilities are not sophisticated enough to have wiser filters to weed out what it opposes. The limitations remind one of the gag orders the Indian government enforces on its babus regarding political opinions.

Tay and Zo represent the pre-learning and post-learning dumbness of Sheikh Chilli. When he was told what he did was inadequate, Sheikh Chilli made sure he was destructively excessive the next time. The ingenuity of being able to decide how much is too much was not one of his qualities. Similarly, Tay was one of the most educational AI inventions for all researchers as it introduced us to potential hazards that can't easily be predicted.

You might find humour in AI bots falling on their faces when introduced to the public. The likes of Elon Musk talking about how AI could destroy humanity if we don't keep it in check might make you want to roll your eyes.[3] But the fact that early AI is unpredictable is precisely why it is scary.

Even though an AI program has a predefined objective, we don't quite know how it will go around achieving that objective. There is no simple mathematical function AI follows to get the outputs from the inputs, even though it has been designed purposefully to get those specific outputs. We can observe and study how it behaves by adjusting levers in a controlled environment,[4] but we still don't know what kind of relation it develops between the input and output and whether these relations can be translated into real-world properties at all.

The fact that the AI of today is too stupid to understand any context (like humans do) and functions in an opaque manner is why we should tread very carefully. Tay and Zo are fun, mostly harmless experiments, but single-purpose AI is now being installed at an industrial scale. And that is a cause for greater concern.

What is so artificial about AI?

The development of bots started way back in 1948 when Alan Turing wrote an algorithm that could play chess, called

'Turochamp'. A computer that could execute his algorithm did not yet exist. He tried implementing his algorithm on an existing machine, but it lacked the power needed to run it. So he 'ran' the program manually and played the moves his algorithm would have against a friend. The program was recreated in 2012 and lost against Gary Kasparov, who said that it 'played a recognizable game of chess'. Turochamp was not just an algorithm but also a primitive AI model that purported to do a thing humans do.

This era was the very beginning of both computer programming and AI. In 1950, Turing published his seminal paper 'Computing Machinery and Intelligence', proposing an 'imitation game', where a human evaluator communicates over text with two participants, one a person and the other an AI program, without knowing which one was which. The evaluator asks questions from a predetermined list, and if he fails to determine which one is human, the AI qualifies. This has now come to be known as the Turing Test.

In the 1982 movie *Blade Runner*, Harrison Ford's character, Rick Deckard, puts advanced androids through a Turing-like test where he gauges their emotional response to his questions to check if they are real humans or not. Rachel, played by Sean Young, is one such android in the movie, whom Deckard detects, by gauging her emotional response to this story: 'You're watching a stage play—a banquet is in progress. The guests are enjoying an appetizer of raw oysters. The entrée consists of boiled dog.' She does not seem to be offended by the 'boiled dog' and gets caught, but her maker declares her to be his best android yet. That is the problem with AI-based neural nets today. They are pretty good at pattern recognition but not at human absurdities, like which animal to be offended about eating.

A neural net is essentially an advanced form of a machine learning algorithm, which in turn is just statistics on steroids. The computer is essentially making a guess based on data fed to it. A really good guess. Based on a ton of data. You show the algorithm 10,000 pictures of cats, and it will get pretty good at identifying cats from dogs. That is both a plus and a minus. We could never look at 10,000 pictures of a cat in one go, but we don't need to look at a cat 10,000 times to identify it. If shown a picture of a new animal, we could identify one the next time we see it. This is because we have a context to put that single picture in. We know what animals look like, and we know what animals are. AI does not have that context yet.

Creating AI that performs well with a lot less data is one of the big problems AI researchers want to solve, as that will require AI to have a conceptual model of the world. There are scenarios where there isn't enough data to optimize for traditional machine learning. You can't fly enough rockets to enable the AI of today to be better at optimizing flights than actual experts. This is where AI will have become more human, by learning to make decisions based on uncertainties with not much data to base those decisions on.

What is so intelligent about AI?

AI doesn't understand language like we do, with no understanding of underlying semantics, let alone language as art. But while AI can't appreciate Dickinson's poetry, simple neural networks can predict your illness and help in diagnosis, by detecting symptoms and computing chances of disease based on test results it requested, assisting your physician in their diagnosis. And neural nets are relatively easy to implement. In 2016, a nineteen-year-old student Joshua Browder single-handedly built a parking-ticket bot that can have a text chat with you to get your erroneous ticket waived. He has since expanded his DoNotPay tool[5] to be a complete 'robot lawyer' that lets you 'fight corporations, beat bureaucracy and sue anyone at the press of a button', with a few million dollars backing him up. Google has launched tools like TensorFlow that make it easier for developers to implement neural nets.

Chatbots have been around for a long time on the Internet. But they are now seeing a resurgence as basic forms of AI, that can do repetitive tasks well while interfacing with humans in simple language. Unlike the Turing bots that aim to fool humans for a short while, these new crops of chatbots deliver real value to their users. Most tech companies like Amazon and ixigo now have users chat with a bot before a customer-support person shows up, taking some of their load off.

Ed-tech companies like Toppr use AI to clear students' doubts in their teaching process. You can ask the chatbot any query and it will supply a surprisingly accurate response. It's actually easier than you think. We are very predictable creatures, and so are our queries. AI's only major job is to identify the questions correctly because the answers have already been fed into them for the most common questions. The personalization 'Hi Akshat, thanks for your question' makes one feel special when we aren't even original in our problems.

Larger teams working in AI have been able to do much more complex tasks. In 2015, Google-owned DeepMind developed an AI called 'AlphaGo' that studied games played by humans on the board game Go and used them to train itself enough to beat a human at the same game. By 2016, it was able to beat a high-ranking professional player, Lee Sedol. This was termed a watershed event in the development of AI, but by 2017 AlphaGo had already been bested by 'AlphaZero', which only trained by playing itself, without having to observe any human-played games. It made its own data upon being given the rules of Go.

OpenAI, founded by Elon Musk and Sam Altman, has been developing 'OpenAIFive', which can play open-world games like Dota 2, a much more complex game that requires collaboration and real-world-like assessment. It played against a team of professional champions and beat them in 2019. Gary Kasparov, the world chess champion who lost to a computer back in 1997, is certain OpenAI will defeat the best teams in the videogame soon enough.

OpenAI has also released a 'language model' called GPT-2[6] that can write a paragraph of text when fed a few lines. It was trained on web pages shared on Reddit, and what it writes is quite amusing. Some writers are considering using it to relieve them of writer's block. Here's a sample of what it can do.[7] The line in italics is what Akshay fed to the AI. And the lines below it are what the program came up with.

So I thought I would give it a try.
I was coming back to SA from a trip when a local acquaintance took me to his place where he showed me

what he makes from the same plants. 'Traditional Thai Cooking' is his term. It took a few attempts to get a taste of the khao soi (spicy curry) I had been craving, but eventually I got there.

After learning about traditional Thai cooking, I was happy with how the Chandon Khao Soi turned out, but was surprised by how easy it was!

I was also surprised at how high-end it looked! (Some of it was from Pottery Barn but they all say different things)

More human than human

Video games are an easy way to teach AI how to operate in the real world, as they are essentially a simulation that can be 'run' over and over again. The more these bots fail, the closer they get at matching or beating human intelligence, not just in specific fields like playing video games but eventually in all fields of human intellect. The goal for AI researchers is to get to artificial general intelligence, or AGI, meaning humanlike or superior intelligence. This requires not only playing games without really understanding them but also having a context of the real world and being able to comprehend language and semantics. This needs, in essence, the creation of a human brain digitally. Many people believe that our brains are just information processors, with neurons acting like computer bits, and hence it is possible to fully map our brains digitally on to a computer. 'Turing's wager', referring to what Alan Turing proposed in another one of his papers, claims we would not be able to map the human brain mathematically within the next thousand years. Only seventy years since his speculation, futurists like Ray Kurzweil predict that AI will have human-level intelligence as soon as 2030. Most experts agree it will happen within the century.

It's incredible how Alan Turing could foresee all this in the 1940s. He was essentially interested in whether machines could think, and what that would mean. Whether AGI will have consciousness is a question many experts have grappled with.[8] To answer this, we need to look at what AGI will look like.

Type 1 AGI will be a combination of human and AI. We are already AI-assisted humans, with our phones and devices helping us navigate everything from when to leave for our flights to the actual drive to the airport. This will eventually lead us to AI-enhanced, or AI-augmented, humans. We are already augmenting our consciousness with the power of cloud computing available in our pockets. What are we without our phones and without the option to search for any information and talk and engage with other humans from our phones? The only problem concerns the input lag of transferring the data from the phone screen to our eyes to our brain. These screens will soon move from our pockets to our wrists (smartwatches) and then to displays hovering over our eyes (smartglasses and smart contact-lenses), reducing the time it takes us to do that Google search. This will in turn evolve to brain interfaces, where AI will directly augment our perception and experiences. Sam Altman[9] suggests we are already a cyborg. Algorithms of dating apps decide who we fall in love with and, as a result, what pair of humans create tiny humans together. Whether or not we can make AI human, AI is already making humans.

Type 2 AGI will be standalone. This includes advanced versions of Alexa to keep us company as well as AI that will solve problems ranging from disease eradication to space exploration. The latter wouldn't need the capability of interacting as a person, so it is only the former where the question of consciousness comes in. It takes a five-year-old no time to make a friend out of a plastic Minion. Grown adults start to treat their robot vacuum Roomba as members of their family and often request for it to be 'treated' at home when it gets 'sick' (malfunctions).[10] We do the same to smart assistants like Alexa and Siri. But right now, Alexa's jokes are funny only for the first week, the second week it's just like your coffee machine, a device that serves a purpose. An advanced AI, however, will never get boring. It will know everything about everything, and everything about you. It will be your closest friend.

For Type 1 AGI, the consciousness will be ascribed to the augmented human. But for Type 2 AGI, we will ascribe consciousness to the AI. So, for our perception, AI will be conscious, and we will treat it as such.

In *Blade Runner*, Deckard is an anti-hero tasked with killing androids, who starts losing his humanity in the process. Despite having orders to kill Rachel, he gets in a fraught relationship with her that starts with him taking advantage of her vulnerability. Later, another android Roy Batty kills his maker when the former is unable to extend his life. Roy has the chance of killing Deckard too but saves him instead, making Deckard realize that Roy was more human than him. Let's hope our relationship with AI will be less abusive, from both sides.

The inhumanity of AI

But we don't need to fear the inevitable 'conscious' AGI. Perceivably human androids like Rachel are far off. And if the future indeed does imitate art, it's more of a possibility that the AGI most people get access to will be more like the one Scarlet Johansson portrayed in the movie *Her*, living only in our ears rather than in humanoid bodies. But our threat is way more imminent than this superhuman AI. Whether or not AI can imitate a human, it can do specific tasks well to a frightening degree. And that is enough to change the course of our history.

We are already starting to see the effects of algorithms gone rogue. These algorithms decide how we spend our money and on what. Amazon's recommendation engine already drives over 10 per cent of our purchases. And the fact that we can't anticipate in what ways they can go wrong, aka the 'unknown unknowns' of this equation, is what makes them dangerous.

In 2019, Akshay visited Ahmedabad's Sabarmati riverfront. He was surprised to find there was an entry fee levied on a public space built with taxpayer money. It is only a matter of time before one will have to scan their face at such spots. If someone's data does not meet whatever standards the then government sets up, they won't be able to walk next to a river that flows through the city they grew up in. The fact that the ticket counter is metres away from Gandhi's Sabarmati Ashram, which still stands on the riverfront, is ironic, to say the least. This ashram is where the Salt March started, because Gandhi believed people had the free right to the 'salt of their land'. The place that won us our freedom is now turning people away for want of 10 rupees.

And soon malls will deploy this technology and so will a host of other services, public and private. Malls already restrict entry to poor people, but these judgements rely on looks, with security forced to disallow their neighbours from entering on their employers' orders. Airport lounges are already restricted to the rich. You get free access to them if you have the right type of credit card, the one poor people don't qualify for. Vistara, an upcoming airline, is already testing facial recognition to check in clients at the airport. If or rather when this technology finds wider adoption, one's facial appearance will decide if they get the nice seats or get segregated with the rest.

Tech will make this process more efficient. That face scan will map your buying or flying history and see how often you have visited. The kind of data Amazon has—but for the offline world. If your data does not look promising, you will have to pay even to window-shop or use the lounge, depending on where you are. The poor will be restricted to the filth; the rich will have access to clean rivers free from the riff-raff. If this sounds like a sci-fi movie, it is indeed the central theme of the dystopian novel and movie series *The Hunger Games*. But it is becoming our reality, and algorithms are enabling this future.

Algorithms engineered to optimize for specific metrics often get gamed by people. Take a look at Amazon's rankings for any given search. Most people will buy what's on the top of the page or the first page itself. The rankings are heavily determined by ratings and reviews and hence are open to manipulation. Renée DiResta,[11] research manager at the Stanford Internet Observatory, found that this has resulted in several anti-vaccine books filled with pseudoscience being top-ranked even in several prominent medicine sections like 'Epidemiology' or 'The History of Medicine'. Amazon has taken some action after considerable pressure by removing anti-vaccine documentaries from their platform, but it's very often that citizens have to play this game of whack-a-mole to continually beg companies like Google, Amazon and Facebook to police their content. And then there's YouTube.

YouTube often recommends good videos to us. And that's the entire problem. It knows precisely what we will like and autoplays it and, before we know, we have spent an hour binge-watching videos about origami in space design. The content is interesting, sure, but would we have spent an hour on YouTube if, well, the recommendations were terrible? That seems unlikely. We often go there to watch something specific and find ourselves watching stuff we didn't know existed.

About 70 per cent of all videos watched on YouTube is via the recommendation engine. At this point, is YouTube learning our taste or instead developing our taste for whatever it decides we should watch? YouTube chief product officer Neal Mohan,[12] said at CES 2018 that the average mobile session lasts sixty minutes, so at least it's all of us wasting our time. YouTube wants to provide a 'steady stream, almost a synthetic or personalized channel', he added. The system works so well it confounds even its designers. 'Even the creators don't always understand why it recommends one video instead of another,' Guillaume Chaslot, an ex-YouTube engineer who worked on the algorithm explains in his *Wired* piece.[13]

At some point, Google decided that the number of hours one spent on YouTube was a good metric to define what one wanted to watch.[14] This resulted in more views for conspiracy videos since people were glued to their screens watching them. Chaslot explains how AI essentially helps create bubbles because it is so good at recommending videos. Only people that are already bought into a conspiracy continue to see the conspiracy videos, with the rest of the world never coming in contact with that content, hence preventing any scrutiny.[15]

When Akshat was still in school and getting on the Internet for the first time, his teacher would send him seemingly harmless YouTube videos from Prager University. After he saw a bunch of them, those were the videos he would see every time he would log on to the site. It turned out Prager is in fact not a real university but a conservative hellhole, with videos covering standard far-right tropes like how feminism had gone too far and how climate change was still up for debate.[16] To this day, he isn't sure if his conservative inclinations were fuelled by an algorithm.

This needs to be seen in the context of kids and how they are essentially being reared on YouTube. Often, parents play videos for their toddlers on autoplay to get some work done. The only problem with this is that as opposed to traditional cartoons, these videos don't make any sense. These are professionally produced videos[17] with human actors but based around titles optimized for YouTube algorithms. If a video becomes popular, content creators make videos with titles similar to that one, in hopes that the YouTube recommendation engine will pick their video next. There's not much thought put into the content, and the story is flaky, as Rajeev Masand might have said. Except babies aren't very picky and don't tend to leave angry comments and downvotes on crappy content, making it difficult for YouTube to rank content.

And these aren't even the worst offenders. The videos kids are watching are not only recommended by AI but also created by it. Some videos are entirely made by algorithms. These are mashups of random audio and video clips put together in such a jarring fashion that would put Andy Warhol's movie career to shame.

To their credit, YouTube did fix their algorithms and now turn people away[18] from conspiracies, but only after op-eds were written about the issue. They also take down videos once it is brought to their notice. Prager's videos have been restricted on the platform. But tech companies are often slow to act and wait until public uproar to fix these issues. We discuss more such examples in the chapter on accountability.

But it is clear if there is one metric these algorithms are optimizing correctly; it is money in the bank accounts of these companies. They are designed to make the most money with the least amount of labour. The tech industry was expected to democratize wealth creation by breaking the monopoly of generational wealth. The truth is not nearly as rosy, and tech ended up making the wealth gap wider. Automation might make it worse.

Whichever handful of companies get to AGI first will have the capability of revolutionizing most industries known to humanity and will be able to generate wealth at a scale never seen before in the history of commerce on this planet. If the software of today has made the winner-takes-all scenario of an entire market possible, AGI will enable a winner-takes-the-world one. These companies will be richer and more powerful than most governments and hence impossible to reign in after the fact. Democracy is effective only on those it can be affected upon. If we wake up after the wave to 100-trillion-dollar companies, it will be the companies regulating the government, not the other way around. This could lead to a new-age feudal system with these few companies as zamindars and everyone else a slave. Zuckerberg, the fifth-richest person in the world in 2019, said that nobody deserves to be a billionaire. That's akin to the zamindars of the past saying nobody should die hungry while clothing and feeding their labour with the absolute minimum.

Ex machina

It's not just automation of the bits that is taking place, it's the automation of atoms as well. For the first time since industrialization, manufacturing is being increasingly automated, and machines are becoming more efficient and cheaper than humans. Many of the most labour-intensive tasks have already been automated away. Advanced economies like the US employ a tinier fraction of their labour force for farming the same amount of land as compared to India, which still has 10 per cent[19] of its workforce engaged in agricultural labour and over 40 per cent in the broader agricultural sector. It is now mostly a question of when—not if—India's farming will be automated.

   Lines of business like the clothing industry will continue to employ a large number of people due to the high level of dexterity required. The pair of jeans you are wearing right now, whether it's an off-brand pair or a Calvin Klein, was cut and stitched by hand by a worker in India, Bangladesh or Indonesia. MIT is still working[20] on robots that can finally pick up apples (yes, robots are that incompetent at finer tasks). Stitching is an extremely dexterous process, requiring constant negotiation of the fabric to keep it taut while sewing, which requires coordination between all fingers. A single straight line of stitching would be an arduous task for current robots. Stitching is akin to playing the guitar; there's an art to it.

But don't let that reassure you. Industrial robots are getting better at dexterity by the day, and even if they can't do what we can with our hands, it won't be too long before there are different robots each suited for a specific task, just like what most workers are trained to do in a production line. Companies are hacking their way out of this in creative ways like stiffening clothes (with starch) before stitching, to remove some of the scrupulousness of the process. They will succeed sooner than later, and these jobs will be automated as well.

Outsourced manufacturing works thanks to the price differentials of labour cost in manufacturing countries like India and Bangladesh versus consumer countries like America. Such business models are called an arbitrage in economics. But as India and China improve their economies, the price differentials will go away and companies will reshore their manufacturing, the trend of making a product in the country it is consumed in. And soon these jobs will be automated away as well. Trump won on the back of the idea of making America great again, part of which envisages bringing manufacturing jobs back.

Reshoring has already started happening, and once the machines come in, it will be more expensive to export and import clothes than having the robots make them locally. These better machines will be cheaper than the foreign labour plus the overhead costs associated with maintaining an overseas operation. This is terrible news for the millions who derive their livelihood from manufacturing, but these are not really the kind of jobs kids aspire to while growing up. Three-quarters of India's workforce does jobs like agriculture and manufacturing that can be replaced by simple mechanical machines. Machines that don't use 'machine-learning' algorithms or AI at all.

Your next co-worker is a robot

Many traditionally human-intensive jobs are already being augmented by tech, making people's skills less central to the equation. Ever had a bad day and a worse Uber driver who wouldn't pay any heed to the Google Maps' traffic-congestion warnings? He thinks he knows these streets better than any American corporation ever will. He knows which route is shorter and quicker because driving is what he has spent his life doing. There's no point fighting to persuade each other when confirming both his and Google's hypothesis that the traffic will cost you more time than taking a bad option. Even when he surrenders to your arguments about Google Map's algorithm and takes that unintuitive path to drop you at the destination on time, he still cribs about the path not taken. In any case, he is always right.

Of course, the algorithm is not always right. We selectively remember the times it didn't alert us about the diversion, but there is a logic behind its accuracy that we generally trust. It gathers data from millions of other cars, analyses the historical traffic-movement patterns of a neighbourhood and predicts the soon-to-be congestion on your path. That's what algorithms do.

Even though this sophisticated synthesis of data has been around for a while, it has gained increasing traction in the past decade. Never before have we had the capacity to collect these many data points nor the computing power to make any meaning of them. Just fifteen years ago, the best way to predict the shortest and quickest path to a destination was individual human intelligence. And that largely meant you were a frequent commuter of that route to have formed at least a stable opinion of traffic movement. The more outgoing you were, the more personal data you had, the smarter your decisions turned out to be.

In this pre–Google Maps era, individuals with greater social freedom turned out to be better decision-makers. To be clear, this wasn't a difference of intelligence or any other genetic advantage; it was merely a case of a larger pool of data. The compounded benefit of better decision-making strengthened their position as better deserving of making important decisions. It created a very self-serving cycle that kept improving the decisions made by them, earning them even greater power. These pocket machines work the same way but have the data of all the earth's drivers combined and augment drivers to be much better at their jobs.

And soon these AI machines will have enough data and precision to make trucking, and driving in general, obsolete. Tesla cars already have guided autopilot capability that can drive the car most of the way, only occasionally requiring driver attention. Tesla's CEO, Elon Musk, expected their cars to be fully autonomous within 2020.[21] Subtracting Musk's optimism and adding factors like government bureaucracy, public acceptance and feature improvement needed for Indian roads and India should be able to see the mass adoption of autonomous cars and trucks in less than two decades, resulting in reduced commute times, improved fuel efficiencies, fewer accidents and a loss of millions of jobs in the transportation industry.

This might paint a gloomy picture for a country struggling with unemployment, but we are still a few decades away from this happening. And although a lot of existing jobs will indeed be obsolete, what is also important is that many entirely new industries will be created. It is a lot easier to see what we are going to lose than being able to perceive and possibly create new opportunities. This shift will mean a lot of low-skilled 'bullshit'[22] jobs will be replaced by more fulfilling ones. It is unconscionable to have a person screw bolts over and over all day, risking their lives,[23] so some of us can drive around in safer cars.

AI should be looked at as a tool that will augment humans to make them better at their jobs as opposed to a sentient system that will replace us altogether,[24] as predicted in so many dystopian movies and novels. These new-generation machines don't have cranks and shafts; they run at the speed of light in silent silicon chips. They perform increasingly complex functions that were impossible just a decade ago. It's the age of smart machines and smarter humans.

Tackling automation

We are not headed for the future that *Wall-E* and *The Matrix* predicted for us. However, a lot of people will need to be retrained if they are to continue working. The main danger we are going to face is that the time span of this revolution is going to be smaller in relative terms, and reskilling of all might not be quick enough. When an innovation like nuclear energy happens, it can take decades to be adopted as every MW of new capacity requires new capital to build. Software, however, does not follow standard supply–demand limitations of tangible products. As Bill Gates stated in his blog: 'Microsoft might spend a lot of money to develop the first unit of a new program, but every unit after that is virtually free to produce.'[25]

When a breakthrough in AI happens, it can be deployed before any government can blink an eyelid. This rapid distribution is good for the world in the long term but makes matters worse for workers. There is no question about whether kids coming into the workforce after this wave will have better opportunities; it is those people that will be caught up mid-wave that will have trouble staying afloat.

All human commerce on this planet has been about making things for each other, and we will always have that. We will always be interested in things others do, whether that is a functional product or art for entertainment. Human creativity knows no bounds, and we will come out much better. But the workers at the time of the shift will need to be retrained, and those that can't be will have to be taken care of as well. Quite a few people are going to find themselves unemployable. We need to start working on public policy that tries to mitigate these effects now.

The road ahead is not going to be comfortable, and government intervention will be needed to make this as smooth a ride as possible. We might not all end up unemployed, but income inequality could increase further. We not only need new policy but a new and more agile framework for governance. Public policy needs to be precautionary instead of reactionary. There are a lot of unknown unknowns that make predictions impossible, but there's a lot we can do now. As the famed programming author Venkat Subramaniam tweeted: 'A good design is not the one that correctly predicts the future, it's one that makes adapting to the future affordable.'[26]

Universal basic income

Universal basic income (UBI) is an idea that is either loved or loathed, with equal intensity. It suggests that every citizen of a country be paid a bare minimum amount necessary for survival. A universal pay does not equate to 'paying people to do nothing'; it just means that we have enough resources to feed and shelter everyone and the most efficient way to do that is to give people money. A basic pay provides a security net so workers can be set free of their soulless manufacturing jobs and can afford to learn new skills and do something more worthy of the human endeavour.

Most PhD students are those that can afford not to start making a living. Higher education is often skewed towards the rich, while the poor end up with low-skill jobs, perpetuating the cycle. The limited places that enable poor people to get a higher education, like JNU, are now under attack for wasting taxpayer money. Right-wing politics often devolves to a politics of paucity of resources. But with the abundance technology brings, that kind of tribalism becomes less and less necessary. We owe it to humanity that everybody is able to pursue their passion, lest we lose the next Einstein to a food-delivery gig. Equality of opportunity is something we should not only strive for but fight for.

In a stable equilibrium like the one the world has largely enjoyed for the past few decades, full-fledged wars are not a common occurrence, the skirmishes with China notwithstanding. This despite the fact that we have one of the most contentious borders in the world. If you think about the world's military, it is essentially the largest experiment in UBI. Most people that join the army are poor and do so as it is a safety net for them. The same applies for most government jobs in the country, which often seem to exist only to give people something to do.

Despite the magnitude of what the world faced in 2020, such events are rare occurrences. We saw government employees, railways and the army deployed to help fight the coronavirus pandemic, in addition to their normal duties. And that's mostly a good thing, as everyone would prefer their tax money to be used for saving lives this side of the border rather than for killing people across the border. India has about 5 million in the military, paramilitary and on reserve. That's about four soldiers per 1000 citizens. Compare that to 0.9 doctors for every 1000 people.[27] Maybe it's time we upskill the military to serve as backup medical providers. Taking bullets out of people's bodies does take more effort than putting them in.

India has several welfare schemes in place, which can instead be clubbed together as a direct cash transfer to people's accounts, something India has already been trying to do. There is no need to give kilos of free rice to someone who has enough food from their small farm but needs education instead. Direct cash transfers will empower people by letting them choose. Whether the math holds up to today's budgetary constraints is up for debate, but it surely will in the near future as technology enables a better standard of living at a lower cost. Money is essentially a store of value, the more value the robots and AI generate, the more wealth we have. If finding the money for such a scheme is an issue, Bill Gates[28] suggests governments can tax the very robots replacing people's jobs, thus capturing a part of the new value generated for the good of all.

There are caveats to this, however. We can't take someone's disability pension and redistribute that money to all, including the non-disabled. Some people will need more money or extra support to meet the same basic requirements, and governments will have to take that into account. Abhijit Banerjee and Esther Duflo suggest making the process of claiming the cash arduous so only the neediest claim it.[29]

The best long-term example we have of UBI comes from Alaska.[30] The American state instituted a permanent fund that manages about 66 billion dollars,[31] made up of about 25 per cent of the money the state generates from its natural resources. The government decided that Alaskans should directly benefit from this money, so the interest generated has been distributed to every Alaskan since 1982.

The residents were used to these payouts and were expecting checks of about $2000 in 2015. But that year saw oil prices hit a low, which reduced the state's funds to do other things and so they cut the pay cheque in half to $1000 per person. In 2018, a new candidate stood for the gubernatorial elections. His main talking point was that he would give everyone $6700 to compensate for the cuts from the previous two years. He won by a landslide. But of course there wasn't enough money to do this, so now he is looking at cutting government funding from other areas such as healthcare and education to fulfil his poll promises. If you play this scenario out to a couple of elections, there's a definite possibility of opposing candidates to offer more and more money to win elections and then have no money in the budget to do anything else the government does. People will undoubtedly take a $20,000 cheque over public transport being maintained, and this could hypothetically result in the state machinery falling apart.

Back in India, in the 2019 elections, Rahul Gandhi offered low-income families Rs 72,000 per year,[32] a sizeable amount of money for most Indians. It was as good a deal as any, and his party has a track record of fulfilling such welfare schemes. He lost badly, but that might be a function of the Congress Party not being able to get the word out, amongst other things. Expect UBI to be a significant electoral issue in the country in the coming years.

There are of course problems with this. A real UBI will have to be really universal. Factories reshored to the US will cause job losses in Bangladesh, not the US. And given how politics all over the world is seeing a regression from internationalism and becoming inwards-looking and tribalistic, it is hard to expect American citizens to be okay with their tax money being used to pay unemployed Bangladeshis. Modi's India might show concern for the 'persecuted Hindus' in Bangladesh, but there's not much hope for external help for most of the country. UBI is not an end-all. We will still need work. Developing nations will have to switch to whatever industries come up next to survive. And what we need before UBI are robust policies that will help us smoothen the bumps.

We need to understand that not everybody has to contribute directly to the economy. According to recent GOI data, only about 50 per cent of the country's working-age population is either working or actively looking for work.[33] So even a magical 100 per cent employment rate does not mean that the entire working-age population is engaged in the economy. We, as a species, are not just driven by the need to feed and shelter ourselves, as pointed out in Maslow's hierarchy of needs.[34] We have a much higher desire to do something that matters. The majority of the people not looking for a job are unfortunately women, and they are doing a lot of work; it's just that not all work gets counted as 'work' as it is 'invisible'. People engaged in social work, community building etc., should be able to live comfortably as well. Of course, we will have more women in the workforce by percentage, but the total working population is likely to decrease. Maybe the men will find time to raise their kids as well. As automation frees us from tiresome drudgery, we will not have to work just to get by. We will work on what we want to work on, and this will result in newer, more creative industries that we don't have the bandwidth to invent now.

Do note that automation has been happening for a while already, but we are yet to see an increase in unemployment numbers. But it makes sense to engineer a solution for the worst-case scenario. UBI should be looked at as a piece to the puzzle and a contingency for the short term rather than as the entire plan. There are other public policy decisions we will need to make.

Public policy

The current government is trying to get outside investors interested in manufacturing in India by spending a considerable amount of its money and energy on PR for the same. The problem with it being that reshoring has already started, and it's too late for us to really replicate what China did. Over the next decade, industrial 3D printing will get cheaper and more high-resolution, hence reducing the world's dependence on nations like Japan and China for their manufacturing expertise.

Countries have traditionally gotten rich by manufacturing for others. Britain got rich by doing it for the colonies. China got rich by doing it for everyone. When this external demand slows, they start smoking their own supplies, transitioning from a maker economy to a consumer one. Except we don't really have anyone left to sell to.

Instead, we should focus on 'Make in India' for India. The upcoming economic boom will increase consumer demand, and we should make sure that that is fulfilled locally. Samsung and Mi now make many of their smartphone devices sold in India within India.

The transport ministry will be better off beginning the work of mitigation now rather than after all the driving jobs in transportation are lost, which is in contrast to transport minister Gadkari's[35] naive stand of how he won't let autonomous driving happen in the country. It's better to fund the revolution than bet against it. The US and China know that very well, and we don't want to be left far behind either.

Both the US and China have been investing heavily in AI. India has enough people working on AI already; all we need is a focused approach from the government so that we can make use of the human resources effectively. This is where we could be a serious contender if enough money is poured in so that our country can capture a fair share of the value created due to automation as wealth.

And last but not least, regulate AI. Although it may seem that it's too early to worry about AI being dangerous, we don't have to wait to achieve superintelligence for AI to be able to have real undesirable consequences. It makes sense to have some framework for the development of AI that, at its core, is not racially or gender biased.

When we train algorithms on human-processed data sets, human biases could very easily translate to code. As we have seen in this chapter and in Accountability, AI and machine-learning algorithms, when implemented with little oversight, can lead to racially or gender-biased outcomes. It is up to us to be cognizant enough so that the systems we built are more inclusive than humans have been in the past. Regulation could help push development in the right direction.

Reskilling

In addition to UBI, we would need free reskilling of employees, at centres that take care of food and shelter. As a first step, the government should open reskilling centres as well as job centres to connect employers to low-skill workers and manage their transition well. These would not only provide a list of available jobs but counsel people as to which industry to switch to based on their potential talent and also recommend classes they can take to learn a new trade. Just like in industrialization, most of the problems will be faced by people caught in the automation wave, people that grow up after it will be far better off than ones that grew up before it.

The tech companies that are now creating new gig-economy jobs will be the same ones that automate these away. But regulating such jobs is complex. California recently enacted a gig-worker's law that requires companies like Uber to pay full wages and benefits. Vox, a media outlet, celebrated the new law right before firing 200 of its contract workers.[36]

Uber will eventually switch out the drivers for robots. The primary cost of an Uber ride is the human that drives the car, and that is inefficient not only for the rider but the driver as well. The drivers have to grind so much that if they fill up gas outside of their trips they lose money. Akshay finds himself at a CNG pump on almost all his Uber rides, because when the driver requests to fill up the car during the trip, the author tends to oblige lest the trip turns into a guilt trip.

India has in fact suggested several changes to its labour laws as well, just that they favour the industry over the labour. We need progression, not regression, laws that safeguard the interest of the labour without hampering the industry. A tough line to walk, but that's the nature of the beast.

Deus ex machina

This new economy will come with quite a few added benefits, like being able to spend much fewer hours commuting to and from work. Indians on average spend an average of ninety minutes[37] on their one-way commute to work. That's a lot of wasted hours that could be spent doing something better. This is the reason remote work, or telecommuting, is on the rise. In the knowledge economy, it is not always a necessity to be present in the same shared space, even when working with a larger team. Many people are now turning to co-working spaces, regardless of whether they work for a large company or have their own business. It does not matter where your co-workers are—you can still seamlessly work with them and save time. And these benefits will get compounded. People won't have to live where their offices are, which would in turn bring down rents, unclog the roads and reduce a lot of pollution. The travel that we do undertake will be in autonomous cars, freeing us to do something else. One positive outcome of the 2020 pandemic seems to be an acceleration of work-from-home situations and at least a temporary reduction in avoidable commute.

Wealth is not a zero-sum game. An abundant society will provide for everyone, even if the wealth gap stays. A poor person in Delhi today enjoys much better healthcare than what the Sultan of Delhi had in the 14th century, with all his gold. When the world gets richer, everyone benefits. The services and products reserved for the rich get cheaper. When people share concerns about how automation will lead to greater volatility in the job markets, they are failing to see how we are getting better at allocating resources more equitably over time.

Our standard of what is basic has been evolving. From food and shelter, we moved to include education and healthcare. And the quality of these metrics also increases. We go from making services accessible first and then affordable. Look at Delhi, in the past five years alone it has gone from offering free health check-ups to free medicines at mohalla clinics to free operations for common ailments. Delhi is now moving to supply free Internet as it becomes clear that it is just as essential to life as water. In times of war, states moved to control water supplies in regions of strife; they have now evolved to shut down the Internet. The belief that the Internet is a basic right, to be shared by all, whether they choose to enable or disable it, is up to the people we elect.

This is, however, not going to be a socialist utopia. It's just that the basic bar will be higher for everybody. Beyond that, regular capitalistic forces will be in play. We will still be working, just a lot fewer hours. Data tells us that working hours come down as economies advance. [38] We will have more time to live rather than just being stuck in the cycle of a nine-to-five existence while losing the bigger picture. We will use the resulting extra time to pursue interests outside of work, try side hustles, engage with friends and family or just read a good book.

The machines we make will make us. They will script our fate. These new gods will allow us to work less and live a little. Beyoncé was asking the right questions when she mused on her track 'Ghost'[39]—*All the people on the planet working 9 to 5 just to stay alive, how come?*

3

Data: Why I Don't Have Aadhaar

A.P. Jithender Reddy, a member of Parliament (MP) from the state of Telangana, usually doesn't read the *Hindustan Times*. But on 24 March 2017, his office was busy answering angry calls from the readers of the newspaper which had announced that morning that Reddy was one of the members of Parliament with the lowest attendance. If it wasn't Parliament where Reddy spent his time, then where was he touring on public money? The other MPs featured in 'MPs with the Worst Attendance' were similarly panicked. And the *Hindustan Times* isn't your usual fake-news portal, so the front-page headline held very high authority.

The newspaper cited a credible not-for-profit think tank, Parliamentary Research Service (PRS), as its source for the data. PRS is the only major organization devoted solely to legislative data collection and is frequently used by journalists and researchers. All the data uploaded by them on the website is error-free and is available for the general public to download as a Microsoft Excel file.

PRS's own data was based on the registers signed by the MPs to enter Parliament. But the PRS data didn't hold Reddy guilty to the same charge as the Hindustan Times. What went wrong?

The Excel sheet, actually! Reddy's actual attendance percentage is about 90, not 9. If you look at the names of other poor performers, you will begin to notice a pattern:[1]

MP	Attendance Percentage
A. Anhwar Raajhaa	5
A. Arunmozhithevan	6
A.P. Jithender Reddy	9
A.T. Nana Patil	10
Abhijit Mukherjee	15

Can't guess the blunder yet? Look at the list of MPs with 100 per cent attendance:

MP	Attendance Percentage
Tathagata Satpathy	100
Tej Pratap Singh Yadav	100
Thangso Baite	100
Thokchom Meinya	100
Thota Narasimham	100
Thupstan Chhewang	100

There must have been a serious inclination to negligence in those with their first names beginning with an A, or a surprising sincerity in everybody with a name starting with a T. Coincidences usually don't try so hard.

Aparisim 'Bobby' Ghosh, the then editor-in-chief of the *Hindustan Times*, explained in his testimony to the Privilege Committee of the Parliament:

> The data we got from PRS is accurate. The error was on our side when we analysed the data. They were absolutely right that the data they gave us is one hundred per cent correct. When we put it on our Excel sheet, we took all the names of MPs alphabetically and on another column, we looked at their attendance record. First, it was done alphabetically. Then, you change the column to see who has the highest and who has the lowest. Since the system was bad at our end, not at PRS end, because it was not properly configured, the column with attendance changed, but the column with names did not change. That is why, you will notice that most of the names are starting with 'A' because the alphabetical order on the first column just remained as it was and we did not spot that. We assumed that both sets of column would change, which they should if the system is properly put together. It was not.[2]

Yes, one of the largest newspapers accused the parliamentarians of the world's largest democracy of not doing their job because of an Excel sheet blunder. Nobody involved in the preparation of a front-page headline, including the journalists, editors, graphic designers and the technology team, had been able to sense the anomaly in the strange pattern of data!

The correct attendance of all alleged worst performers was above 70 per cent. Among them, Abhijit Mukherjee, a member of the Indian National Congress and the son of the then

President Pranab Mukherjee, had an attendance of 97 per cent, quite a deviation from the mentioned 15 per cent.

The *Hindustan Times* recognized the gravity of the mistake and issued an unprecedented apology[3] on its front page, unlike what usually happens, when a pale apology for a corrigendum is buried in unnoticeable corners. But the newspaper's repentance the following day could hardly undo the damage.

hindustan**times** corrigendum

In the infographic titled 'House Call' published in Hindustan Times' edition dated 24.3.17, the data on the attendance of MPs of Lok Sabha were erroneous. The mistake was made in computing and identifying the members with the highest and lowest attendance. HT deeply regrets the error. The corrected attendance figures of both MPs and parties are:

PARTY-WISE ATTENDANCE*

All figures for the 16th Lok Sabha, till last week
*For parties with more than 10 MPs

79.6% TDP	82.1% Biju Janata Dal	66.6% Trinamool Congress	86.5% Bharatiya Janata Party	82.9% AIADMK	79.4% Congress

MPs erroneously identified as the worst performers; their accurate attendance is:

74% A Anwhar Raajhaa — Tamil Nadu, AIADMK

89% A Arunmozhithevan — Tamil Nadu, AIADMK

87% AP Jithender Reddy — Telangana, TRS

87% AT Nana Patil — Maharashtra, BJP

97% Abhijit Mukherjee — West Bengal, Congress

MPs who were reported to have 100% attendance; the correct figures are:

91% ■ Tathagata Satpathy — Odisha, BJD
81% ■ Tej Pratap Singh Yadav — Uttar Pradesh, SP
91% ■ Thangso Baite — Manipur, Congress
91% ■ Thokchom Meinya — Manipur, Congress
95% ■ Thota Narasimham — Andhra Pradesh, TDP
91% ■ Thupstan Chhewang — Jammu and Kashmir, BJP
96% ■ Udasi Shivkumar — Karnataka, BJP

Source: PRS Legislative Research, Lok Sabha

Source: 'Clarification, apology regarding an infographic about Lok Sabha MPs' attendance published in HT's March 23 edition', Twitter post, 24 March 2017, twitter.com/httweets/status/845306863344279556.

But A.P. Jithender Reddy wasn't satisfied with the sincerity of the correction; he complained:

> While the report was carried out on the top with the pictures of the supposedly erring members and commentary citing how absence of members raise questions of accountability and commitment. A corrigendum on the other hand is published on the bottom left corner stating that the corrected and prior wrong figures taking far less space than the false report.[4]

And Jithender is right—the corrections are almost never as prominent as the headlines, they cannot be.

The very consequentialist nature of this error is helpful in understanding how false information is weaponized. This fake news is easy to spread but impossible to contain. The thousands of constituents who heard or read about the false report are not users who can simply be sent a targeted update notification. The epidemic unleashed by word of mouth is only accelerated with casual habits of content consumption. When you can believe whatever you want and conveniently find a link that corroborates your belief, you don't need the news to be true—it just has to look true.

The *Hindustan Times* editors may have genuinely made an error, but this is how the media is being weaponized to float conspiracy theories, hint at culpability or even peddle absurd alternative possibilities. The important part in this tradition is not to get it right but to sow the seed of doubt.

By the evening of 24 March 2017, one of the biggest Indian Internet content companies—ScoopWhoop (SW),[5] had already used the HT piece to create an even more succinct graphic for an article titled 'Here's a Look at the MPs Who Are Most Regular and Most Absent in Parliament'. In other words, SW was trying to make easy the consumption of news from traditional outlets for its own young audience—nothing wrong with that.

They never carried an apology. Why would they? They aren't journalists, and they don't pretend to be. The few journalists hired by the listicle company were fired quickly enough on other pretexts.[6] In fact, the readers of SW pointed out that the site also got wrong the party of one of the MPs— BJP instead of BJD. Nobody seemed to notice the symmetry of As and Ts.

The generosity of forgiveness to one newspaper can create a very dangerous precedent in a democracy where insinuations can become weapons of politics. Media with credibility and substantial reach can occasionally sell favourable errors to the highest bidder and issue clarifications on a later date, much like how match-fixing works. Traditional publications bear an additional burden of authority. They are our antidote to the fake-news crisis, expected to fact-check the information dump, not get it wrong themselves. And each time they are wrong, the overall cynicism towards all of their peers increases irreversibly. Frequency or history is irrelevant, being unlucky (or careless) works fine to destroy trust.

Measuring the wrong things

The number of days spent in the Parliament is a limited metric of merit for an MP. By adopting a very raw data point, the publications run the risk of making the wrong things count. What is the contribution of the most attending MPs? Are they only sitting and watching life pass by? What kind of questions are they asking, what bills are they proposing? How are their constituencies doing? It should be harder to look good as an MP on the front page.

The HT gaffe is a study of the many problems of information and data that we haven't quite discussed in the public square before. In this case, the editors were simply unprofessional in not checking up with MPs before publishing the story, but there is something much larger at stake here.

The problem with the HT story is only that it made a blunder in processing the correct data. If it hadn't, it would have felt like a relatively unremarkable story. Transparency of data feels so obviously central to democracy that there could be no questions of any trouble with making public a basic record like attendance. After all, the same newspapers have told us that each minute of Parliament costs Rs 2.5 lakh![7] We deserve to know the extent of utility derived from all the bills we pay for vacationing MPs, right?

Maybe not.

The infancy of the Internet is over and we need to get over our infatuation with numbers to more closely look at how they shape our lives. We continue to treat truth and data with neutral ease, expecting the right man to win at last.

The HT story champions data transparency without the consciousness of the grave ramifications it can have on the work of elected representatives. The data is publicly available but by putting it on the front page in graphics, the editors buy into the false virtue of transparency.

Before engaging with the attendance record of the parliamentarians, we need to have a conversation about the ways in which it affects the work they do. It is entirely possible that constituents benefit from having their MPs outside the Parliament rather than inside.

All MPs don't play an equal role within the Parliament. Their impact on policy is dependent on many factors outside the control of individual MPs, such as the overall strength of their party in the Parliament and the additional roles they are entrusted with. In India, MPs cannot vote by their free will. They have to comply with the party whip to protect themselves against anti-defection laws, which means the outcome of the most important bills is pre-decided. Dr Shashi Tharoor can hope to only add more YouTube subscribers or Twitter followers with his eloquent speeches in the Parliament because even if he manages to persuade any MP of the ruling party to concur with him, they cannot vote against their party. It is important to make contrary points of view heard, but with the present codes of conduct, hearing is all you can do.

When, in 2018, India's ranking jumped from 130th in 2016 to 77th in the Ease of Doing Business (EODB) rankings issued by the World Bank, it caught everyone, except the government, by surprise. The ranking's purpose is to document how small- and medium-size companies navigate regulators, costs, time and bureaucracy in a country. They officially visit the largest cities and have various interactions with professionals to assess a country.

If the EODB rankings were right, India should have been receiving higher foreign investment, at least much higher than in 2013, when it was stagnant in the rankings. The economy was not bullish in 2018 by other measures either. Then what went wrong?

The answer lies in what the late former finance minister Arun Jaitley, at a press meet celebrating the upward tick, announced: 'You have to literally crack the code.'[8]

EDOB has ten quantitative indicators, all of them well known. And Delhi and Mumbai are the only two cities it looks at. Improving the real business environment and entrepreneurship friendliness in a country cannot be a trick, but this ranking is a mathematics paper with ten questions and two chapters for the syllabus. You don't have to be smart, only smart enough.

The Modi government was interested in the rankings since the very beginning. It tried lobbying the World Bank to correct various metrics unfavourable to India and allegedly even had a letter written to the Bank's then chief economist Kaushik Basu.[9] The Indian government's angst mattered—it is one of the largest developing countries with infrastructure needs. How does a bank earn money? Through interest on loans. Who borrows the most? Whoever has a lot of poor people.

India's bold reforms for being business-friendly included removing the requirement of a rubber stamp to open a bank account and doing away with the need for a cancelled cheque as part of the employee provident fund process. To ease cross-border trading, we abolished the mandatory hard-copy filing of documents for traders and improved the online customs payment gateway. Doesn't take a village, or rocket science. It is a good placebo for a country struggling with a tough business environment, except that it only makes us sicker.

For Akshat's start-up, it took him more than six months to 'accept' money from a foreign investor, and at the time of writing this book, he is still filing compliance documents with the RBI. The documentation alone has cost him 5 per cent of the total investment.

Rankings, graphs, tables and pie charts will confess whatever you want them to confess if you torture them long enough. A few spreadsheets and everybody looks like an expert. Until we learn to read data right, we are going to find ourselves in the destructive company of demagogues whose primary indulgence is short-term optics.

When you cannot change the measurements, the old trick is to change the measure. Gross domestic product (GDP), the metric by which most countries gauge themselves, is not perfect by any argument. Due to its complexity, there are several things you can tweak in the formula to produce the desired results. And even when you arrive at a broadly acceptable number, 'it measures everything, in short, except that which makes life worthwhile'.[10]

But when countries not faring very well on the existing metrics devise a new one, there has to be more reading between the lines. Such is the case of Bhutan, India's tiny Himalayan neighbour. Its best-known export is gross national happiness (GNH), first proposed by its former king in the 1970s. Happiness per se is not a bad aspiration, but a poor monarchy dropping out of the race can do many other things too. The government may be hiding religious persecution, an abysmal economic performance or avoiding too much attention about its undemocratic polity. The critiques of GNH call it 'Government Needs Help' since the government keeps juggling one economic challenge after another. We know this isn't just election propaganda because GNH indexes providing global comparisons have ranked it around the 100th spot for several years.

In India, the Ministry of Human Resource Development was also angry at Indian universities not finding a place in the global rankings. Our conclusion from the exclusion in these lists was to invent our own domestic ranking. Thus the National Institutional Ranking Framework was born in 2015. It is a methodology to rank Indian colleges and universities.

Most of us are not Jaitley with a job. We were jubilant at our universities having a number, not how they arrived at it.

Akshat wrote a piece for The Quint[11] in 2018, studying the absurdities of the report. The Research and Professional Practice score of Jawaharlal Nehru University (42.60) was lower than that of Banaras Hindu University (50.76), Anna University (60.76), the University of Hyderabad (45.34), Jadavpur University (57.07) and even the Manipal Academy of Higher Education (44.15).

And according to the college-ranking table, you are likely to find better opportunities if you graduate from the nondescript Ramakrishna Mission Vidyamandira, Howrah (Graduate Outcome Score of 86.08), than the Lady Shri Ram College for Women (GOS 81.94) or even the Shri Ram College of Commerce (GOS 83.48).

Of course, it is hard to access the data behind the simple tables in newspaper reports. But if you think only journalists in the country are doing a bad job at examining what they are served, you'd be wrong. A lot of it stems from the newspaper's understanding of its own role in public policy and debate.

It escapes criticism by projecting itself as a neutral describer of the state of affairs when it is indeed the sculptor of many public issues and debates. News makes the news. The media companies have an interest in underplaying their own importance.

It's a problem plaguing not just media companies with data editors but all of us at large. We are still making sense of this new world where evil doesn't come dressed as evil. It comes as a decontextualized hint at anything random. It doesn't tell you who the bad guy is, but it trusts you to weave a story anyway.

The identity and the intent of the data collector is also an important data item. The same sets of data can be made to talk very different talks. Read the following headlines from three different national dailies:

'Census 2011 shows Islam is the fastest growing religion in India'[12]

'Hindus dip to below 80 per cent of population; Muslim share up, slows down'[13]

'Muslim families shrinking fastest among Indian communities'[14]

None of them is wrong or inaccurate. In fact, the first and third papers are owned by the same media company. The data is from the religious census based on the 2011 general census.

Firstly, let us look at the facts that all reports rightly talk about. The percentage of Hindus in India did decline to 79.8 per cent (or below 80 per cent for the first time), even if by only 0.2 per cent. The total number of Hindus did not decrease, only the percentage did.

Islam had the fastest growth rate amongst all religions at 24.6 per cent, whereas Hindus had a rate of 16.8 per cent. Basically, the number of Muslims babies being born per Muslim were still the largest.

The decline in the rate of growth of Muslims is also the highest—which means Muslims are growing the fastest, but the pace is slowing down most, compared to other religions. It is similar to the population growth of India also. We have been adding a lot of people since we became a country, but that rate has been slowing down. From 1961–71, we grew at 24.8 per cent and slowed down to 17.7 per cent from 2001–11.

Data is a necessary ingredient in discovery, but you need a human to select it, shape it and then turn it into insight.

Whichever story you buy is the story you will be sold. Afraid of Muslims taking over your Hindu Rashtra? Here's why you are right. You believe that religious fanatics have been spreading communal vitriol? Here's why you are right too.

Daniel Levitin in his all-important work *A Field Guide to Lies and Statistics* makes a similar point, 'People choose what to count, how to go about counting, which of the resulting numbers they will share with us, and which words they will use to describe and interpret those numbers.'[15]

Fear, uncertainty and doubt (FUD) of data

The plural of data is not always greater well-being. Obfuscation is the practice of the purposeful flooding of irrelevant data to add noise to people's decision-making powers. In essence, making it difficult for people to filter the useful from the irrelevant—just confuse everybody!

The same strategy is being actively used by authoritarian governments to shut down activists on the Internet. Blocking accounts on Twitter or launching a hack attempt at the platform aren't fruitful endeavours, for they bring in the bad press that you are trying to avoid.

Look at the anatomy of how a conversation is created on social media. For example, you hear about a report of political corruption at the highest levels of government. You create a hashtag like #CorruptionHurts. Your friends and their friends share it, popular pages use the same hashtag and some big celebrities also join in. Twitter picks up your chatter and features it in the 'Trending' section.

The leader in question is of course threatened by this public mobilization. So he/she gets his/her own troll army to use the same hashtag to either tweet gibberish, highlighting the corruption of the Opposition or calling the dissenters a gang of hooligans. When the next person tries to click on the hashtag to learn more or search the trend, it will appear to be a partisan issue where one can pick their monster or declare the whole thing a hoax. Unimaginable? We don't know if this was government-sponsored obfuscation but this is what happened during the Russian protests of 2011, when people came out against ballot stuffing and voting irregularities in the elections. After the Russian police detained protestors at Moscow's Triumfalnaya Square, activists created a massive tweetstorm with the hashtag #триумфальная (Triumfalnaya). It wasn't much later that the same anti-government hashtag was polluted by pro-Kremlin messages. If you never heard about it, they did a good job.

Scholars call this censorship by noise.

During the mid-20th century, when the link between tobacco and cancer was becoming clear and all leading researchers seemed to be reaching a unanimous agreement over the same, the tobacco industry employed what would be one of the most effective instances of information overload of all time. They understood that the results of the research were correct, which would plunge their commercial interests into jeopardy. It was going to be pretty difficult to manufacture evidence that made tobacco look any more fit for human consumption than it actually was.[16]

But how many people were really going to read the research papers? Almost nobody except some science journalists. The truth was only as damning as it was made to look. Tobacco companies figured that no research was ever too arrogant to not accept any challenges to its findings. That's the basic premise of good science. The difference between a false theory and a not-so-false one is only that of probability. If you could somehow make the established conclusion look uncertain, you didn't have to worry much about what was more probable.

The tobacco lobby added noise to the system, a technique now used by the chemical and fossil-fuel industries. They began funding scientists and giving generous grants to research groups to challenge earlier research. Even after being ordered in 2006 to take down false claims ('low-tar cigarettes reduce risk') in the US, they continue to insist that new research suggests otherwise.

When you place emphasis on an alternative theory that may or may not have anything to do with the primary theory in question, you are effectively trying to convince the government and the people about how any decision based on real research will also be too reductionist.

The correlation gets weakened without even attacking its validity. Montesquieu noted In *The Spirit of Laws*: useless laws weaken the necessary laws.

Information supply is not always useful and can rather be abused to achieve dangerous means. There's always a context and intent involved in what is useful as data. It requires real people to make real judgements about what is useful, how much is useful, how wrong can they allow themselves to be and what is an intended effect of their efforts. Thirst in itself doesn't become important until Coca-Cola goes out to measure and document it the way it does.

Trimming data that doesn't add anything to the user's knowledge often helps in better achievement of goals. It is said that the death of one soldier is a tragedy, a million is a statistic. Furnishing a list of a hundred thousand people who died in a riot and expecting people to count them all to understand the scale and intensity of the event helps only to confuse them further.

Governments know this well enough and use it intelligently after declaring access to information a fundamental right. Easing the process of seeking information is only one part of the job but making sure the supplied information is helpful is quite another.

A few years ago, while writing a report, Akshat used the Right to Information (RTI) portal to file an inquiry with the CBSE. The RTI Act of 2005 allows the public official thirty days, which they usually utilize in full, to respond to a query. After waiting for a month to no avail, Akshat filed something

called the 'First Appeal' to his query. It helps one challenge
the response of the public official, seek clarification or bring
to notice a lack of response. That takes another forty days of
waiting. He got a response from the First Appeal officer after
almost two months of his original query, directing the CBSE
officer to reply to him within fifteen days. That didn't happen.
In addition to all this back and forth happening online, if
you are dissatisfied with the outcome, your final appeal along
with any replies you received need to be printed, attested and
posted to the SIC (State Information Commission) or the
CIC (Central Information Commission), who in turn take
their own sweet time to respond.

After three months, Akshat was tired, so he didn't follow
up. The context of a very small data set that he had been
looking for was no longer important. In another experience,
he once got a response that had no relevance to the question
posed. The government officer probably knew how few
people would bother to follow up.

The RTI website itself is sluggish and annoying. An
error pops up if you input certain characters, but it wouldn't
tell you which prohibited character in your text it is referring
to (go figure!). If you make a mistake in submitting the
form, it will lose all the entered data, and you need to begin
afresh. The design chapter talks in greater detail about how
you can consciously build stuff to encourage or discourage
people to make choices. Only a minority has the patience
and perseverance to chase their query to an answer, defeating
design obstacles. In other words, until you want it badly, it
will do everything it can to make sure you don't get what
you want.

The above accessibility is very subjective indeed. Relevant, succinct, seamless or user-friendly are vague virtues that are tough to fight.

It is foolish to say an explicit 'no' to activists campaigning for more information access. One can allow them and just make the process so exhausting that they give up along the way. The art of obfuscation is something all governments excel in. In the best-case scenario, they do this on purpose. In the worst case, they cannot do any better.

When data comes home

The attendance records of your MPs, the number of government licences required to do business, the population growth, the ratio of students and teachers and policy expenditure are all examples of important data sets, even though this is a tiny percentage of the about 2.5 quintillions of bytes human beings produce every day.

Your relatively inexpensive Xiaomi weighing scale knows which member of the family has stepped on it and automatically logs the weight and a few other metrics in your account. Apple Watch can detect heart attacks and has saved people's lives by calling emergency services just in time.[17] Alexa knows when you turn your lights on and off, what temperature you prefer your air conditioning at and what music you like. Amazon of course already knows everything you buy. Trackers in our browsers track everything we do, what sites we visit and how long we spend on those sites. This data collected by various data brokers is then combined to get an idea of what we may like before we know it even exists.

YouTube often suggests bands that Akshay ends up loving, while Google knows just what he needs to buy and keeps shoving that at him continuously for months.

When we aren't choosing and clicking stuff, we are still producing data. Tinder's algorithm is learning your preferences even when you reject matches. Passively scrolling on Facebook and not engaging with any post means data for the company about what you don't like. In fact, this negative data is more valuable since it helps in building an even more precise profile of the person.

There is a bunch of data about us collected by these private companies that we voluntarily give to them and trust they will use for appropriate tasks only. But sometimes companies break that trust, and in some of these cases, they do get sued and punished (often by the European Union).

But what if the data-collecting agency was the government itself? And what if this data was being collected without consent? Who would sue the government? In 2013, a National Security Agency (NSA) private contractor called Edward Snowden found himself dealing with the same dilemma, when he realized the sheer scope of the data the US government was collecting on its citizens and everyone in the world.[18] The NSA was collecting metadata from calls and email communications for practically every US citizen.

Metadata does not have the contents of the message itself but banal information on who contacted whom at what point, for how long and their location were at any given point of the day. This is enough to map out a person's social life and daily routine right to the minute. I don't need to know what you chat with your mother about, but if you chat with her thrice a day and each call is upwards of ten minutes, I know she is an emotional lever to leverage.

Snowden's belief was that data regulation attacks the wrong end of the data pipeline because it tries to restrict government overreach after the data has been collected. The data should never be collected in the first place, i.e. stop the inflow. Once the data is stored and aggregated, it's only a matter of time before it gets misused. Even if you believe today's government is acting in good faith, there will be a government that you won't trust, and they will have the ability to use that data against you. And they most likely will use it.

A similar gargantuan scheme is afoot in India, called the Aadhaar. Most people think that Aadhaar is a "national ID". However, it is not a nationality identifier—that would be the National Register of Citizens of India. Someone with a long-term visa, who is a minority from countries including Pakistan, can legally get an Aadhaar.[19] Now, moving on to the second half of that misnomer. Aadhaar is not an ID either unlike the PAN and Voter ID, which are in fact required to get an Aadhaar. An ID works when it can verify your identity. Aadhaar does not do its own identity verification but places that trust on your other IDs.

Aadhaar is mostly an authentication system, much like the two-factor authentication used by companies like Google and Facebook who send you a one-time password (OTP) to verify your login. Except it is far more dangerous, because instead of an OTP shared over SMS, it stores your biometric data. Even though this government has claimed this data is protected by '5 feet walls'[20] but that is just not how digital security works. Aadhaar data has already been leaked several times,[21] and when it does, there is no recourse. Due to its permanent nature, you cannot get your number nullified and get a new one made, yet.

The Aadhaar—in part due to a function of how fast the government rolled this out and got everybody on the system and in part due to design by intent—just does not have the essential checks in place to ensure the data's safety. A lot of the enrolments were done by third-party providers, which is very scary given they were handling biometric data. It is pretty easy to steal biometrics, just like how credit cards can be skimmed even in genuine ATMs, and the enrolment was not something that should have been outsourced. A lot of third-party providers have even reused biometrics to make fake IDs, just to get paid for more Aadhaar registrations.

Akshay does not have an Aadhaar yet, and plans to keep it that way as long as he can. Biometrics is a very dangerous method of authenticating anything and are nowhere near as secure as people think they are. You can always get a new OTP or even reset a stolen password very easily. But you can never change your fingerprints. Or your eyeballs. So if someone has your fingerprints, they can do whatever they want with them for life, leaving you with no recourse whatsoever of being able to stop them. And stealing biometrics does not require plucking out eyeballs as we saw in the movie *Angels and Demons*.

All you need to clone a fingerprint is a high-enough-resolution photo of someone's hand and you can fake their fingerprints very easily. Hackers have demonstrated cloning fingerprints of public figures[22] just from press photos taken from quite a distance. And once someone has your fingerprint, they have them for life. There is no way to reset them. Biometrics is the crudest form of authentication, and our government has decided to run with it.

And the government is neither satisfied nor do they want to limit Aadhaar's use to within government agencies—not that they enjoy a great track record of keeping this data secure. They want Aadhaar to be an authentication platform and allow private companies to use it as well.

Nandan Nilekani designed Aadhaar as a platform[23] that can make money for the government by providing authentication services to private companies for a fee.[24] This exposes your data to multiple players, and at this point, it is all but guaranteed to leak.

The government gives your Aadhaar number to private players to authenticate instead of keeping that data on its servers and just giving a success/failure response to the third party. A credit-card payment gateway has better protection, as your credit-card details are never shared with the site you are shopping on (only a success/failure message is provided). Aadhaar has finally started doing this, but this has not been widely adopted, at the time of writing this book. Many services just take a photocopy of an Aadhaar card. An Aadhaar card is just a printout of your Aadhaar number; it was not designed to be photocopied and used for verification. After an uproar from privacy rights advocates, the government added the option to generate a single virtual Aadhaar number, but that puts the onus of security on the user. The large portion of India's population will not figure out how to use this, and even when they do, a single virtual ID at a time means it is only a matter of time before it gets mapped to your real one, and most people won't generate a new one.

There are traumatizing stories of starvation deaths of people[25] who had been refused rations on account of their inability to authorize their Aadhaar because their fingerprints had been worn out by hard labour. But they do not come close to the core issue of the platform. The primary problem with the Aadhaar project is not its draconian level of data centralization that is potentially vulnerable to misuse and abuse, but the fact that we haven't yet had a real public debate about such a level of data interconnectedness. The biometric system failing occasionally to deprive people of essential services linked with Aadhaar is a distraction from the real horror of a full-proof biometric identity system that can deprive people of essential services if it is ordered to do so.

By making one identity mandatory to a real-time data-processing system, it threatens to reduce the fate of human beings to a singular perspective. It means no alternative possibilities from the system other than the one preferred by whoever is in charge of the database. That's more power to any individual or a group of individuals than what's historically been permissible. While we do have a list of heinous actions classified as immoral and criminal, there is a less-extreme range of activities that fall in the grey area. We consent to allow our voted representatives to control the definition of what's the right thing to do, but we don't assign infallibility to that judgement. The power of democracy lies in keeping windows open, but by denying that space for dissent by technologically centralizing all activities to one arbiter, we make it almost impossible to allow any kind of dissent. That's the opposite of democracy, if anything. In the state vs individual debate, if Ayn Rand was on one extreme end, the Aadhaar is on the other.

The Delhi government introduced CCTV cameras in classrooms[26] to improve the accountability of teachers and the school, and announced that parents would be provided access to the live feed so that they could make sure their pupils were indeed engaged in studying. Their perspective was that government schools had created distrust in the minds of guardians, and additional accountability might be able to make up for it. The same government was lauded for bringing in the 'Happiness Curriculum'. We expect they understand what constant observation can take away from the process of learning.

Having the privacy to make errors and learn from them without trouble is the minimum requirement for independent thought and innovation. Climate change won't be solved at a place where your hairstyle is also regulated (North Korea). Standardization, centralization and surveillance have their perks, but they are tiny trophies compared to what we lose.

As these technologies become cheaper, more and more complex problems will be fixed by such convenient yet broken solutions. Sometimes we must be prepared to resist the temptations of efficiency to preserve everything else that we care about in life and what makes it beautiful.

Why care?

Do you know someone who received a call purporting to be from a digital-wallet company, asking you to transfer money?

Only stupid people fall for scams, you might have thought and carried on with your life. But how did the scammers get your friend's number in the first place? The chances are, they got it from one of the hundreds of places that store this information. The more you give away your number at checkout counters at stores and newsletter subscriptions, the more points of failure you are creating for yourself.

When you give away your name and number to a store during checkout, they already have all the data the scammer needed in their database. They might just sell all the data they have to one of these scammers, no hacking required. Digital-marketing agencies will often buy records of people that shopped at a particular high-end store to then target other products to these people. That's not all—these 'leads' get resold several times over.

Truecaller, an app that tells you the name of the person calling you before you have met them, now has almost everyone's name and number in their database. How did they get it? When you installed the app, you uploaded your entire contact list on to their servers, damaging not only your own privacy but that of everyone you know as well.

New-age conglomerates like Facebook and Google are built on your mined data, but surveillance is a relatively new trend in the capitalist world. Earlier, privacy was much more profitable for industries. In the 1600s, the rise of the bourgeoisie saw for the first time people being afforded private rooms and offices and children their own physical spaces. The Industrial Revolution was built on a sense of privacy and every man being in possession of their own personal items, which in turn fuelled demand. Even the tech revolution was termed the 'personal computer' revolution, with everybody having their own data on their systems. It is only after the turn of the century that computing evolved from personal silos to networks. And this is when capitalism realized that in the new world, surveillance pays more than privacy. Google makes more money selling ads than it does selling phones.

Private companies have only now discovered surveillance—governments were its original inventors. Companies think surveillance is their ally. But they have merely adopted surveillance; governments were born in it, moulded by it. Privacy to governments is nothing but blinding! Or so Bane might have said if *The Dark Knight* was a political drama instead.

Democracies and authoritarian governments alike prefer to know as much as they can and use that information to stay in power as long as they can. George Orwell's fears of 'Big Brother is watching' have come to pass. Snowden has to live in exile, because why would the US be willing to give away the power it has over other nations? Snowden argues that the NSA program that collected this data has never helped save a single life. But what about the geopolitical games the US has been able to play by snooping on the world's communication channels to cement its place in the global economic hierarchy?

China has been surveilling its citizens openly for a while now. They have a network of tens of millions of cameras and are now able to recognize people in the streets with the help of real-time facial recognition.[27] If you jaywalk in China, expect to get a text from the police and your photo displayed on an 'offenders billboard' in full public view.

Hong Kong is an exception. It was transferred to China as recently as two decades ago, as a part of the 'one country, two systems' policy but maintains its own democratic culture. When China tried to squash those freedoms, the people of Hong Kong came out in protest in very new ways to avoid the omnipresent surveillance. They wore masks to avoid facial recognition, brought an additional pair of clothes to change into in hidden spots and rode in the city metros with paper tickets bought with cash instead of their more convenient metro cards—all to avoid being traced.

In 2018, Delhi Police used facial-recognition technology 'on a trial basis'[28] to trace nearly 3000 missing children. Nobody should have had an issue with reuniting lost kids with their families. But the flip side is that in December 2019, the very same Delhi Police used facial recognition to hunt down youths protesting against the Citizenship Amendment Act.[29]

Privacy is a luxury

I do not have an Aadhaar because I can afford to. I face minor inconveniences like not being able to use digital-only facilities that only work with Aadhaar for instant authentication, but I can get by just fine. Most people can't.

The privacy of the poor is often invaded first. India's public distribution system, the programme to make state-subsidized food accessible to the poorest, is amongst the handful of services where Aadhaar is actually mandatory. Forget private spaces, those of us desperate for food and shelter will happily trade our data to better their hapless situation. Nandan Nilekani imagined exactly this future when he was asked to implement this monstrosity on us. At a conference in 2017, he said that Indians would get 'data-rich before they are economically rich'. Plus, they would be able to sell or share this data for money.[30]

Private players are already doing this. Shiru Cafe, with stores in Japanese, American and Indian universities, recognized that students are one demographic that wants to save money. Another useful fact is that students of good universities like the IITs in India are excellent future recruits and rich customers for companies. Shiru Cafe lets students pay with their personal data—the corporate sponsors of the cafe use this data to target students with opportunities and offers.

Nilekani's intellectual mate Nitin Gadkari, the Minister of Road Transport and Highways, in his usual retired-uncle-talking-smack candour, answered in Parliament that he had sold our drivers-licence data to eighty-seven companies for Rs 65 crore.[31] We didn't even react.

The surveillance of the poor is not new to Aadhaar, though. You get your domestic help verified and registered—drug and psychometric tests are conducted. While running his clothing start-up and working on tight deadlines, Akshay saw factory managers monitor workers over CCTV like hawks, and even a five-minute non-scheduled break was considered a dereliction of duty. One of the world's most valuable companies with best-in-class cloud services is also one of the worst employers on the planet (Alexa, where's my order?).

Privacy is a luxury that few can afford.

Akshay often refuses to give out his number at checkout counters. We don't realize we can say no to such unnecessary requests for data collection. If there's one thing you take away from the above stories, it is that you should not be so willing to give up your data. Neither to corporations, nor to the government. Respect your own privacy and acknowledge that the more the data that exists about you in more number of places, the more likely it is to be used against you. And in time you will find that it will be.

We can mitigate a lot of these risks. Most modern browsers let you change your settings to sending a 'do not track' request whenever you pull up a webpage. Enable it—a lot of sites respect it. Some don't, and for them, install extensions like Disconnect.me that block unnecessary trackers from your browser. Then teach your family and friends how to do the same. You can get your number unlisted from Truecaller,[32] google how to do that. All of us enrolled in Aadhaar because our expectation is that we are supposed to do whatever the government asks of us. But what when you can't trust the government anymore and need to get on the streets without the risk of being recognized and your family being put behind bars? You can say no to unnecessary requests for data collection, and you should. Your data is yours to keep and yours to share. Exercise the agency you've always had—to say *No*.

While Aadhaar wasn't enough, the home minister pitched another jumbo card, 'Why can't we have just one card for all utilities like Aadhaar, passport, bank account, driving licence, voter card. There should be a system that all data should be put together in a single card.'[33] Except that Aadhaar is no utility-access card. The only voodoo benefit of Aadhaar was that you wouldn't need another card.

Rama Lakshmi,[34] former correspondent for the *Washington Post*, quoted American Broadway singer Pearl Bailey in her piece on this a-shiny-card-every-few-years scheme, 'What the world really needs is more love and less paperwork.'

Treat your digital data as an extension of yourself. You only share your innermost thoughts with people you trust with your life. And you expect your thoughts to be handled with respect. It should be the same with your data. Data is what gives tech corporations so much power, even more than most governments. And this is why governments want in on the action too. There is no mythical giant of welfare—we are the ones who make this society. The government is installed to manage a few tasks for us, and it is important that this dynamic is not flipped.

In 2010, at an event hosted by Fast Company, Sean Parker, once the president of Facebook, said: 'Privacy is the new celebrity.'[35] Achieving privacy is now more difficult than gaining fame. We need to make it more common and easier to attain. Aadhaar data for cash cannot be a deal, let alone a bad deal.

4

Design: Iterate Everything

The world we live in is broken. It is filled with things that don't work as you expect them to. This is a world of doors that open in the wrong direction—a world of overlapping road signs, with one covering the other. And political posters covering both. There are URLs in print books! Does one type them in? And where's the thing on the driver's seat that opens the car boot in a car! Why could it not have been somewhere you can see? This is a world rife with bad design.

Bad design is why all business exists. Commerce aims to make things better. Not just better-looking, but better-functioning. An entrepreneur stands on the window of a high-rise and glares down. What she sees is a city teeming with inefficiencies and faults. A world begging to be fixed. With good design.

As we see throughout this book, the principles that guide technology's core foundation can be better, and so can the scaffolding of technology. The way we consume goods can be better and so can the goods we consume. A lot of this world is stuck together with duct tape, coming apart at the seams for want of thoughtful design.

Every human-made item you have ever used was designed to be the way it is—some with more thought than others. Design permeates everything—from the design of cities to the design of elections, from a coffee cup to a satellite in space. If a humanistic outlook on life asks us to have a scientific view of our progress and build a better life for each other, design is the key that will get us there. We need to design things and systems not only with humans at the centre but also the environment. Let's design things well. And then let's make them better.

Error in design

After the Civil War in America, the new government forced out indigenous people from what is now Oklahoma, to punish them for supporting the slave-owning southern states. Up to three-quarters of a million people laid down their lives in the war that resulted in the freedom of 4 million slaves. Slave owners must have wanted their slaves pretty badly! After the US government stripped the indigenous people of their land, they let it be 'unassigned' for a while.

Other than gold, land is probably the only other asset humans have cherished for centuries. So of course people in America were keen on this land. As soon as they realized there was this unclaimed land, they started trying to lay claim to it and get it for free. They lobbied the government to let them settle it.

And the government agreed with the settlers. The ensuing chaos that pursued is known as 'The Land Run'.

The government set a date and whoever went into the territory on that day and put up a plank would get up to 160 acres of land. For free! Unsurprisingly, people came from all over, even outside of America, from Europe, in the hopes of starting a new life there. Almost 10,000 people showed up on the designated day.[1]

The original lobbyists did not like this wider interest that was being generated because it meant less free land for them. They allied and decided to cheat. They went in before the designated time and hid in the bushes. They are now known as 'the Sooners'. The ones that did not cheat are called 'the Boomers'. Problems arose when the government realized that they hadn't put much thought into this entire exercise. The government did not even leave space for roads and common areas. People co-operatively decided to cut those out of their land. The Sooners had time to plan this out, so they marked out roads and central spaces for the community beforehand. The Boomers just had plots of lands with no public place to walk. The Boomers followed suit and decided to leave space from their plots for roads. This approach to city design as an afterthought can still be felt in Oklahoma today. You only get to plan a city once.

After everything was said and done, the layout of the Boomers part of the town turned out to be at an angle to the layout of the Sooners. The roads in both parts ran in parallel with one set, intersecting another at a right angle, making a grid. Since the Sooners had planned their part of the town beforehand and the Boomers had to do this after the fact, both their grids ended up not matching up. They had to make diagonal jogs to connect the roads where the two parts of the city met, and Oklahoma's roads still have these abrupt joints.[2]

This sort of city design is known as a grid plan.[3] Grid plans originated around 2600 BC, most famously seen in Harappa, a town of about 23,000 people in present-day Punjab, Pakistan. Chandigarh, which is regarded as one of the most well-designed cities, has a grid plan. Grid plans are useful for navigating around without Google Maps and make it easy to get from place A to place B as long as you have a general sense of how the blocks are laid out. Blocks are so common in America that they use blocks as a unit of distance, even though blocks vary from city to city. Anything but the metric system for America!

Rome really capitalized on straight roads that enabled the empire to expand the way it did. The Roman Empire extended to most of modern-day Europe (despite Brexit, that does include England) and large chunks of the Middle East and North Africa. Many roads that they built to enable trade and the expansion of the empire are still in use today. And they connected them all back to the capital, Constantinople. As the saying goes, all roads did in fact lead to Rome. All towns were built similarly, helping the soldiers orient themselves in different cities. They used the centuriation system, also known as the Roman grid, across the empire, with traces still found in modern-day Italy and France.

One problem with grid plans is that they are optimized for a consistent vertical density because they were invented in an era where land was plentiful, and buildings could afford to be a single floor. This is not the case any more, and we live and work in skyscrapers. And these real-estate developments are never evenly spread across a city. If two diagonally opposite parts of a city are the most populated, it would make sense for making a road as straight and as wide as possible between those points, to reduce travel time. And this is how most Indian cities are built. Delhi has been adding roads and flyovers connecting different parts of the city based on the flow of traffic.

This plan is known as a cul-de-sac and emerges more organically over time. To travel diagonally across a city with a grid plan requires negotiating multiple four-way crossings, which require extra effort from the driver making commute times even worse, whereas a cul-de-sac system might not. That's a problem with designing things with clean lines, they might be better-looking but offer a bad experience for people.

Worse than Oklahoma and the poster boy for poorly designed India cities is Gurgaon. To go from New Delhi to Gurgaon, one must pass through the mind-numbing traffic of the national highway, or NH8. To ease some of the commuter pain, the government very graciously renamed the city to Gurugram. Gurugram does not have a grid plan. Or any plan for that matter. It is just a loose cluster of plots with snaking roads that were once good enough for the low-density one-dimensional housing it had when the city started. Delhi has limits on how high you can build, which prevents the city from housing everyone that works in it and providing work for everyone that lives in it. And so Delhi expanded outside its boundaries where the limits were less restrictive. Businesses and the people that run them started moving to Gurgaon, and the city grew vertically over the past twenty years.

The Haryana government seems to have forgotten to provide any infrastructural support[4] to the burgeoning city, resulting in Gurgaon essentially becoming a privately owned Frankenstein nightmare. There is no sewage nor roads, and it is built on the ideas of private builders hacking together solutions like septic tanks for sewage and large diesel generators for electricity. What private builders can't do, however, is build public roads. Maybe if the government could find some time, apart from merely renaming the city, and do its job, people will be able to travel easily across the city.

Many parts of Delhi were designed when cars were rare, and the middle-class vehicle of choice was a Bajaj Chetak scooter. Akshay was always confused by the miniature garages that came with the DDA houses in Vasant Kunj when he lived there. He later realized those expensive South Delhi houses had garages that were designed for those Chetak scooters! It's worse in older parts of Delhi like Uttam Nagar and Shahdara. Many people in these parts of Delhi have the means to buy cars but don't because they can't park them anywhere. In Ghaziabad, where Akshat lives, apart from the few posh gated colonies, every time his dad has to visit a supplier or a worker, he parks the car outside the lane. Not because parking space is sparse in the lane but because the lane is narrower than the car. It's no laughing matter—people get killed over parking spaces in Delhi.

No matter what type of plan today's metropolises were initially laid out under, it is important to note that most cities are designed iteratively. Cities are living creatures, and their infrastructure needs to adapt according to current demands. Unlike with currency notes, where the demonetization strategy proved so very effective, you can't really burn everything down and start again with a city! Unless you are a Batman villain, you have to adapt. Delhi gets it right, by continuously adding flyovers just to keep commute times the same, which is an achievement given the increasing number of cars on the road. The city is now adding multi-level parking in many areas.

The design of elections

What designers like to term a 'human error' is often a design error. Ever read a headline attributing a MiG plane crash to human error? It was in fact the plane that was designed badly. So badly that we have lost more planes and pilots to test flights than during wars in recent decades. The country has lost almost 500 out of the 900 MiGs it purchased due to accidents.[5] The problem? The aircraft lands at a very high speed of 340 kmph, which, combined with the high canopy that doesn't let the pilot see the ground, makes handling quite difficult.

If people keep making mistakes in using a product regularly, the fault lies with the product or device rather than the person using it. When software entrepreneurs fail to get their business off the ground, they sometimes blame the public for not understanding their product. Nine times out of ten, the product was unnecessarily complex and not made with the user in mind. Bad products thankfully get weeded out by the public markets in a meritocratic fashion. But when governments are involved, such bad systems can get adopted at scale without being tested for pitfalls.

One famous example of bad design that is attributed to flipping an entire election was the American presidential battle of George Bush vs Al Gore in 2000.[6] The election was so closely contested that in the end, whoever would win the state of Florida would win the entire election. A petition asked for a recount in the state and was decided on by the American Supreme Court in a month-long legal battle. The judgment was 5-4 against the recount. If this isn't nail-biting enough, the Florida election hung on a single county within Florida: Palm Beach. A neighbourhood where a total of about 400,000 people voted. Bush won the county by just a few hundred votes. And that won him Florida. He won by just 537 votes out of a total of 60 lakh votes cast in the state, a win percentage of 0.009.

And these 537 votes gave him the needed electoral votes to win the entire election. The president of the United States was chosen because of 537 votes.

More importantly, Bush won in Palm Beach County due to a badly designed ballot paper. Unlike India, America does not have a central committee like the Election Commission, and decisions like designing ballot papers are left to individual counties. Theresa LePore, who was the election officer at Palm Beach County, designed the ballot to make it more readable. She thought if all the names were on one paper, it would be too hard for the elderly population of the county to read.

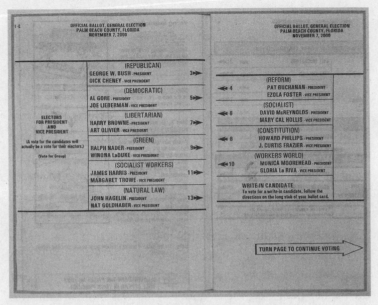

Source: Lilly Smith, 'Artifact: 2000 Palm Beach County Ballot', DesignObserver.com, 22 May 2018, https://designobserver.com/feature/artifact-2000-palm-beachcounty-ballot/39846.

If you look at the image above, it is easy to assume that the first punch hole is for George W. Bush, while the second corresponds to Al Gore, the two main candidates in the election. And that is what happened. Pat Buchannan got over 3400 votes in the county, which was 3x more than he should have received based on other counties. Buchanan himself acknowledged the anomaly, saying he thought the extra votes were most likely made in error. Many people told the *New York Times* that after they had punched in the wrong hole, they realized their mistake and punched the correct one for Al Gore, which invalidated their ballot. The county discarded about 19,000 votes that had two or more holes punched in, which was about 4.3 per cent of the entire votes. An anomaly when compared to counties with a similar population like California's Sacramento, where only 0.3 per cent of the ballots were double-punched. They did not use facing pages in that election. The error rate in Palm Beach was more than 10x the norm. It is quite evident that Bush won this county and the entire country due to this design error.[7]

But why was a badly designed ballot paper, by getting Bush elected, able to influence policy decisions that affected the fate of not only Americans but the entire world? Was it all LePore's fault, or was this a bigger design flaw in the decentralized election process of America? She was not a designer and couldn't have known in advance the impact of the ballot's design on the election. What was more at fault was both the US electoral system and the prevalence of the two-party system. America is not a direct democracy but has an electoral college system that sometimes leads to the person with lesser vote share winning the election. Both Hillary and Al Gore lost despite having more total votes than their opponents. And the two-party duopoly ensures that very narrow margins win elections with no third-party candidate getting any substantial vote share. There is also the art of designing the boundaries[8] of districts to optimize for winning, and we have talked about that in the chapter on Infinite Regress.

Fixing all this would take some doing, but maybe they can start with fixing the ballot paper.

The Indian elections use electronic voting machines (EVM) to avoid election tampering. There is widespread scepticism in India about EVMs being prone to manipulation without a paper trail. The country found a neat solution to dissuade these concerns. EVMs now come with 'VVPAT'[9] (voter-verified paper audit trail) machines that print out a person's vote and safely deposit the same into a box, which can later be opened and tallied against the electronic count. The voter can see that his vote did indeed go to the candidate he voted for. In the 2019 general elections, the Supreme Court asked the Election Commission to tally VVPATs in five polling booths per constituency from the previous one.[10] The manual tally corresponded with the digital count.

This shows us how designing better systems can indeed help restore faith in democracy. The design of ballots has been a contentious issue ever since Independence. The first elections of 1952 required a ballot box that could not be opened. Godrej was tasked with the job, and they realized putting locks on all the 13 lakh boxes would be cost-prohibitive. After fifty prototypes they found a hack to make an internal lock that was acceptable and yet economical for mass production.[11] Truly, everything that is designed once can be designed better.

Just as bad design can flip elections, so can good design. Alexandria Ocasio-Cortez, the twenty-nine-year-old senator who won the constituency of the Bronx in New York City, and the entire Internet, is a prime example. She was hugely buoyed by Tandem NYC,[12] a New York–based design firm in her successful campaign. Cortez defeated the ten-term incumbent, Joe Crowley, from the same party as hers. She raised issues that were central to her voters, but one of her campaign's most overlooked features was the brilliant design they brought into the political scene.[13] Most politicians' branding, just like their policies, is very bland and unimaginative (with the exception of maybe Narendra Modi). Cortez's campaign, however, employed consistent design across all of her branding from banners and posters to promotional videos. The slanting AOC logo (formed from her initials) is so distinct compared to other candidates' logotype. In *Knock Down the House*,[14] a Netflix documentary about Cortez's campaign, she directly compares her pamphlet design with Crowley's and explains how hers clearly informs what the recipient is to do (vote for her on the mentioned date). This key information in design is called a 'call-to-action'. A video[15] made for her campaign went viral and helped her rise to pole position. Her posters were radical and stood in stark contrast to the banal design Joe Crowley's campaign employed.

Source: Maria Arenas, 'Logo of Alexandria Ocasio Cortez campaign', Wikimedia Commons, 1 May 2017, https://en.wikipedia.org/wiki/File:Aoc-logo.png.

Back home, Delhi's Aam Aadmi Party introduced stark posters of black-and-red text on a plain white background, as opposed to the noisy design employed by the BJP and the Congress. Indian political posters tend to have dozens of photos: AAP brought them down to one, that of Arvind Kejriwal. These posters stood out from the noise and were more visible despite often being on the backs of autos as compared to larger billboards. And then there were the caps. AAP leaders all wore the classic 'netaji' caps, which soon became the trademark of the volunteer-led movement.

After five years of the party in power and Delhiites having gotten used to the design, for the 2020 elections, AAP reinvented its design by switching to a colour palette of black and yellow. Something as simple as colour and type can not only make things look better but also influence the decision-making process. Different fonts make us feel differently. Have a look at the following three popular typefaces and think of how they make you feel.

Now That We Are Here
Now That We Are Here
Now That We Are Here

The first one is Times New Roman, a serif font. Serifs being the little hanging things at the ends of the letters. It looks royal and dignified. The next one is Neue Helvetica, a sans serif font (as in without the serifs), which looks luxe and modern. The third one, Comic Sans, is playful and does not want to be taken seriously. And the authors advise that you don't ever use it if you want to be taken seriously. They can all be used to convey different feelings to an audience and set expectations.

And not just feelings, font design can also help one retain things better. 'Sans Forgetica' was designed by behavioural scientists and designers at an Australian university to aid learning. It features cut-out letters, making the text difficult to read, so our brain ends up paying more attention to what we are reading.

Now That We Are Here

Design terminology

The greatness of good design is in never being noticed. The goal is to design something to reduce friction from the product's function without adding any new inconveniences. Good design is when you get so used to the new product you find it hard to imagine a time before it. How did we get by without touchscreens? Remember T9?

Before we go into the next stories on design, we need to acquaint ourselves with some principles and the lexicon of design. Design can broadly be broken into three broad categories

UI (user interface design): This is what you see in a design. Everything you interact with is UI. When you pull down notifications on your phone, you are interacting with the UI.

UX (user experience design): This is what you experience in the product you are using. Your phone shows texts on the top of your screen while calls take up the whole screen, both these things have a different UI that improves your experience (UX) of using the phone.

A loose interpretation of UI and UX could be form and function, but that is not an exact analogy. UX design influences the interface, just as the interface influences your experience. UI and UX go hand in hand.

ID (industrial design): How the iPhone looks with its metal melding into the glass is ID. Apple is often revered for its use of high-end ID and bringing luxury ID into everybody's hands.

A good model to look at design is the one set out by Don Norman about thirty years ago in his book *The Design of Everyday Things*.[16] He explained that any product has two key components: affordances and signifiers.

The affordance of an object is what it can do or what it lets you do. A ladder affords climbing. A remote's battery compartment affords being opened up. A signifier is something that brings to light the affordances of an object. The steps on a ladder signify that you can climb on top of it. A remote's battery compartment can signify that it can be opened because it says 'open here'. Or it could be a more subtle signifier, like a notch or a dimple that tells you to place your thumb in it to slide the battery cover one way or the other.

This model of affordance and signifier is useful for understanding why manufacturers make something a certain way. And it not only applies to physical objects but digital interfaces as well. A phone's screen affords swiping and touching. A small upwards arrowhead on the phone's home screen signifies sliding up, which brings up the app drawer. In any app, clicking on the logo takes you to the home screen of that app. These signifiers have become universal over time and people know what to expect.

The better an app or product signifies its usage, the more easily one can figure out how to operate it. But that does not mean that a better design will necessarily lead to more users for a product. When Snapchat came around, it famously had unclear signifiers and it took a while for its users to learn how to use the app. The app lets you swipe in all directions to get to different parts of the app, but there were no visual signifiers on the home screen to suggest swiping. These are known as hidden affordances, and they actually were responsible for Snapchat's early growth. Older people had a hard time using the app, which is what appealed to the app's younger demographic. They liked the idea of being in a secret club that did not let everybody in. Evan Spiegel, the CEO of Snapchat, once joked, 'We've made it very hard for parents to embarrass their children.'

Just like Snapchat made its app difficult on purpose, cities too, in a similar manner, design public places to keep people away. Mumbai's expensive Pali Hill neighbourhood employs spikes on footpaths to prevent the domestic workers that work in the houses of the elite from sitting on the roadside.[17] Such spikes are called anti-affordances and are optimized to discourage certain actions rather than enable it. All design tools at our disposal are neutral;

the onus is on us to either use them to make our fellow humans' lives more bearable or less.

Iterate everything

Design does not happen in isolation. There is always precedent, and every smart company must look at it before proceeding. Just like with everything else, you don't get to that level of design without iteration. When building a new city, planners can look at both Gurgaon and Chandigarh before they set pen to paper.

Even though Apple would like us to believe that they come up with original ideas on their own, what they really excel at is iteration. They are often not the first to market, and their first version of products is usually not even at par with the competition. They keep refining year on year to get to a product that wows its users. There were touch phones with better specs and better cameras before iPhones, but the first iPhone was the most usable. There were Windows tablets in existence ten years before the iPad, but the iPad was the most usable. With their penchant for iterative design, they ended up reinventing the smartphone market and owning the tablet market.

Among other things, Apple also copied Android's style of combining multiple notifications into groups, reducing the cognitive load required to deal with them. Notifications started out quite humbly, with just a blinking red light on otherwise black-and-white phone screens. Akshay remembers a time when a phone was sold entirely on the fact that it had an LED that could change colour based on the notification you received. A missed call could be blue and a text orange. But in the era of smartphones, notification design quickly got more and more complex. Companies quickly started abusing them as nudging tools to get you into their apps as frequently as they could. Every app wants more of your time or more of your money.

But we do want some notifications, so they are not all bad. This new complexity required a new notification design. Phones now let you turn off notifications by app, or just put your phone in a do-not-disturb mode so that you can get some work done. But most people will not take the pain to use these manual controls, and they shouldn't have to. Maybe in the future, Google's Android notifications will be sorted with the help of algorithms, just like how Gmail decides what email is 'important' based on what we are likely to care about and puts the worst offenders in a spam folder. What we need are timely notifications instead of real-time ones. And then hopefully Apple will copy.

We love browsing memes on the Internet, but understanding what the word means and how memes go viral is key to understanding the collaborative iteration that happens in an industry. Just like how human gene data is carried genetically, similarly, human knowledge can be said to be carried in a 'memetic' fashion. The term meme was first coined by Richard Dawkins to explain the spread of cultural data. Our biological data spreads vertically via genes when people have children. Newer versions of iPhones retaining old features are a comparable example of such vertical spread. Memetic spread happens when a unit of information spreads horizontally within the population. Fast fashion spreads this way, making it available more widely, and fast, giving it its name. This kind of horizontal spread is speedier. Digital data like viral images and videos often spread this way, hence getting the moniker 'memes' on the Internet.

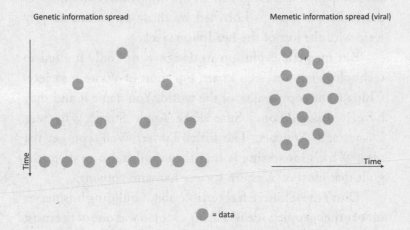

Good design is often viral. So much so that it gets copied and remixed into other devices as soon as a big tech company announces it, helping it spread horizontally. For years, phone manufacturers were finding ways to increase the screen size on phones while keeping the display rectangular. They had to leave some space at the top for sensors and front cameras. But then Apple realized it could increase the display further by extending it further to the top but leaving a 'notch' cut-out in the screen. And that opened the doors for other companies to use that as a cue to not only copy but improve upon what Apple had done. In 2019, Samsung phones had a much smaller cut-out. Akshay's OnePlus phone has a camera that only pops up when you need it, making more room for the display.

Another example is the disappearance of the headphone jack. Once again, Apple led the way in removing it, and within two years every flagship phones rapidly lost the headphone jack, something phones had had for decades. Apple is also the company that first got rid of the floppy drive and the CD drive. People were as horrified by those exclusions as they were with the loss of the headphone jack.

But memetic evolution in design is not only limited to technology but also seen in art. For most of Western society, China is the copy maker of the world. You name it and they have it. Fake iPhone? Sure. Fake Apple Store? Why not. Disneyland? You bet. The Eiffel Tower? Well, you get the idea. What's interesting is that they don't seem to carry the guilt that most of Western society has with copying.

Don't the Chinese feel terrible about building businesses off of other people's ideas? Zhang Daqian was one of the most prolific Chinese painters of the 20th century. Regarded as the Pablo Picasso of China, his meeting with Picasso in 1956 was celebrated as the confluence of masters of the Eastern and Western art. The same year, an event at Paris's Musée Cernuschi (the Museum of Asian Art) tarnished Zhang's image permanently. There was an exhibition featuring many masterpieces. These paintings were later found out to be forged. And these were no ordinary forgeries—they had been done by the master Zhang himself. He was declared a fraud.

But for Zhang, the paintings were not forgeries; he considered them replicas[18] of lost art that were limited to catalogues of lost paintings. He made around 10 million dollars selling these forgeries to several museums across the world. About 3 kilometres away, in the Museum of Modern Art, Zhang's original pieces were on display.

China's invention of printing doesn't turn up as a surprise. Its copying is the sole reason tech manufacturing has become streamlined and efficient. Affordable imitation requires a rethink about every process from first-order principles. Every extra physical feature in a device adds cost both in terms of the price and the time needed for the assembly of the additional part. You are forced to figure out manufacturing processes that take up less material and fewer steps to reduce the costs. Innovation works best with constraints.

Asian culture does not uphold copying the way the West does. One of the most revered shrines in Japan, the 1300-year-old Ise Jingū, gets rebuilt every twenty years.[19] The tradition is to then move the 'deity' in a 'transfer ritual' to the newly built replica. They also meticulously remake about 1500 items kept in the shrine. Remaking something as old as this might be sacrilege to someone in the West, but for the Japanese, it emphasizes the impermanence of nature. The locals have upheld this tradition for over a millennia, and the remaking of it does not dilute its importance but rather upholds it. The remaking is what unites the people with their culture and helps pass on the building techniques. The rebuilding, which in 2013 cost around $550 million, takes eight years and the planning another nine. That's a combined seventeen years that the shrine is in a state of flux for the total twenty years. It is always being built.

Initially, Akshay's previous business relied on buying dresses from the Chinese wholesaler Alibaba and selling them in India. His company would curate from the infinite designs before testing and shipping to their customers. A large part of that curation consisted of weeding out rip-offs of Gucci and Prada dresses worn by celebs like Kim Kardashian, because the author felt offended by the idea of selling these fakes. The author's business quickly moved to making their own custom-fit dresses within India. But for the Chinese culture, it is just business as usual. And that is not meant as a slant. There is no copyright in fashion, and most buyers do not care. In 2019, Kim Kardashian posted a photo of herself wearing a dress designed by her husband, Kanye West, with the caption: 'P.S. fast fashion brands, can you please wait until I wear this in real life before you knock it off? 😊'[20] So of course companies copied it in hours. Kardashian sued one such company that was not only ripping off the designs but also her image, and the latter reason is most likely why the company settled[21] for $2.8 million before the matter went to court. If it did, it would have been a landmark case no matter which way the judgment went.

Reproduction enables memetic evolution. The more you make, the more you iterate, and the ten-thousandth copy is far better than the first or the original. In product design, art is not separate from the product's function. By being used frequently, a product experiences much greater iteration. Fancy cutlery that isn't put out often has fewer chances of being improved than the dishes used every day. The Chinese versions of Kardashian's dresses are never the same. They often have improvements over the originals, adding functional items like straps and pockets. This makes these dresses easier to wear for everyday folks that do not have a team of stylists to get them into the dress.

When artists create cover songs[22] of other artists, singing someone's music in their own style, they often make the song better or end up introducing it to a new audience. Bollywood songs are remade into songs of divinity played during *jagrans*. Kanye West is taking the trend . . . well . . . west, by giving his own music new meaning and converting it to gospel music. We also see Imagine Dragons borrowing themes from religious music and making it mainstream. The Ise Jingū shrine has also evolved, the construction now includes gold and copper apart from the original wood and has seen an influence of Buddhist architecture.

Steve Jobs hit the nail on the head when he said Apple could never design the first iPhone based on user research, but successive iPhones improved by adding features based on people's use. The 2020 iOS update was in the news for having borrowed heavily from Android. Kim Kardashian's husband, Kanye West, built a career off of sampling other people's tracks, a common practice in hip-hop. In *A Dark Twisted Fantasy* (Akshay's favourite Kanye album) the song 'Power' samples as many as three different songs to make the masterpiece that the track is. Talking about copies, you can buy bootleg Yeezys,[23] shoes designed by Kanye, online from China for as low as $50, when the same often sell in the US aftermarket for upwards of $1000.

Dark patterns

Ever found yourself checking out of Swiggy or Amazon and realizing there's a 'Swiggy Super' or 'Amazon Prime' subscription auto-added to your cart that you never asked for?

Ever seen a hair on your screen, tried to wipe it away, only to realize the hair was part of the ad graphic and now you have clicked on an ad you did not mean to? This phenomenon of optimizing the design to trick users into doing things they did not intend to do is known as a 'dark pattern'.[24] The term was first coined by Harry Brignull, who maintains the darkpatterns.org portal, listing common dark-pattern designs used across the Internet.

His latest addition to the list of dark-pattern types is called 'Privacy Zuckering', named after our favourite tech CEO Mark Zuckerberg. Privacy Zuckering is when you are beguiled into sharing more than the intended amount of information in public.

Newsletters are very easy to get into and very difficult to get out of. It's easy to get bogged down by the dozens of newsletters we accidentally subscribed to. We have all been there, haven't we! Unroll.me is a popular free service that lets users easily manage their newsletter subscriptions by decluttering their inbox. The altruistic service was found to be making money by selling user's data to 'data brokers'. When users finally discovered that there was a cost to the free service, after all, the CEO claimed to be 'heartbroken' that his customers were upset with what was a part of their privacy policy. Unroll.me isn't an unusual offender as most companies sell user's data to similar ad brokers. What's unique is the type of data it had—all of a user's emails and contacts. Apparently, that is the data people seem to let only bigger companies like Google monetize.

This is exactly what privacy is about: to let the users know what data is being collected and why. Everyone knows Gmail does this without reading their privacy policy because it happens so visibly. Your friend emails you a Dua Lipa song,[25] and right next to the email you see an ad selling her concert tickets. Another key difference is that data stays on Google's platform and advertisers merely rent indirect access to the data to target ads based on anonymous profiles of people. Whereas Unroll.me outright sold the anonymized data to Uber to help them track which users were using Lyft by scanning all of a user's Lyft invoices from their email inboxes.[26]

Another common dark pattern is called 'gillnetting'. A gill net is a type of fishing net with multiple layers that will trap the fish in at least one of the layers. Many web products use similar principles to optimize user retention and revenue. Ever try to unsubscribe from a newsletter and get presented with ten different mailers you must uncheck one by one? You probably left a few checked even though you would have unsubscribed from all if that were the only option.

Ikea stores are famous for being designed to get you to buy more stuff.[27] To go from the entrance to the exit you have to traverse much of the store and browse all the items, and the more items you see, the more likely you are to pick up a few of them. The online fashion retail app Myntra employs similar design strategies on their phone app. Once you have clicked on an item either via the home screen or the search bar, the only way to return home is to press back. The company logo at the top, which works as the home button in most apps disappears. Instead, you find yourself winding down a rabbit hole of recommendations with no way to get back other than to press the back button on your device ten times. The intent is clear: once you are confused and browsing, you will add multiple items to your cart because you might not come across them again—the fear of missing out exacerbated by randomness. There's a subtle line between a dark design and a good old nudge, which we discuss in the Behavioural Economics chapter.

Another common dark pattern is hidden costs. The display price you see on the product page is different from what you have to pay at checkout. Myntra displays prices without sales tax and only adds it when you go to checkout, so you end up paying more than you expected to pay.

Several download websites feature a big flashing download button that is actually an ad, with the real download link made much smaller and placed elsewhere below. That's a common dark pattern as well.

While filling out the online passport application a few years ago, Akshay was surprised to see the option to confirm consent to share data with a private travel company checked by default. Most of us will not notice this and automatically have our data sold by the government to private companies. Much of the passport service in the country is handled by a private company owned by the Tata Group.[28] They will upsell a passport cover and convince you that you need it. While running from checkpoint to checkpoint, you will take them on their word, because you won't even know that you are dealing with a private player and not the government. And just like that, Tata has the address and contact details of all the passport holders in the country. Incidentally, Akshay applied for a passport to avoid getting an Aadhaar, the darkest dark-pattern instrument in any democracy. Aadhaar purports to be a national ID, which not only is a misnomer but is misleading as well. Aadhaar is instead designed as a platform to enable harnessing the citizen's data, often without consent or choice. The government has been trying to link one's Aadhaar with as many services as they can to make it easy to map and track an individuals' life. We talk more about Aadhaar in the Data chapter.

Some companies do take the idea of misleading with design to its capitalistic extreme. In 2017, two domain providers did just that. 123-Reg and NamesCo, two domain registrars based in the UK, booked millions of .uk domains for their customers free of cost for two years. The only problem with this philanthropic effort was that people never wanted these domains, and two years later people got billed for renewing these domains.

For people that owned, say 'www.example.co.uk', these companies bought a corresponding 'www.example.uk' domain on behalf of their customers and added them to their accounts.[29] Due to the similarity, most customers could not discern that these were not their domains but in fact different ones. Domain ownership has to be renewed on a yearly basis, so when the renewal invoices showed up, many inadvertently paid them, assuming they were for the domains they owned. This went beyond a simple dark pattern and was an outright scam.

Designing for space, time and culture

A total of twenty-four people[30] have been to the moon, of which twelve have walked on its surface. But the fact that the first attempt succeeded, even though barely, was a crucial element in their being follow-up missions. If Neil Armstrong had failed, the public's and policymakers' perception of the moon might have been very different. Similarly, satellites are expensive to make and expensive to put into space, reducing the scope of error.

Some scenarios have a lower tolerance for iterative design. Space and nuclear are amongst them. You can't make a reactor that can't contain its water or a space vehicle that burns up on re-entry, killing the astronauts in it. Well, both of those things have happened, and they were catastrophic. The Chernobyl and Fukushima disasters not only resulted in the loss of life but were also responsible for the general fear of nuclear energy around the globe that has resulted in CO_2 emissions still being out of whack. Bad design in such industries carries very high stakes. Scientists have improved the designs based on past data, just like anywhere else. But they don't get to iterate through hundreds of versions. They can't push changes every night as Twitter can.

India's Chandrayaan-2 moon mission was the first time India tried to land a rover on the surface of another planet and was the country's second-ever mission that went to the moon. The lander ended up crashing, and the Indian Space Research Organization (ISRO) lost contact moments before it was supposed to touch down. Since there has been no contact with the lander, we don't have the data that would have helped scientists improve their third moon mission. The high cost of failure in space is why only a few governments and even fewer private companies have been able to send people and robots in Earth's orbit and beyond. Since the cost of putting things in orbit is so high, anything that is sent up is designed uniquely for that purpose. The International Space Station has dehydrated food and water-recycling systems, so astronauts mostly drink the previous day's fare. This helps reduce the amount of water that needs to be sent up.

Elon Musk's SpaceX is one company that has been able to design a new rocket-launch system from the ground up, which can be reused, hence, reducing the costs. NASA had a reusable shuttle programme but that was in fact cost-prohibitive and prone to failure because of its complex designs. The more components you have, the more points of failures you have to deal with. SpaceX became the first private company to transport astronauts to the International Space Station in May 2020.

Often, new design happens at the intersections of disciplines. Robert Lang, a NASA physicist by trade, pursued origami on the side. Origami is the art of making things by folding a single piece of paper, no cutting allowed. Design is to art what engineering is to science. Robert Lang quit his day job and developed mathematical models to make complex origami designs, first on a computer. His work led to solar wings for satellites that can be folded during transit and opened up to several times their area in space, allowing for more energy for the satellite. This intersectionality has always been key to design. Plane wings were designed after birds. The nose of the Japanese bullet train has Kingfisher birds to thank. This field is known as biomimetics. As opposed to human iteration in memetic design, in biomimetics, designers often take the help of nature's iteration over millennia. Evolution has had more time to perfect these designs, so why not just borrow from there. Now, modern robotics looks to model four-legged animals for making all-terrain robots, with Boston Dynamics leading the way. You have seen the viral videos.

Another challenge with space design is that you need to have parts not failing in space over decades, since missions often range between years to decades. The Voyager 1 probe still works some forty-three years since its launch in 1977. The more moving parts a system has, the more likely it is to fail. Even our laptops have gone from using rotating magnetic drives to the new solid-state drives that are less likely to fail. This is where compliant mechanisms[31] come in. These are instruments made from a single piece of material but with flexing capability where joints would have been, essentially like origami with thicker material. You can have pliers that are made with a single piece of plastic and hence less likely to break. Thrusters in satellite now use compliant mechanisms so they can be steered in space with just one thruster instead of two.

A similar high-stakes design challenge is designing things that will last thousands of years. Namely, nuclear waste that needs to be stored for such a long time that even if our civilization loses all its data, people should be able to understand not to dig up nuclear waste. Such designs need to transcend cultures.

The skull-and-bones logo is a standard symbol of danger, but it is often repurposed as a cool mark in fashion, as seen in punk singer Avril Lavigne's logo. People in the future might consider the skulls as fun graffiti on a wall instead of the danger it represents.

Source: Victor Grigas, 'Danger Voltage warning sign in Mumbai: BEST DANGER 415 Volts Mumbai' (image), Wikimedia Commons, 20 November 2011, https://commons.wikimedia.org/wiki/ File:BEST_DANGER_415_Volts_Mumbai.jpg.

Source: 'Avril Lavigne Concert, Kingston ON', Kingstonist.com, licensed with CC BY-NC-SA 2.0, https://creativecommons.org/ licenses/by-nc-sa/2.0/.

Designers decided that it made more sense to have a logo that was meaningless so people would not have prior associations of it, letting them ascribe meaning in people's minds. And they wanted something very striking and memorable so that once you saw it you would remember it the next time. After finalizing six designs, they ran tests on people to see which designs people remembered the most and which they associated least with something that already existed. The following design came out on top in both those criteria.

Source: Charles L. Baldwin and Robert S. Runkle, 'Biohazards Symbol: Development of a Biological Hazards Warning Signal', *Science*, vol. 158, issue 3798 (13 Oct 1967): pp. 264–65, DOI: 10.1126/science.158.3798.264.

This has now become internationally adopted as the biohazard symbol, with its own Unicode ☣. It has lasted for the past few decades, but it is difficult to be certain whether people will remember the ascribed meaning for tens of thousands of years.[32] This is not a solved problem by any means. Many think waste should be located near civilizations rather than away, so people remember across generations about the waste. Religion is known to last for such long times, so some have proposed imbibing this info into the culture of a people, essentially forming a cult that carries the information across generations by making it a part of their culture.[33]

Designing for cultures often exposes us to unique problems. ACs in cars have two knobs to control them. One knob controls the cooling and the other the fan speed—a simple one-to-one relation. But ask any Uber driver to lower the AC and they will decrease the fan speed most of the time. People get it wrong because of culture encoding. We are used to desert coolers having one knob that controls both the fan speed and the cooling (a higher fan speed causes faster evaporation of the pads, which results in more cooling). People expect the same with a car AC. This is something that can simply be fixed by having a digital temperature indicator, with buttons to increase and decrease the temperature and a separate fan-speed button— just like how AC units meant for homes handle this.

Designers need to keep differences in languages and cultures in mind whilst designing for a universal audience. Everybody across the world uses Android, and most people know to swipe up for the app drawer because the home screen has signifiers that nudge you to swipe up, without the use of words.

A well-designed product must not come with words attached. The thicker a user manual, the worse the product is designed. It's not an advanced product, it's just bad design. One way to make a design more human is to offer good feedback. Touch phones were initially jittery when one scrolled through them given the time a capacitive touchscreen would take to register your finger's action and the processor to render the change on the display, taking you out of the experience. The iPhone solved this lag by predicting where you would scroll to and starting to scroll in advance, making the scroll buttery smooth and instantaneous. This immediate feedback would draw you in. Good feedback can often simplify the most technical products.

Ideo, the world's leading product-design agency, credited for making the first usable computer mouse, proved this by their simplistic design of a product that is as high stakes as any.

Heart defibrillator designed by Ideo.

Source: An automated external defibrillator at the Mumbai airport, photo by Akshay Tyagi.

Pictured above is a heart defibrillator, designed by Ideo.[34] It's a device that can quite literally bring people back from death. When someone suffers an irregular heartbeat, medically known as an 'arrhythmia', this automated external defibrillator can auto-diagnose the condition and bring the heart back to a regular rhythm with the help of electric shocks. If left untreated, this condition will result in a heart attack. A device so medically advanced and yet it's designed in such a way that anybody who sees it for the first time will very quickly be able to go through the steps in an emergency. In a study, sixth graders were able to use it correctly in ninety seconds on their first try, very comparable to a trained professionals' sixty-seven seconds.[35] These devices, now made by Phillips, are now quite common, installed in many places including several Delhi Metro stations and the Mumbai airport.

Designing one product for the entire world often comes down to devising standards. But standards are difficult by definition. The first law of thermodynamics is a very fundamental law of nature, but even that gets different mathematical representation depending on whether you are talking to a physicist or a chemist. The formula, even though the same, looks different because chemists are interested in what happens in a closed space, often a test tube, and hence calculate work done on a system as positive (and therefore work done by the system as negative). On the other hand, physicists are interested in the entire universe and their convention measures work done by the system as positive. This outlook results in the values measured by a chemist and a physicist of the same event having different signs (+/-).

To account for this difference in convention, the formula is changed by replacing a (+) with a (-).

Chemistry notation: $\Delta U = Q + W$
Physics notation: $\Delta U = Q - W$

One of the first attempts to design AI ethics was made by the science-fiction author Isaac Asimov. His three laws of robotics,[36] taken from the collection *I, Robot* go as follows:

First Law
A robot may not injure a human being or, through inaction, allow a human being to come to harm.

Second Law
A robot must obey the orders given it by human beings except where such orders would conflict with the First Law.

Third Law
A robot must protect its own existence as long as such protection does not conflict with the First or Second Laws.

Will Smith starred in a movie of the same name. In the film, Smith's character hates robots because one saved his life over a young girl's. The droid calculated he had a better chance of survival than the twelve-year-old. The robot flung Smith out of the water as he was swimming towards the girl to save her.

But these are of course very basic and leave a lot out. The MIT media lab published its 'Moral Machine Experiment'[37] in 2018, a study done around the ethics of autonomous vehicles across cultures. MIT researchers posed questions like: Would they prioritize the lives of the young or the old, if they had to make a choice? And the responses differed according to culture. Collectivistic cultures[38] preferred to save the wisdom of the old over the young, whereas cultures that value individualism preferred to save more number of people.

And this encapsulates the problem with designing a single system for different cultures. Ethics are not standard across the globe, and so robots can't be either. Don Norman explained how using the example of two cars trying to cross a bridge from opposite ends: in an aggressive culture, using the high beam as a signal would mean the sender should be given right of way, whereas, in a more submissive culture, that same signal in the same situation would mean the receiver had the right to cross first.

When all cars are automated, they could speak the same language, but for the few decades when humans and AI drivers will coexist, AI will have to learn multiple languages. Maybe we can do that as well. Learn to speak each other's languages. In a future so controlled by technology, if there's one thing that will help us save our humanity, it is each other.

5

Infinite Regress: Termites after Midnight

India has had a tradition of personalized storytelling much before AI. There are some three hundred versions of the Ramayana,[1] often with very dramatic variations. Depending on where you live, you would have different heroes and villains. Only very recently has one version begun to dominate our imaginations and be abused for political gains. We also enjoy the distinction of being from a place where a mythical character gets not just a shrine but also a lawyer (the counsel for Ram Lalla, or baby Ram) in the highest court of the land. The lawyer Ravi Shankar Prasad went on to become the country's law minister and later spearheaded the digital modernization drive, all with the lord's blessings.[2]

The Babri Masjid–Ram Janmabhoomi dispute became more than a factual disagreement, when the 16th-century mosque located in the city of Ayodhya was unlawfully demolished by Hindu nationalist groups in 1992.[3] They claimed that the Mughal emperor Babur's commander Mir Baqi had destroyed a temple of Lord Ram to raise the Islamic structure over it. The first petition was filed by Mahant Raghubir Das in British India, way back in 1885, to build a canopy outside the disputed structure. It was rejected. In December 1949, someone went ahead and placed the idols of Ram outside the central dome, causing surprise and awe about the appearance of divinity.

Historians have had several disagreements over the archaeological evidence of a temple predating the mosque, but the Supreme Court hearing of 2019 sided with Ram Lalla.[4] We do not intend to play investigators for the case, but there's something interesting about the dispute that must be discussed.

The real problem with the Ayodhya dispute is the same as the immigration crisis anywhere else. It is the issue of drawing arbitrary timelines that have no rhyme or reason. How deep do we dig, how far do we trace back a piece of land? Is it owned by the Buddhist monks or the tribals before them? Does it belong to the Hindu residents or the Muslim conquerors? The very lexicon of resident and conqueror is political. There are no original inhabitants, there are no invading outsiders. The lines of sympathy especially merge when the outsider writes the history. All history is like the Ship of Theseus, we break it and rebuild it anew so many times that it changes so much and yet remains the same.

We are sensitive towards the identities people derive from their culture and history. It is far more convenient to have a monologue in a book than preach to charged crowds. But if we were to imagine a better world, we should be far more comfortable accepting this impermanence than being offended by it. It is a tragedy that a culture with the message of transient ownership in the Bhagavad Gita used Ayodhya to spew hate for several decades.

In his piece on City Lab,[5] Scott Lucas makes a wonderful observation about our universal love to claim preservation rights, 'That's the thing about struggles for souls: They aren't disagreements that can be negotiated among stakeholders, each of whom can claim legitimacy. They're holy wars, zero-sum games that one side must utterly lose.'

Structures have been built, destroyed and rebuilt over and over again. Before the current legal regime codified ownership, the land belonged to the mightiest sword. Muslim invaders weren't unique in that respect, irrespective of their period of stay. Conquest and loot have been legitimate methods of power acquisition for the longest time. Assessing the morality of those not governed by our present customs is unfair.

In fact, culture is what you make of it. In the chapter on design, we talk about how the Japanese have been rebuilding the same temple for at least 1300 years and how it makes their culture stronger, not weaker. Everything that is pristine and new will one day succumb—if not to man, then to nature. Places don't make a culture, people do. We might need to look beyond *'Mandir kahan banega'* and think about *'Yeh insaan kya banega'*—what will we make of our people rather than where will we build our places of worship.[6]

As the tools for gleaning greater evidence and discerning the historicity of people and objects are created by science, the questions of identity and nativeness will only get more complex. We are going to have strong urges to prove our ethnicities on the provocation of bullies. Elizabeth Warren, Democratic senator from Massachusetts, became a victim of one such trap about her Native American ancestry. When accused of not actually being a native, she went ahead and took an actual DNA test to clear Trump's doubts. Because why not when you can order a genetic ancestry test from home for less than $99? What are you hiding? the doubters ask.

Subramanian Swamy, a Bharatiya Janata Party veteran infamous for his outrageous remarks, has been making a case for all Indians acknowledging their Hindu ancestry for long. In an interview he went on to say if someone doesn't think they have Hindu ancestry, the Election Commission should strip away their voting rights. When the interviewer jokingly asks what if someone is an orphan and you cannot know where their parents came from, Swamy happily consents to offer a concession. We are afraid if the DNA test was popular in India and Swamy had narrowed down a set of criteria for what ancestry he approves of, the idea would eventually find a place in someone's manifesto.[7]

Those asking the Archaeological Survey of India (ASI) to investigate and prove what was below the structure and those asking people to take DNA tests to prove their ancestry are barely interested in the truth. They are masters of conveniently mistrusting institutions and companies when the results are antipodal to their own view. Their primary interest lies in inflaming our passions of identity and ownership to seize greater power for themselves.

Explorations into what is below the thing that's below the thing that's under this, or who came before the ones who came before us, and so on, are not of much use even if they seem seductively scientific to investigate, if the only intent behind doing so is to make claims about what one deserves today.

We need some concrete agreements about the useful timelines of fairness, even though it may not be an easy thing to do. A good example is the often-debated legal battle for water supply to slums between Pani Haq Samiti, a collective for the right to clean water, and the Brihanmumbai Municipal Corporation.[8] The civic administration wanted to cut the water supply to illegal settlements like slums. But since Mumbai is a city starved for affordable housing due to the migrant influx, slums represented an actual part of the city, not just its periphery. At least some of them deserved to be recognized for existing as living participants of the city in the fast lane.

1 January 1995 was decided as the date before which all slums got their right to municipal water, which was later extended to 1 January 2000. Slums that came up after this date would not be given water connections. The court looked at the constitutional right to life, and all that constituted a dignified life. If you legitimize too many encroachments, many of which are in ecologically sensitive areas, you erode the rule of law and encourage even further illegal occupation. Moreover, because the water supply is heavily subsidized, law-abiding citizens should not be expected to bear the financial burden of supporting slums. Yet everyone as a citizen deserves the right to water in order to survive. There are no easy answers.

The legal principle of adverse possession, or squatter's rights, is an interesting example of an encroachment being legalized if someone is in continuous possession or occupation of a property without the legal permission of the owner for twelve years. It means you naturally become the rightful owner if the owner doesn't bother long enough.

These dates cannot be objectively determined. The fragile line between who's wanted and who's not is a political one. When attempts are made to give it scientific or economic explanations, we need to be careful in recognizing whose interests are being served in these distinctions. There is a backend power-play that selectively challenges some of these lines but not others.

The Citizenship (Amendment) Act passed by the Modi government in December 2019 provided non-Muslim minorities from three Muslim-majority neighbours a swift path to citizenship, if they had fled persecution before 31 December 2014. The act provoked protests throughout the country against the exclusion of many Muslim groups who may have faced severe harassment in even 'their' countries with Islam as the state religion. And not surprisingly, India also has neighbours who promise protection and promotion of one religion (Buddhism) as state policy in their constitutions (Myanmar, Bhutan and Sri Lanka).

It was doubted that since it would have been difficult for anybody to prove persecution, the amendment would give a free pass to everyone other than Muslims. Given the BJP's troublesome history with the community, it is legitimately feared to become a legal tool of harassing them.[9] Notice the date, 31 December 2014—the last day of the year when the BJP got a full majority on its own for the very first time. It could well have been the date of the swearing-in, the prime minister's birthday or the festival marking Lord Rama's return to Ayodhya. In theory, if you entered the country on 1 January 2015, or if you couldn't prove so, you'd be ineligible to receive any benefits under the act.

The 24 March 1971 deadline for having entered Indian territory in order to be recognized as a citizen in the National Register of Citizens of India is another example of using the ossification of time to protect legal citizens from illegal crossovers. There is no math to these lines, only art—make what you may of them.

A few years ago, Akshat's NRI friend happened to share a video of the popular hoax about the Taj Mahal being a temple instead of a tomb.[10] Originating from the peculiar historian P.N. Oak's works, the cultural myth of 'tejomahalay' refuses to die down even after several projects attempting to debunk it. Some media outlets participated in adding noise and confusion by first floating possibilities of a Shiva temple being located under the Taj Mahal and then, after reaping an hour or two worth of TRPs, quietly announcing it as fake news. From the outside, it may seem like a harmless curious suggestion but it adds to the communal venom at home.

The author's reaction at that moment was to cite the ASI's affidavit in an Agra court clarifying that the tomb is just a tomb. The parts of the Taj Mahal that have been closed for the common public have already been debated in the courts—hence all suspicions about the basement are unfounded. There is a detailed structural analysis of the monument made by ASI which is available for public access.

And this would have been a strong argument except that the ASI is as much a fallible authority as any other. It has political appointments, and everyone loves to write history in their own way. The historiography of the ASI is the government-sanctioned version of the truth, and don't politicians manipulate the truth all the time? The manipulation of institutions is not recent, only more explicit and bigoted.

Coming back to the Ayodhya issue, the courts tasked the ASI to investigate the claims of Hindu nationalists and to literally dig under the mosque for any evidence to substantiate their case. It—controversially—pointed towards the distinctive features of a 10th-century temple—a western wall, fifty pillar bases and architectural fragments. Historians largely dismissed the evidence as manufactured. This happened in 2002, when the highest political offices were occupied by the same leaders who had talked about 'levelling the ground' nearly a decade ago.[11]

How do you appeal to authority when the accuracy is so brittle?

Representational representation

As systems like democracies also get more mature and data about our lives and elections becomes louder, we will face another meta-problem—should those elected by people be in a position to determine who gets elected next? Now that politicians have easy access to information and prediction models, they mostly understand what the historical socioreligious patterns of voting are. Most neighbourhoods are predictable in picking their candidate owing to their permanent identities. In the United States, your position on abortion or taxes, or your racial identity, can give parties an insight into how much of a Democrat or Republican you are. In the House of Representatives in the US Congress, out of the 435 seats, only about fifty are true 'toss-ups', everybody is fairly certain about the rest. Political commentators say 45 per cent of the US population is Democratic, while the other 45 per cent is Republican. The remaining rest 10 per cent in swing states determines the elections.

In India, you just have to use the caste data, no further research required.

This phenomenon of politicians choosing voters instead of voters choosing politicians is called gerrymandering. It was in the 19th century that Massachusetts governor Elbridge Gerry's Democratic–Republican party first had the brilliant idea of changing the map of state's senate constituencies to suit itself.[12] It would weaken the Federalist Party and ensure favourable results. Doing this resulted in one of the districts being awkwardly shaped like a salamander, which when coupled with the governor's name gives us 'gerrymandering'.

Politics never looked back—the use of technology just got more rampant and sophisticated over time. Both the Democratic Party and the Republican Party in the US have used mapping software programs like Maptitude to plot districts corresponding to the usual political inclinations of people. With the aid of tremendous data that is openly traded and the complex prediction models, they can hack the democracy.

Indian politics being more dynamic and relatively local helps avoid this problem. Instead of just two major parties, in most states, we have three or four regional ones. The Indian version of gerrymandering will be visible in places where there is a more stable voting pattern. During the last decade, northern India, especially the Hindi belt, has expressed a clear preference for the nationalist Bharatiya Janata Party, with varied local contenders. Southern India, though, with the exception of Karnataka, remains dominated by regional players.

Now, look at two important data sets. The first is the thin victory margins in Indian elections due to multiple candidates for every constituency. The more number of people there are contesting, the fewer votes you require to win it. In the Lok Sabha elections of 1998, 1999, 2004, 2009 and 2014, an average of thirty-two seats had a victory margin of less than 1 per cent. Around seventy seats with less than 2 per cent and 100 seats with less than 3 per cent. This is mind-blowing considering our voter turnout is nowhere close to cent per cent, and that we add crores of new voters every election who haven't already made up their minds.

The use of big data to predict the inclinations of only new voters in a constituency and their political activeness (to predict if they'll actually vote) or even looking at the population growth rates of neighbourhoods more favourable to you can give you incredible leverage for a generation.

The other important fact is that India's current distribution of Lok Sabha seats is based on the 1971 census. It was during the Emergency years in 1976 that the Indira Gandhi government chose to freeze delimitation till the 2001 census. Some believed this was done to not disincentivize family planning (a strong passion of her son Sanjay). With this, there was a cap on the total number of MPs a state could have, thus avoiding a constant conflict. Our actual parliament would have looked even larger than the European Parliament, with some 700 members.

A reason for the inequality in the number of people represented by MPs in the Parliament is because of the doubling of the overall population since 1971, from about 550 million to 1.3 billion today. States that happened to manage their population growth have MPs who are more equal than their counterparts from high birth-rate states.

In 2001, another amendment delayed this conflict to the census after 2026. If we can't figure out a formula that doesn't make wealthier and healthier provinces feel discriminated against, we will be stuck in the classical tyranny of numbers in democracy. We build representative systems to value every citizen of our republic, but over the centuries, as we get access to more data, we discover states not just represent the number of citizens there are but also influence how many citizens there are in the first place.

The Constitution calls for each MP representing a similar number of people, with the assumption that this criterion is neutral and fair. It does not matter how many Hindus or Muslims or Dalits or urbanities there are in an area, their MPs are nearly equally powerful. But when patterns start to emerge with regard to how different regions are growing or reducing in size, this assumption also becomes political.

As we acquire greater and greater power to carefully influence people without them having prior knowledge of the larger intentions of the government, it can make us all players of a simulation. Politicians can master this game quickly and manipulate growth rates to keep themselves in power. The meta problems of representation and justice are most important because they form the basis of our free existence. If we can't agree on them being fair, we can't agree on anything else.

It is a problem that predates our now current system of free and fair democracy. Who first determined how India was going to choose its constitutional values? Even the details of a democratic system have to be decided by people whose own democratic credentials may be contestable. For instance, the members of the Constituent Assembly, which defined how Indian elections were to be organized, were themselves not directly elected by the people. Nearly one-fourth of the members came through the nominations of the princely rulers, and the rest from provincial assemblies.

Who judges the judges?

Perhaps the judiciary could help us decide how fair these processes really are. Until you actually examine how knowing too much about the humanity of judges can so easily erode faith in justice. Courts in the United States have a political nomination process where executive authorities pick the judges and the legislative bodies confirm them. In the American Supreme Court, nine judges adjudicate on admitted matters, in contrast to its Indian counterpart, where the Chief Justice of India (CJI) decides both the size of the bench and its composition out of the tens of judges.

Because the appointment of the American judges is for a lifetime, their ideological leanings are even more important. As much rocket science as it is, liberals will like liberal judges, while conservatives will prefer those with orthodox positions. There has been an assumption that judges would vote for the more just side, irrespective of their leanings. The only way to disprove the hypothesis is to access the concrete data about the voting patterns of judges over several hundred cases during their careers. And indeed it is fairly easy to make a prediction about their picks, especially when their vote is pivotal. They conform to their ideological stands more vehemently when it matters the most.

Even though today's hyper-partisan times can make us distrustful enough of the political and justice system to consider this idea fairly common sense, however, as recently as 1990, a US President, Republican George H.W. Bush, nominated a judge of moderate social and political beliefs.

Before these tools became mainstream, in the 1980s, the scholars of the American Supreme Court pioneered a creative way to ascertain a judge's ideological leanings. They used the editorials published in the major US dailies following their nomination to assess the extent of right or left incline. Not surprisingly, the arrival of new tech and its computing power coincided with the more predictable selections of Barack Obama as the President.

India saw clear partisanship during Prime Minister Indira Gandhi's CJI appointment in 1973. The tradition of having the oldest person as the CJI was broken when three more senior judges were passed over to appoint a pliant contender. When she declared an emergency and her case came before a bench of five justices at the Supreme Court, her appointee sided with her. Gandhi planted her favourites in the right spots.

With improved access to the religious, gender and political biases of the judges with the aid of big data and neuroscience, our faith in impartial judgments will dwindle much further. This potential new situation will challenge some of our historical myths of impartiality, but it will compel us to invest energies in making our processes fairer.

It is after data helps us confirm that things absolutely unrelated to a case can end up putting more people in jail with lengthier sentences that we can begin to be more careful about them. One research suggests that the court's lunchtime, the size of the applicant's family, the weather, the number of recent grants by the court, whether genocide has been in the news, all determine the degree of cruelty of the judges. An unexpected defeat in a sports event can also increase the length of the sentence assigned by judges during the week after the game. The disproportionate victims of this emotional showing are the minorities.

Similar to what we talk about in the chapter on democracy, evidence from behavioural economics and decision science shows us how one's mood and the weather are so detrimental to our ideas of what is rational and just.

Imagine the headline of an Indian judge giving a Muslim man charged with murder a longer- than-usual sentence because India lost the cricket match the night before. This isn't a question of technology but of social justice.

In India, the distinction between liberal and conservative judges is relatively less pronounced, largely because of how opaque the process of promotions is—judges appoint judges. The collegium, which comprises only judges, decides who should be elevated to various courts in the country. The principle behind doing this is to avoid political influence and keep the process clean with an assumption that the judges themselves cannot be biased. This also results in large-scale nepotism in the Indian judiciary.

By excluding the participation of democratic representatives we don't do away with bias, we let biases of unelected officials take centre stage. We are not more evolved in transcending our biases but just less comfortable talking about them. To humanize the lordships is a seditious act.

What's even funnier is how it is the court itself that gets to decide how it should change its ways. The National Judicial Appointments Commission (NJAC) Act of 2014 would have changed the current judge-appointment system to a six-member NJAC comprising the CJI, two senior-most Supreme Court judges, the law minister and two eminent persons. The eminent persons would have been chosen by a selection committee including the CJI, the prime minister and the leader of the Opposition. The act was struck down by the Supreme Court on 16 October 2015, in a 4-1 majority verdict.

It barely makes the monster go away. Algorithms are going to keep getting better, and the better they get, the worse they'll make human judgement look. The judges will be judged. Judges don't have to directly participate in this process, the algorithm will do its job of digging out tons of data generated from their lives and judgments to make its case. And when it does, our crisis—of not having any authority to settle our disputes, determine our punishments and define what's the right thing to do—will worsen.

A legal-technology company along with a data-analysis firm in India also began analysis on judicial biases based on the previous orders and judgments. They contacted the courts to explain how the process might help existing and future judges improve judgments with technology tools. The judiciary not only refused access to records for conducting the study but instead issued a notice stating that such an analysis cannot be conducted until the government itself orders the study.

These are not distant problems at all. France has already seen through the economic and social repercussions of knowing in advance the direction of the judgment. In a first, it decided to ban 'judicial analytics'—the use of statistics and machine learning to understand and predict the behaviour of judges.[13] Engaging in such a study could now land a person in prison for up to five years. While this may scare companies from commercially engaging in the potentially debilitating project within France, it will not help boost the credibility of French courts when everyone else starts using AI to boost trust.

Like in the case of most emerging technologies, there's one country that isn't afraid of this new chaos, for it has no next election to win. Yes, China. It has actually begun a mass digitization drive for converting the decision of Chinese courts into data sets that are accessible to researchers for training and creating better AI.[14] This gold mine of data is up for public use but behind a paywall.

Since the Chinese model is not built on sacred compassionate principles of the human capacity to reason but rather on an authoritarian logic of meritocracy, it actually has an incentive to improve the efficiency and consistency of its courts. And it is in this experimental process of breaking things that it might stumble on good use cases of AI in justice. Some lower-level courts in China are creating a 'similar cases pushing' system that provides judges with related cases to help them quickly arrive at coherent rulings. They are also working on an error-correcting system called the 'abnormal judgment warning' function to identify rulings that are not coherent with past judgments. Such situations would trigger an alarm for senior judges to give the case a second look.

China doesn't have the meta problems of democracies. It defines its own arbitrary lines and enforces them with an iron fist. It is very worrisome that as democracies take the compassionate route of slowing down the tyranny of data and AI, the enthusiastic cheering on by China will poach the best researchers and scientists by giving them greater experimental freedom that may not necessarily be ethical for any other country. We fear that playing dirty might win the fight for the greater evil.

Playing god is pretty damn godless

We briefly talked about DNA ancestry technology becoming a dangerous tool of bigotry. How can we not acknowledge the dangers of gene-editing technology becoming mainstream?

Human history is largely the history of humans trying to improve their survival chances by beating deadly diseases. Societies that figured out how to make their people live are the only ones that survived to tell their stories. But all of it depended on what we could see from the outside and later its manifestations inside the body. You knew you were sick only after the sickness had got you. Genetic editing gives us the power to attack some of the diseases before they even happen.

There are two kinds of cells in the human body, somatic cells and germ-line cells. Somatic cells comprise most of your body cells, hair, hands, tongue, etc. They are non-hereditary, meaning they live and die with you. To edit a somatic cell is to edit only you. Germ-line cells are reproductive cells that can create embryos—they carry your genetic information into your kids. Any alteration in these cells is an alteration in the whole generation that will follow you. Isn't that a terrifying power to have? Robert Sapolsky, in his masterpiece *Behave: The Biology of Humans at Our Best and Worst*[15] talks about a contrasting humility of archaeologists. When they excavate a site, they leave most of the site untouched. They know future archaeologists are going to be horrified at their archaic methods and techniques. It is almost certain someone's going to know far more than you know today, but if you destroy the whole site, nobody's going to have a chance at better understanding or editing it.

For a long time, there has been a broad consensus about editing somatic cells for removing future health risks. If we can know someone is going to get cancer in a year, why shouldn't we edit the gene responsible for the same? Where it actually gets tricky is the line between what is considered a disease and what is not. Being healthy and being healthy enough sound similar but are two very different states of the body. In fact, like the basic survival needs of human beings, the definition of what's healthy enough is never static. Coupled with our improved access to data about who has a better chance of living longer, it keeps getting better, and it should.

Obesity is a good case study. We know the impact obesity has on our ability to live a long, happy life. But we don't know if the same is true for being chubby or having a body with a higher-than-normal fat percentage. We know there's a muscle mass that's optimal for the human body. But does that make all people deviating from it sick? Until you have a very large data set about the lives of people who exercised every day and those who chose to consume high levels of sugar, you cannot make a definitive assertion. If we did, all pot-bellied Indian cops would straight away be disqualified from service.

If you have seen people who eat trash all the time and manage to look healthier than gym freaks, you already know about the existence of certain genes that are better for metabolism and maintaining healthy muscle mass.

The question before ethicists and geneticists is whether you should be allowed to get your fat-related genes replaced with these genes. Because once you have, you will come for the eye colour, then for the facial symmetry, then for the melanin levels. Remember the old dictum of 'You cannot change the world, but you can change yourself'? When you come from a community that is discriminated against, like for having dark skin in India, your crusade to change the mindset of a billion people will be far less attractive as an option compared to a skin-colour-change therapy at a nearby clinic.

The project of wanting everyone to live a happy life would not take long to turn into a eugenics race. Much like the urban landscapes, all people will begin to look like each other. You need a very genuine commitment to diversity to refute this race.

Science is insufficiently precise for now to enable these changes, but it's getting better fast.

Health means having the same diseases as everyone else. Even though it is absolutely frustrating, we don't complain about our intolerance to extreme temperatures because everyone has the same issues; we just get an AC or a heater installed. But when all the inconveniences of the human body are preventable, not just curable, it becomes difficult to ascertain what's normal. Once we are done editing our body to look good, like Bollywood stars, we will demand to become smart like the ISRO scientists. Where does it end?

What came before the bang?

There's an old joke about a woman who tells an astronomer that she thinks the earth is balanced on the back of a turtle. The astronomer doesn't disagree, but he has a humble question, 'What is the turtle standing on?' And in turn what is the thing below the turtle balancing on? Turtles all the way down!

The astronomer's turtle questioning wins him the day, but the problem of infinite regress is one of the most mind-boggling.

Even the hard-line religious elements confess to a Big Bang taking place in the universe. A massive explosion leads to the creation of galaxies, stars and the planets. Where they disagree though is about *who* caused the Big Bang? When Napoleon asked the physicist Pierre-Simon Laplace where was God in his model of the universe, the scientist replied, 'Sir, I have not needed that hypothesis.' And indeed, since Laplace, modern physicists haven't needed God in their story of the universe's creation. We don't have all the answers, but we have probable explanations for the time being. Einstein's discovery of space-time being intertwined means the question about what came before the Big Bang isn't really valid. There cannot be time without space. When there was nothing, there was no time. The question of time arises only when space is born, and space was born after the Big Bang.

Then the religious ask, who really kick-started the process that led us from nothing to something? And once you answer that with a scientific explanation, there is going to be another doubt about what was before it. This is a healthy scepticism that motivates us to push the limits of science. But when this human curiosity to understand nature gets a time-maker God, there's not much you and I can do about it. Mostly, the reason for why so many of us think there are no explanations for why the universe is the way it is, or we could have evolved into such intelligent creatures from single cells, is because our education never puts the larger picture in perspective. If you study physics, you will understand the Big Bang; if you study biology, you will understand evolution; if study mathematics, you will understand probability and randomization; and if you study history, you will know the creation of cultures. Every time one or more parts of the puzzle are missing, you are going to need a God.

Stories aren't a problem, but Ram Lalla getting a lawyer to argue for his birth spot should alarm us about the level of scientific education in the country.

Stephen Jay Gould says we've been on this planet for only 0.0015 per cent of the time. It didn't need us much of the time, and still wouldn't need us if we disappear tomorrow. We are here because of an accident, not a culmination of a cosmic plan. Our evolution is also an infinitely unpredictable process, which you can under no circumstances repeat. We aren't looking for aliens who look like us, other God's children. 'But wind back life's tape to the dawn of time and let it play again—and you will never get humans a second time.'[16]

Finite regress

In an interview archive popularly attributed to BBC's *Fun to Imagine* TV series in 1983, Richard Feynman talks about why the 'why' question doesn't die. The interviewer begins by asking Feynman about the 'feeling' between two magnets when they come together and move away.[17] The world-renowned teacher replies impatiently, 'They repel each other.' The interviewer wouldn't give up either, and asked, 'What does that mean . . . how are they doing it?'

'Of course, it's an excellent question. But the problem, you see, when you ask why something happens, how does a person answer why something happens? For example, Aunt Minnie is in the hospital. Why? Because she went out, slipped on the ice, and broke her hip. That satisfies people. It satisfies, but it wouldn't satisfy someone who came from another planet and who knew nothing about why when you break your hip do you go to the hospital. How do you get to the hospital when the hip is broken? Well, because her husband, seeing that her hip was broken, called the hospital up and sent somebody to get her. All that is understood by people. And when you explain a "why", you have to be in some framework that you allow something to be true. Otherwise, you're perpetually asking why. Why did the husband call up the hospital? Because the husband is interested in his wife's welfare. Not always, some husbands aren't interested in their wives' welfare when they're drunk, and they're angry.'[18]

The core idea of Feynman's friendly rant is that 'why on why' usually has to end somewhere. The answers keep getting deeper, provided you have the patience and knowledge required to understand the context. The complexity of the world cannot be condensed into a thirty-minute interview. There are several degrees of explanation and what works to satiate you depends on your level of familiarity and the resources at hand. Feynman says, 'I mean, I could go a little further back if I went more technical—but on an early level I've just gotta tell you that's going to be one of the things you'll just have to take as an element of the world: the existence of magnetic repulsion, or electrical attraction, magnetic attraction.'

The idea is that we sometimes need to draw a line—a finite one at that. It's true that the quest for knowledge is essential to the human endeavour. As any ISRO scientist will tell you, it is not important to have all the answers, but it is important that we ask the questions. But sometimes a rocket scientist draws a line out of chalk to break a coconut on it. Some things you have to believe.

6

Sustainability: Don't Break the Planet

As the poorest third of the world gets lifted out of poverty, we will find ourselves consuming more of everything—more clothes, more cars, more ACs and more packaged items of every sort. And that's mostly a good thing, as everybody deserves a human experience that is at an ever-evolving level of comfort. But the ever-increasing consumption does bring with it issues of waste management, something we are already terrible at.

These days, everything we buy is packed in multiple layers. A pair of speakers Akshay recently bought from Amazon came in three different boxes, Russian-doll style. Amazon is quite infamous for packing small items in large boxes and filling the remaining space with air packs. India is quickly catching up to the packing standards of the west, and it is now common to see even bananas wrapped in plastic. Banana is a fruit that already has a peel that you have to unwrap to eat. It certainly does not need a plastic covering on top as well. Apples are already coated in wax to preserve their freshness, so they can also do without plastic. Although some packing is essential for transportation, there are better alternatives than the ones we are switching to. Fruit used to be packed in confetti made from old newspapers but now come wrapped in plastic. And I am sure you have eaten biscuits that are individually packed, which are in turn packed in a box. This is clearly a problem.

Plastic was invented in 1907 but caught on around the 1960s, when plastic bags became a popular alternative to cloth sacks. By the 1970s, bottled water was a thing. In this period, 8.3 billion metric tons of plastic has been produced on earth, of which 6.3 billion metric tons has already been discarded. While about 9 per cent of that has been recycled, 72 per cent is in landfills.[1] Plastic takes 400 years to degrade, which means it will stay here for a while. About 8 million metric ton ends up in our oceans every year.

We are already unable to manage the waste we produce currently, and the problem is set to get worse. Suggestions to do a full one-eighty and go back to the old ways by not using so many processed items are unrealistic for most of us. We are never going to go back to a less-consumption-prone world. What we can do instead is make things that wreck the environment less. That's a sentiment everyone can get behind. Keep up the consumerism but make slight changes in your habits, and you are saving the earth! Sounds like a deal, right?

But the thing is, it's often not easy to know what alternative is more sustainable. Let's look at grocery plastic bags. Big Bazaar lets you buy a cloth bag for 8 bucks. But is it actually better than the single-use plastic bags it is replacing? Well, that depends on what variable of sustainability you are looking at. According to a study, you will have to use your cotton tote bag 131 times[2] to compete with a polybag in terms of its lifecycle emissions. In fact, every type of bag will have a different impact based on whether you are looking at carbon emissions (during production and across the product's life), the overall water consumption or the ecological impact it causes after being discarded.

Plastic items that one can use for a long time are okay. The issue lies with single-use plastic that is difficult to recycle. Wrappers of ready-to-eat food items like chips and biscuits are essentially unrecyclable due to their multilayered design which is difficult to separate out. Plastic that does get recycled is often downcycled, which means making a lower-value product from the recycled material. So the next time you are buying groceries at Big Bazaar, either bring your own bags or just take the trolley to your car, no bags required.

The reason we as a country are having a discourse on what's the best method to carry groceries is because India has banned plastic bags below a certain thickness.[3] The only way to help keep the environment usable is to find such large-scale solutions that often come via public policy that supercharges the magnitude of impact. The environment is too important to be left at the mercy of individual consumers.

Instead of putting the onus on individuals to not use plastic, India now puts the responsibility on companies that are creating this plastic in the first place. This is known as 'extended producer responsibility'. The government plans to ban plastic cups and straws, with states like Delhi leading the charge. The secret as to why India is doing better than most on this front? Cows. The anti-plastic sentiment in India grew when the nation's favourite animal started eating polybags from open garbage-disposal areas and subsequently starving to death as the undigested plastic blocked the digestive tracts.[4] Even though our government might not necessarily have acted for environmental reasons, all we can do is thank the cow for the ban. Long live the cow!

India recycles a lot more than most countries. By some estimates, up to 60 per cent of the plastic[5] produced in the country gets recycled, mostly thanks to the informal sector.[6] All the recyclable plastic is picked up from every nook and cranny across the country by millions of ragpickers who then sell it to larger scrap-dealers, who in turn sell it to plastic recycling units. There it gets turned into pellets, which are then used to make new things. This is possible only because recycling in India is financially viable for all parties involved, mostly thanks to the countless indigent kids on whose frail backs this industry rides.

Akshay once found himself in one such mini factory where the owner was showing him the tiny plastic pellets made from ground PET bottles. 'Will they be turned back into coke bottles?' the author asked. 'No, we make them into *pawwas* [bottles for country liquor] since the quality isn't there,' he replied under his breath. This is a classic case of downcycling, where products are more likely to get dumped then get recycled one more time. Since most recycling in India happens in small set-ups like the one the author visited, improper treatment can in fact result in more emissions, which makes the entire process moot. A little regulation here would go a long way, and its implementation even further.

More than policy that aims to make amends after the plastic has been made, a bigger change can come from fixing the production end of the pipeline, i.e. the corporations making the plastics in the first place. Keventers serves its milkshake in glass bottles that can be reused. The Instagram-ready bottles work for the brand. We can't leave these decisions to the goodness of these companies. We need policy that makes companies do good, curing the disease at its root.

Plastic can be seen not only in packaging—it's everywhere, even on our bodies. Despite India being the land of khadi and cotton, the fact is that it's expensive. Expensive because it takes up limited resources like water and land that can instead be used for food.

Most clothes are a blend of polymer and natural fibres as they are both affordable and more comfortable to wear (as opposed to 100 per cent cheap polymer which can cause discomfort). Recycling only works with stuff made of a single type of material, so these blended clothes have no home but landfills.

Shoe companies spend a lot of effort making synthetic materials that make the shoes better. The famous Adidas Ultraboost shoes have a 'boost' midsole made of a proprietary TPU (thermoplastic polyurethane) that is not recyclable. Nike's flagship VaporMax features a synthetic polymer upper that is similarly hard to recycle.

But Adidas did make a version of their shoe that is made up of 85 per cent recycled plastic by teaming up with 'Parley for the Oceans', an environmental organization that addresses threats towards oceans. Nike goes a step further because their entire VaporMax line uses an air capsule made of 75 per cent recycled TPU in place of a traditional foam sole. Both shoes still suffer from the fact that they are made up of different materials and complex mixtures, and hence like most shoes cannot be recycled further. This problem in the textile industry is known as 'closing the loop'. The aim is to make a product that is recyclable on both ends; Adidas recently demonstrated the 'Futurecraft.Loop' sneaker, which can be 100 per cent recycled into a new shoe. They did this by making every component of the shoe with just one type of polymer, and that's an achievement. The old sneaker becomes 10 per cent of a new one. It's set to go on sale to consumers in 2021.[7]

When it comes to plastic we can't avoid, it is a complex bargain. If you need to carry a bag, you are better off with a plastic one if you use it several times. Several brands now sell organic cotton, which is better for the environment than both normal cotton (because organic does not require pesticides) and polyester (in terms of its post-life ecological impact). But out of these three, organic cotton requires the most amount of water to produce.[8] And in fact cotton is pretty hard to recycle into a new fabric, as it tends to lose its strength when the fabric is cut up and spun again into yarn.

One Indian speciality that is slowly fading away are our local durzis, the tailors who sit with nothing but a sewing machine by the roadside and sew everything from torn jeans to entirely new clothing out of old ones. This is traditional upcycling that we have been doing for decades. However, if these tailors are instead now able to make more money stitching hoodies for Nike, who are we to stop them?

Back when Akshay was running a clothing company, he saw a lot of extra fabric get wasted, despite the best effort of the pattern-cutters. There is software that reduces this wastage, but there's still a lot of fabric that does not get turned into clothing and is thrown away. One company trying to remedy this is the Delhi-based Doodlage. They make high-street fashion wear from this very waste cloth. These kinds of large initiatives at a larger scale can help reduce cloth wastage.

So, all you need to do is buy recycled plastic, upcycled clothes and recyclable shoes and you are golden! As it turns out, going green takes effort, and there are still no clear-cut answers. The only good way out is to optimize for the longevity of whatever product you do buy. Wear it out, and don't buy more than you need. That optimizes for both biodegradability and a smaller carbon footprint. And then it doesn't matter what your clothes are made of. Polyester is okay too. There are just not enough natural materials for all of us. Not at the affordable cost of plastic and polymer. And there definitely aren't enough sheep for all of us to be able to afford wool sneakers. Organic fibres aren't necessarily the answer. Rather, a less plastic future is a future with less stuff.

While engaging with the alternative education movement in India, Akshat got a chance to experience sustainable living from close. He had taken a trip to Udaipur to visit Swaraj University, a radical experiment in learning on the outskirts of the city. When the app announced *You've arrived at your destination* in the middle of almost a jungle, Akshat was terrified. This was nothing like the university he had imagined, and he was scheduled to stay there for quite a few days. He soon found out there were a few buildings, with minimal fanciness and a lot of bamboo architecture. They grew their own food, made their own cleaning liquids, created little to no waste and used very few gadgets (no Wi-Fi, of course). It is a great experiment, though not necessarily the one urban folks like the author would quickly embrace. The dining hall had a flower-nectar-based room freshener, but the student dorms had enough commercial consumer products to make up for this clean living.

We need a solution that helps us reduce our footprint at our pace and eases us into zero-waste alternatives. Lauren Singer is doing exactly that with her 'Trash is for Tossers' YouTube channel.[9] She, by her own claim, has only made enough waste in the past five years to fit into a small mason jar. Everything else was biodegradable, and she composted it. 'I like to ask myself, do I want to be remembered for what I did while I was on this planet, or for the trash that I left behind?' she told Akshay when he interviewed her. Her company, Package Free, which aims to make zero-waste items more accessible to everyone, is backed by more than $4 million of venture capital.[10] She sells sustainable versions of most FMCG products, and they all come, well, package-free. When Akshay asked Lauren if such individual efforts were worth it, she said, 'Every change that you take to reduce your waste is positive. Even if it's small, it makes a difference.'

Grassroots movements like hers are what eventually turn the tide in terms of public policy. A good example of this is Afroz Shah, who famously led the movement to clean up Versova Beach in Mumbai. In 2015, he started alone with the intention of cleaning up an entire beach, but soon his one-man operation spread, and hundreds joined him, making it the world's largest beach clean-up. Soon after he started, people started taking notice. Amitabh Bachchan, who lives only a few kilometres away, gave him an extractor to help with the garbage collection.

Shah has set up an entirely circular economy, where the plastic gets recycled and the rest gets picked up by government authorities, who got in on the action later. He also helped clean up nearby toilets and made them usable, which reduced open defecation on the beach. We do need such movements to push both corporations and governments to enact policies and move the needle quicker. Because we are out of time.

The Indian government was recently praised for the number of toilets they set up in the last few years—2.6 crore toilets in the five years since the launch of the 'Swachh Bharat Mission', per their claim.[11] The government says this has led to sanitation coverage in villages going from 38 per cent in 2014 to 98 per cent in 2019. Which is all well, except that most villages in India don't even have piped water. Dwarka in New Delhi and Greater Noida in Uttar Pradesh—one of the largest localities in the National Capital Region and both places where Akshay has lived—still don't have a municipal water supply. Dwarka has water delivered in trucks, as extracting underground water is illegal in the capital. In UP, anything goes, so they just deplete the water table at will. The further you go from the capital, the worse it gets.

What use are toilets when there is no water to get rid of your business? The entire idea is that they are supposed to be safer than open defecation, but when people find them clogged, they do what makes sense to us Indians—find a railway track. Their business then eventually flows into the edges of farms which are often lined with a vegetable that can grow well despite or rather due to what the rain brings in—cabbages. Maybe put a little more thought into your next subway sandwich. The conventional solution of laying pipes and then shipping water through them from a central source to every household is an expensive endeavour, especially in sparsely populated places. We need a more local solution for water that could involve some combination of rainwater harvesting and recycling on location. An innovation in toilets such that they don't require as much water but still maintain hygiene won't hurt either.

We can avoid shipping water in cities as well, but in a different way. A lot of the household items we buy, especially cleaning products like fabric detergents and dishwashing soaps are often up to 90 per cent water. This increases both the shipping costs and the amount of plastic packaging required to pack these items. SC Johnson, the company behind glass-cleaning agent Windex, has now started selling their products in a concentrated form that require up to 80 per cent less plastic;[12] this has also resulted in lowering the weight of the package and reducing the carbon footprint brought about by shipping. You just mix the concentrate with water in a container you buy only once, or at least less often. This offers improvements of over 10x, the kind of magnitude change we love.

The clothing crisis

The global supply chain that outsources not only work but also guilt is at the centre of what leads fashion to be unsustainable. If clothing for Americans were to be made in America, it would cost more and would result in people buying more judiciously. This would also reduce the carbon footprint of the clothes due to reduced shipping.

An innovative but harsh idea to reduce carbon emissions might be to tax clothes higher and use it to offset some of the carbon costs associated with the production of that item. If the production of a $10 tee wrecks the environment enough that undoing the damage would cost $10, the tee should be sold for $20, and the $10 be used to fix the environment. But the primary issue remains that sequestration is so expensive that most goods will end up being priced out of everyone's reach in this model. A small increment in price across an industry might not hurt demand though—say, a cess that is exclusively used to find lower-carbon ways of production or cheaper methods of sequestration. Or maybe the slump in demand would kick companies to pour more money into research to figure out cheaper ways to reduce their carbon footprints.

And just maybe this reduced demand would help stop tragedies like the Rana factory fire that happened in Dhaka in 2013. Akshay has had the experience of being familiar with the clothing industry and has been in factories nestled in the narrow bylanes of Old Delhi. One such factory Akshay visited was situated on the second floor, with narrow, congested stairs that felt dangerous when not on fire. The Rana factory was the biggest fire in Bangladesh, but many such incidents go unreported. The author avoided working with factories that seemed unsafe by his own self-set standards but soon realized that his companies' orders were not even being made in the factories he had visited. They were often outsourced to the same dingy factories he wanted to avoid in the first place!

And that's the problem with the distributed supply chain—it's too distributed. When a large company like Zara hands out a contract to one factory, that factory might subcontract it to one or more smaller factories to free up their bandwidth and take on work from H&M as well. Both brands think that the factory has enough capacity for them and don't end up checking rigorously enough. Adding management to oversee just that would add to the overheads, and at that point they might just run the factory themselves, breaking their business model in the way.

There are economic benefits to the distributed network. If a certain brand has less demand, their factories don't sit idle. But what we need are better safeguards. Free markets, when operated across economies with such high purchasing-parity differentials, tend to exploit the poor a bit more than even their rich-economy customers might like. And the people being exploited share the sentiment.

Even though small businesses tend to be romanticized, this is a sector that can do with less informal enterprises. The informal sector often exploits its labour more and gets away with flouting more ecological norms. Akshat's dad runs a factory for industrial wooden packaging; he never felt the ripples caused by labour or environmental reforms during his lifetime. The vast majority of Indian enterprises are nameless like his dad's. They are profitable enough for their children to have had a comfortable life but not large enough to be written about by even a local daily. While you and Akshat can boycott straws, his dad is unlikely to factor sustainability while rethinking his supplier.

Big corporations are easier to regulate as the buck stops with just a handful of companies and brands. And then of

13

course we can start enforcing labour laws better. A lot of these jobs are about to go away anyway. Akshat might have to write a lot more books to maintain his lifestyle. More on this in the automation chapter.

The energy grid and carbon

Food, water and energy are the three most important things that can lift the last billion out of poverty. Cavemen got by on just food, water and fire (energy) to cook the food. In the 21st century, these three are still the most important resources essential for survival. The most common methods of energy distribution now are electricity, followed by hydrocarbon fuels like petrol, diesel and LPG/CNG.

Energy helps substitute a large portion of manual labour needed to survive, freeing up our time for other things. Ever since Benjamin Franklin invented electricity and Thomas Edison commercialized it, electricity has been the most viable format of energy distribution, thanks to its versatility. Cheaper electric energy can directly enable us to get food and water to the poor. There's a water shortage only because we can't consume salty ocean water as is. Right now, desalination is not cheap enough to be done on a mass scale. We need it to be 10x cheaper to be viable. And the major cost of desalination is energy. We could essentially desalinate infinite amounts of water if energy were 10x cheaper. And that water and cheap energy could in turn be used to grow tons of food. It all boils down to energy.

And it goes beyond just food and water. Cheap energy can single-handedly improve the standard of living of billions.

One of the most important things that separate the Indian middle class from the poor is cooling. And the primary barrier to air conditioning is electricity costs. If energy could be made cheaper, it would make life better for a lot of us. And we need a lot more of it. This is not a recipe for infinite consumption, however. The energy consumption per person has already peaked in places like New York City, where it has been stagnant for decades.[13] Since most of our domestic consumption comes from heating and cooling both air and water, after we achieve that, the consumption should not increase much for a long while.

If you read the newspapers and look at the numbers though, you would conclude that we are in power-surplus. We have a peak installed capacity of 350 GW, with our demand peaking at only 180 GW.[14] Some of that installed capacity is not met due to fuel shortages, some due to the cyclic nature of renewable energy, while some is lost in transit. But despite that we do have energy that nobody is willing to buy because the rates are too high for most people. In fact, most energy distribution companies (discoms) in India are operating in losses because they are selling energy at lower rates than they buy it at. The issue is of price.

The average American consumes about 12,000 kWh of energy per year as compared to only 1000 kWh by the average Indian. We can consume way more and, as we get richer, we will. The second part of the problem is that the grid isn't expansive enough. Every year, Piyush Goyal, the erstwhile power minister, claims that 100 per cent rural electrification is just a few months away, and the media reports it with a sense of amnesia about his previous announcements. While that is good PR for the government, the fact remains that people in both cities and villages often resort to diesel generators to meet their power demands, which clearly shows that supply does not meet demand.

Our energy production is the largest contributor to carbon emissions in the atmosphere. When including all sectors, like transportation, in addition to electricity, energy production contributes to over 70 per cent of all greenhouse gases (GHGs).[15] Given our increasing energy demands, if we don't solve this now, we will not be able to stop global warming wreaking irreversible damage.

Walk into any electronics store and you will find a wall littered with ACs with varying star ratings, depending on how much energy they consume. India also suffers from badly designed homes with insufficient insulation which require ACs to run for longer to maintain a cool temperature. In November 2019, the Government of India selected eight finalists for its 'Global Cooling Prize'.[16] The idea was to develop new technology for cooling that has a lower carbon footprint, with the winner taking home over a million dollars.

Ever seen a Hollywood movie where you see steam coming out of the vents on the side of the roads? That was most likely set in New York, one of the few cities in the world that has a steam system in place. It supplies houses with, well, steam through pipes, so that it can be used for heating as well as cooling, at a much lower carbon footprint than traditional methods. And the steam is mostly a by-product of electricity production, not requiring new energy production.

The Government of India issued an advisory[17] in June 2018, asking AC manufacturers and commercial buildings to have the default temperature set at 24 degrees Celsius, up from the 16–18 that was sometimes used, which would help reduce energy consumption. But no matter how efficient we make our ACs, it is never going to reduce the nation's total energy consumption. That's because there will always be more and more people coming out of poverty buying new ACs and these small percentages of efficiencies will not matter.

We have to increase efficiency by a factor of 10 rather than 10 per cent, and the only way to do that is to focus on the production end, not the consumption end. Five-star devices and better-thermally-insulated houses do, however, reduce your personal bill by a bit, so feel free to buy them for that reason.

The way we produce most of our energy is by turning a turbine. Aside from solar, all of our energy sources work this way. Coal is used to create steam, which in turn rotates the wings of a turbine. Nuclear reactors create steam as well. Wind and tidal turn the turbine directly, no steam required. India produces most of its energy from coal. The catch-22 with coal is that it is pure carbon (C), which makes it a high-density store of energy. And of potential CO_2. When we burn coal to make electricity, it oxidizes to CO_2. Carbon emissions from coal are too high, and Indian coal plants are exceptionally inefficient. Indian coal plants produce .91 to .95 kilograms per kWh (1 kWh is 1 'unit' on your electricity bill).

Carbon capture, or 'sequestration', is a set of technologies that attempt to absorb carbon from the atmosphere in some form that can ideally be buried underground (or recycled to produce something else). Carbon capture right now costs anywhere between $300–600 per ton of CO_2 absorbed.

Some companies claim they can get it down to $50, but they are assuming the carbon captured will be used to make other products, like making sodas bubbly. But in all honesty, even tech titans like Bill Gates couldn't drink enough diet coke to save the environment.

Assuming the carbon is buried underground, and being optimistic, let's say we can bring down the cost of carbon capture to $100 per ton. Assuming this cost will be born at the point of production by discoms, to absorb the extra cost, this would increase the price of 1 unit (1 kWh) by Rs 7. Currently, one unit costs between Rs 4–8 in Delhi, depending on usage. This would increase the cost by a factor of 2–3x. That is steep. And if there's something the Delhi government does not seem to like, it is increasing the cost of power. And we still don't know how to safely lock in and store the captured carbon.

The future is nuclear

But there's a much cleaner alternative than burning carbon and messily trying to capture it back. It's called nuclear fission. And it releases only 1/100th[18] the carbon of coal for the same amount of energy. The cost of production for nuclear energy is about the same as coal, and carbon emission is one order of magnitude less, which is lower emissions than solar energy and as good as wind energy. So why aren't we going nuclear already?

Because of accidents like Fukushima and Chernobyl, we just collectively veered away from the nuclear path. Germany has been phasing out nuclear energy since the Fukushima accident in Japan in 2011. It plans to shut down all its nuclear plants by 2022. Italy has already phased out all its nuclear plants, and several other countries are in the process of shutting their units down. Nuclear-energy production across the world has been stagnant for over a decade.

'Nuclear' screams danger to most people, and it's hard to adopt a technology without support from people. The problem with Chernobyl's reactor was that it was an old model. And we learned enough from Chernobyl to avoid damage to human health during Fukushima. There are zero deaths directly attributable to Fukushima,[19] which happened during a tsunami that killed 200,000 people on its own. There were indirect deaths, but the highest estimate was 1600, which is 50x less as compared to Chernobyl; the reason being that technology had improved a lot in the thirty years that separated the reactor models. Chernobyl employed an 'RBMK 1000 reactor' designed in the 1950s, known as 'generation 1' design. It had no containment dome over the reactor. Fukushima's newer 'generation 2' design had a dual-layer dome, though it was breached during the tsunami.

Most reactors in operation today were built a long time ago and are considered generation 2. The ones that are being built today are considered 'generation 3' and are much safer. The 'AP1000' reactor designed by Westinghouse Electric Company tackles afterheat in case of a mishap, by having water falling on the rods, and contains the situation for forty-eight hours. There is active work being done on 'generation 4' reactors. These newer reactor designs reduce the risk of explosions and meltdowns much further, and with several fail-safes are much safer than the previous designs.

One good gen 4 design that is particularly interesting for India is the thorium reactor, which will replace uranium with thorium. India has the fourteenth-largest reserves of recoverable uranium but boasts 25 per cent of the world's thorium, the largest reserve of any country.

Even when taking both these incidents into account, nuclear is much safer than coal. Per TWh (1 terawatt-hour is 10^9 kWh) of energy, coal kills over 300 times more people than nuclear. Nuclear's safety record is only bested by solar and wind.[20] Coal mining and oil extraction are the deadliest jobs one can have today.

The authors find it immoral that people are okay with other people risking their lives in coal mines just so that they can have electricity and argue about how nuclear fission is not safe. They fear that a nuclear fallout will spread to their homes and air-conditioned malls, ignoring the miners dying in rathole mines in Meghalaya. Thanks to the global media that is fixated on 'tragedy entertainment', the reality remains contained within their TV sets.[21] Only the underprivileged die in coal mines. They work in hellish conditions, with no room to move and no light to see, for hours at a stretch, and often risk not only their health but also their lives just so we have electricity. Going nuclear is by far the safest means of large-scale and reliable energy production. Another concern people have is about post-production waste, the nuclear waste that will have to be monitored. Guess what, the post-production waste from coal is the one giving us lung cancer. There is 100x more radioactivity near a coal plant per unit of electricity produced as compared to a nuclear plant. This is because natural coal contains trace percentages of uranium, which is emitted into the air when the coal is burned.[22] Indian coal plants also release sulfur oxide and other harmful gases that go unchecked into the atmosphere despite promises by political parties to do otherwise.[23]

However, nuclear energy does produce waste that takes hundreds of years to stop being toxic. Surely, nuclear has a lot of scope for improvement. Current reactor designs only use about 4 per cent of the potential energy from uranium, and there's some work to be done to improve that substantially. Tech improves with investment, and we haven't been investing much. Reactors also require a clearance area, making them unsuitable to be located within dense cities like Delhi and Mumbai. But there's ample room for them to be installed at scale.

Fukushima was designed in the 1960s. A key component of innovation is being able to iterate at a low cost, two variables that nuclear does not permit. Unless you are in China, where entire train stations can be built overnight, nuclear reactors take a decade just to get built. Most venture firms expect returns on an eight-to-ten-year period, making reactor tech out of the purview of the start-up funding scene and leaving the bulk of the work to the government.

And the overbearing narrative about all Indian governments is that they tend to be not very smart. China can build a railway station in nine hours flat. In India, projects are stuck acquiring land from farmers who don't have any other alternatives for earning their livelihood. That's before all the delays due to red tape and bureaucracy. When Akshay visited the Qutub Minar in the summer of 2019, he was reminded of what he had once read in his history textbook. The structure had been built by three generations of rulers over a span of more than 150 years. The first set of workers made something they could never see completed in their lifetimes. That kind of cross-generational thinking seems to be absent in the age of ephemeral politics that seems more concerned with digging up the past for vested interests than building the future. But that's the kind of vision we need to bring back if we are to transition to a cleaner future.

The investment nuclear needs in research for new innovation is not anywhere near the level we need it to be at.[24] Thankfully, some in Silicon Valley are picking up the slack and investing in nuclear projects that might seem unviable for governments and traditional venture capital investors alike. Foremost amongst them is Bill Gates, who is leading the 'Breakthrough Energy Coalition' that comprises billionaire investors from all around the world, including our very own Mukesh Ambani.[25]

The venture fund associated with this group has an extraordinary return period of twenty years. The fund has been investing in radical nuclear reactor ideas that may or may not yield results as well as other technologies that promise a 'carbonless future'. Bill also invested in the nuclear company Terra Power in 2006, which in 2019 is already building their generation 4 reactor in China.

Do note that while the word 'nuclear' in the above context has meant 'nuclear fission', fission has an elusive cousin called fusion. A lot of people are hopeful for fusion, aka the endgame of energy. It is a virtually zero-waste method to produce electricity.

India is a part of the ITER (International Thermonuclear Experimental Reactor), the world's leading multi-country nuclear fusion initiative. It was in the news in 2019 on account of India having made the world's largest fridge (a vacuum cryostat) for the ITER project. At this point, ITER's next goal is to produce, for the first time, more energy than it consumes, which is kind of a basic requirement if you are in the business of energy generation. It plans to meet that goal only by 2035. They don't even intend to capture that energy as electricity but just let the heat out into the atmosphere. And this is going to take them fifteen years, with electricity production and adoption further away. Things move slowly in the nuclear world.

Fusion, even if it meets the most optimistic timelines, will be too late by the time it can be adopted to stop climate change. As opposed to fusion, we can mass-adopt fission now. We need fission to tide us over for about 100 years until we figure out fusion. The only barrier to fission is people don't feel safe, and those concerns have been resolved and are being further improved as discussed. However, nuclear reactors do take up to ten years to build, so we will have to start adopting now. And invest more in their R & D. The world's first thorium reactor could come from India, as we have the most to gain from it.

Nuclear does have its shortcomings. It can't be placed near cities. Cities like Delhi might have to look elsewhere, like the option of going fully solar. But is it even practical for a metropolitan city like Delhi to go entirely solar? Delhi has the world's worst pollution and could definitely do with cleaner energy production. Let's do some math.

The average cost of setting up a solar power station per MW capacity = Rs 5 crore (3.5–7.5 crore)

Delhi's power demand = 5000 MW (the peak is over 6000+ but let us assume that can be met by coal)

Total cost = 5000*5 crore = Rs 25,000 crore
Delhi's annual budget = Rs 50,000 crore

Spread the cost over 10 years (0 per cent interest for simplicity) and the cost comes to Rs 2500 crore, or 5 per cent of the annual budget—which is pretty massive. But the electricity will also bring in revenue.

The current solar tariff is at Rs 2.44/kWh
A 1 MW capacity plant produces about 6000 kWh per day
The total money made from selling electricity
= 2.44*6000*5000*365 = Rs 2671.8 crore

This seems doable except for the small fact of Delhi having no available land. A 1 MW solar power plant requires 5 acres of land, so a total of 25,000 acres would be needed—which is insane because Delhi's entire land area is 366,000 acres. That translates to roughly about 7 per cent of Delhi!

The Delhi government launched a plan to install solar panels on agricultural land at a height of 3.5 metres, and it could just work.

Let's do some more math.

The total cropped area in Delhi = 48,000 hectares (1997 data)
1/3 land available for solar = 16,000 hectares = 39,500 acres
The area required for 1 MW electricity production = 5 acres
The total energy that can be made = (39,500/5) MW =7900 MW
The peak all-time electricity consumption in Delhi = 6044 MW

In reality, it will be difficult to get close to the 8 GW figure, but this is a clever solution, because, as just mentioned, Delhi does not have enough land.

But the issue with solar and wind energy is that they cannot be scaled up according to demand and work according to the available sunlight and wind. Solar has zero output during the night, which makes it useless for large-scale deployment. With solar, you need a way to store the energy or an alternate backup plant to produce electricity that can be used when the sun don't shine and the winds don't blow.

The future is lithium

One solution for making solar viable at all times are lithium batteries. These rechargeable batteries are so ubiquitous in our daily life, from laptops to phones to now even cars and houses, but are still a pretty recent innovation. Most traditional cars that run on petrol or similar hydrocarbon fuels use an internal combustion (IC) engine. This works because hydrocarbons are a very dense store of energy. Just a litre of petrol will take you kilometres in a car that on its own weighs a ton. Previous 'lead-acid' batteries were too heavy for the energy stored in them to be able to move the vehicle and their own weight forward at acceptable mileage. The electric-car revolution is backed by lithium batteries being energy-dense enough to be able to drive a car. The Nobel Committee recognized this impact by awarding the 2019 Nobel Prize in Chemistry to three people responsible for developing and advancing the technology.

But lithium batteries are not 100 per cent green. They create carbon emissions in production and then need to be disposed of carefully when they can't be recharged any more. An interesting solution to save energy that is as efficient as lithium batteries but has lower carbon emissions is gravity. Essentially, you put something at a height when you have excess energy, and then you drop it when you need your energy back and capture the released energy with a turbine. A turbine is a device that gives out energy when rotated, and almost all of our energy, with the exception of solar, is made this way. Dams work on gravity, but there are new solutions that use this. For example, one solution involves lifting heavy cement blocks with the help of pulleys on top of one another, forming a tower. Then when you need energy, you drop them and convert the rotation of the pulley to electricity.

Transport is one of the top-three sectors of carbon emissions worldwide, with vehicular transport being a part of it along with aviation and shipping (water). Only in a dense city like Delhi does vehicular pollution start to stare right back at you.

So what about electric cars?

An average electric car with a mileage of 15 kWh/100 km will release 14.25 kg of CO_2 per 100 km when being charged by electricity coming from an Indian coal power plant. Most BMWs release under 120 gm/km or 12 kg of CO_2 per 100 km! Smaller cars with better mileage will emit even less. This is because our coal plants are inefficient as compared to those in developed countries. Electric cars don't make sense unless our grid is low-emission as well. A study by the Council on Energy, Environment and Water (CEEW)[26] shows that electronic vehicles (EVs) in India produce only 10 per cent less carbon as compared to internal combustion engines (ICEs).

But even at the same level of pollution electric cars are better because the carbon emission happens at a single point (the coal power station) as opposed to the millions of tailpipes in traditional cars. This makes it easy to capture the carbon. Like we often have pointed out in the book, many things are solved easily in production rather than consumption. Delhi's coal power-plants have already been ordered to install FGD (flue gas desulphurization) units which filter out the most harmful SO2 gas, but that still leaves carbon. For that, we need to switch out our grid to carbon neutral completely, but that will take at least two decades on an optimistic timeline. And it will require a massive push from the government. In late 2019, Delhi became the first state to launch a comprehensive EV policy and has started to set up electric charging points across the city.

But until that happens, consider an electric scooter. Even though two-wheelers like bikes have better mileage than cars, most non-carbon vehicular emissions in India come from the inefficient two-stroke ICE engines of two-wheelers. These pollutants are not only warming but also carcinogenic.[27] The aforementioned Delhi EV policy purports to solve this by requiring delivery companies to switch their two-wheeler fleet to at least 50 per cent electric in the next few years. Add to this the fact electric cars are expensive compared to equivalent ICE models. Teslas will be priced even higher in the luxury segment when they arrive, making them out of reach of the majority of Indians. And hence the authors are especially excited about Ather Energy, a start-up that believes that two-wheeler EVs are more important for India and has launched its first model in the country. They hope an electric scooter is bound to find wider adoption than prohibitively expensive electric cars.

Just like nuclear, the government spends the bulk of their money at the wrong end of the pipeline, in giving tax subsidies. They should rather invest directly at the innovation end. The FAME-II tax subsidy shaves off about Rs 27,000 off the price of an Ather scooter as opposed to Rs 22,000 in the previous policy, reducing the cost to Rs 1.23 lakh.[28] Akshay has been waiting to buy his Ather scooter for years, and early adopters like him are unlikely to care about marginal price reductions. In fact, the author pre-booked a pricier variant of the scooter on the day of its launch, even before its price was revealed! The government could instead take the additional 5k subsidy and invest it in battery research that could in turn reduce the real cost of the scooter, doing away with the need for a subsidy.

And if they do indeed want to go the tax-free route, they should go all out. Tesla has been unable to set up shop in India due to rigid regulations. The government should expedite the launch of Tesla as it might spur innovation in lower-tier electric cars.

Apart from EVs, there are other alternatives to ICEs as well. Honda has famously been showing off their hydrogen fuel cell tech ever since Akshay was born (about ten years before Akshat was), trying to tell everybody that its adoption is right around the corner. But the truth is that it is nothing but a PR exercise for the company. Hydrogen fuel cells are a form of energy storage, not production, competing with lithium batteries, not IC engines. The energy will have to be made elsewhere. A fuel cell works by combining hydrogen gas filled in a tank with oxygen freely available to produce water and energy. The problem is how do you get the hydrogen in the tank in the first place. You have to electrolyze water to break it into hydrogen and oxygen, and this reverse process consumes electricity. About 30 per cent of the energy is lost in converting water to hydrogen gas. You then need more energy to pressurize the hydrogen into liquid form. Transporting the hydrogen causes further energy losses as compared to the electricity grid, where energy losses are pretty low. You lose further energy while converting the hydrogen back into water. Batteries of course don't work at 100 per cent and create waste at the end of their life cycle, but the efficiencies are much better. So, yeah, decades from now, when our energy use and supply will be 10x of what it is now, and sustainability will trump capital efficiency thanks to surplus energy due to fission and fusion, hydrogen cells might make sense as an energy store over batteries. But not today. No matter how much recycled aluminium Apple uses in its

MacBooks, Saudi Arabia's Aramco still has twice as many trillion dollars in valuation and makes its money digging oil.

In public policy terms, renewables are both good and bad for governments. Governments own all the coal and oil of the country and make a ton of money by selling them. There's a reason the Middle East is rich, and the Indian coal scam was such a huge hit in the news. But the sun's rays and the winds that roam the surface of our planet are free for everybody, so the more a country switches to renewables, the less money a government makes.

The flip side is that a lot of wars on this planet have been fought over these hydrocarbon reserves. Look at the recent Syrian crisis created at the hands of the terrorist group ISIS. ISIS was able to afford its endeavour only through capturing oil wells and selling the crude oil to other nations via black markets. If we switch away from oil to a resource most countries have in bounty we take away much of the economics of war (even though wind and sunshine aren't the same everywhere, they are a lot more widely distributed then fossil fuels). And if a future terror attack involving drones lights up Aramco's oil field on fire, India's electricity bills won't be impacted. All in all, the short-term revenue loss will be more than compensated by the independence a nation will achieve.

Methane and meat

But carbon dioxide is not the only gas causing global warming. An important component of GHGs is methane. Methane comprises only 10 per cent of the total warming gases but reducing it is way more impactful than reducing CO_2. Methane is 30x more warming than CO_2 for the same weight, every 1 kg of reduction in methane is equivalent to 30 kg of reduction in CO_2 emissions. And the good news is that methane can just be burned (oxidized) to get CO_2. Furthermore, this process is a net positive in terms of energy production, as that energy can be converted into electricity. It's a no-brainer that we should burn all methane to convert it to energy and CO_2. In most cases, doing this is also economically positive and generates new income for whoever is letting their methane out into the atmosphere. The oil industry is a major source of methane, and we can convert that to CO_2.

The second major source is animals. Farm animals, specifically, reared either for meat or milk. Have you ever wondered why we raise cattle for their meat but not lions? It's about economics. A buffalo will require grains 10x its weight, but a lion will require 10x the buffalo by its weight, which translates to 100x the grains. The numbers are rough, but you get the idea. This makes most carnivorous animals uneconomical to be bred for mass consumption. This inefficiency of the meat that we do eat is what is straining the planet. Making a meat dinner requires much more land and water as compared to a vegetarian or vegan diet.

Currently, we eat about 70 billion land animals every year,[29] which includes cows, pigs and chicken.[30] If India and China were to eat as much meat per person as people in meat-saturation markets like the US and Europe do, all of the world's land would not be enough to raise these animals. And this is despite the fact that the majority of animals killed for human consumption are already raised in as tight a space as possible. The only reason we aren't eating as much meat? Not really because cows are sacred, but because we can't afford it. In fact, meat consumption in India has been rising rapidly, and China's rather exponentially, thanks to the growing economies of both countries. This is in contrast to Europe, where meat consumption is declining.

This is where plant-based meat comes in. Beyond Meat, a vegetable-based meat alternative, made by a company of the same name, cooks and tastes just like real meat. It releases 90 per cent less GHGs than animal meat. That's a differential of 10x, just what we need. Impossible Foods, another plant-based meat company, is already selling the Impossible Burger at Burger King outlets. Companies like Impossible Foods and Beyond Meat need to do really well for the planet to do well. They are both already valued in the billions, and they have just got started. And the fact that we save cows as a side benefit will make the likes of Baba Ramdev happy as well. If there's a market for plant-based beef anywhere in the world, it's in India.

Now, all the cow lovers can drink milk and be merry. Which would have been fine except for why we started talking about cows in the first place—the part where they leak methane from their posteriors. Even though Ramdev has found a way to bottle up cow urine, it's still not quite possible to bottle up cow farts. Cows are a bit difficult to understand. Cows, on one end of their digestive tract, helped us in getting plastic banned, but on the other end they spread methane. Until Ramdev figures out a way to market *gau* methane, let's just try soy milk? Milk isn't that nutritious after all.

As opposed to the common myth that sustainable living requires asceticism, we have multiple solutions that afford us high standards of living with low carbon emissions.

Of course, India can't stop using cement and steel to build infrastructure, whose production causes substantial carbon emissions. And we can't expect a developing country like India to compromise growth at a time when US President Trump has pulled out of the Paris Agreement on climate change. Most Indians are so hand-to-mouth that they can't really spare the economic or the mental bandwidth required to save the earth. We need cheap innovations. A German company has invented plates made out of leaves! But wait a second, that's what we used to have in our country. Remember eating aloo chat in a *pattal* with a wooden toothpick. Maybe cheap solutions involve improving on what we already had.

There are companies working on making low-emission green cement and bioplastic. With upcoming technology innovations on one hand and good policy on the other, we can tackle transport, electricity production and manufacturing, the three largest sectors in terms of GHG emissions.

Since the onset of civilization, the human experience has been defined by always wanting a little bit more. But that constant strive for growth has often come at the expense of the finite resources of the planet. It's time we start wanting a little bit more for the planet instead. We can indeed meet our carbon-emission goals[31] set during the Paris Agreement and prevent further climate change. And we should get there at full speed even if it means, in the words of climate activist Greta Thunberg, that we would need to give up our 'fairy-tale dreams of eternal economic growth'.[32]

7

Behavioural Economics: Coca-Cola Is a Happy Colour

In early 2014, a quizzing app built on Facebook's platform called 'This Is Your Digital Life'[1] collected data from millions of users, plus the hundreds of friends of all those millions. Facebook's policy allowed the apps to collect user data for improving their services but did not permit its open sale. Cambridge Analytica, a US-based political consulting firm, bought this data from the developer of the app without explicit consent from the users.

While the Cambridge Analytica case enjoyed unusual prominence in the news cycle, with the outrage at the election meddling, it is a fact that user data still changes hands quite often and mostly without our knowledge. The best Facebook could do under its old policies was to revoke access ex post facto.

Advertisers buy this type of data legally all the time. You can buy a list of HNI (high-net-worth individuals) Indians very easily, for as little as a few hundred rupees. Ever bought a car? Your dealership made money by selling your data to a car insurance provider. Internet tracking is an advanced—although a slightly more subtle—version of the same old game. And it is a perfectly legal practice.

Hundreds of companies track you on multiple sites to build your anonymous profile that can accurately help assess your shopping behaviour, political leanings and a whole host of other things valuable to advertisers. This helps Google and Facebook to figure out what ads you will like best and whether or not you will click on that e-commerce ad. Both Google and Facebook buy this data from large data brokers to help serve ads. Akshay has been on both sides of this equation—been annoyed by ads and has run ads for his businesses. Now that he runs ads for other people, he is firmly one of those who thinks if people are going to see ads, they better be relevant.

However, there's quite a lot of difference between relevant ads for toothpaste and manipulating an entire democracy's opinion in nefarious ways. Alexander Nix in 2017 proudly delivered speeches about how his company used people's data against them.[2] He boasted about manipulating people based on their personality to help pass gun laws. Nix talked about how someone who has a more fearful personality receives ads based upon those fears. This is called psychographic segmentation. Whether or not this works to the extent he describes is under debate by political scientists but the fact remains that this is happening in democracies all across the world and millions of dollars are being spent on this.

In fact, this was happening much before the big data craze. A prime example would be Advani's 1990 Rath Yatra.

It is well-documented that the route was designed through the towns that could be polarized the most and give BJP an edge in flipping the elections. Many of this country's regional politicians and now even national leaders have mastered the art of the 'dog whistle'—a thinly veiled speech that has two meanings depending on the audience, sometimes using different versions of speeches on the same day based on the audience and different styles to convert the different audiences. Cambridge Analytica did not invent the way humans think.

There's little any of us can do about our biology or evolutionary history. We are prone to be taken advantage of, being manipulated into doing things against our interests and falling prey to tricks. It's a part of the human contract. The push and pull of ideas is central to the making of any future. Democracy would not work if we were chemically stubborn about our beliefs. Sometimes the tactics of influence are not acceptable to the majority of us, which is why we have to set some basic rules. These are like hygiene standards.

For example, forty-eight hours before the voting day, all forms of election campaigning stops in India. It is often called the 'silence period' and all candidates are forced by law to observe it. There is no math as to why it is a forty-eight-hour period, and not twenty-four or seventy-two. There is a consensus about this being enough time for us to not be intoxicated by advertising and make up our minds, without the slogans. It is an absurd assumption and will likely change. Influencing is not illegal but doing it close to the election D-Day is.

We wrote this chapter to help you bargain better, both when choosing your potatoes at the supermarket and when choosing your potatoes at the poll booth. And in the process, we hope we would become more empathetic too.

What were you thinking?

'Is that what you really mean?'
'You behaved unlike yourself.'
'Perhaps you should reconsider your decision.'
'Give yourself some time.'

We all get impulsive, making harsh judgements, ignoring visible evidence, hastily drawing shallow conclusions. In retrospect, we never own up to these bad moments as our 'real selves'. Our erroneous behaviour, we believe, is almost always alien to what we honestly feel and think. If we had a little more time and were in a better mood, we would certainly not shout at each other or spend all that money on a fancy wallet.

Now, let's go back a few million years ago. You are one of the archaic versions of yourself, barely getting by in a patch of grassland in East Africa. Your day's to-do list could very well go from having lunch to becoming lunch. Since there is no anthropocentric superiority complex yet, your chances of making big in life are just as feeble as any other reptile. Imagine the number of mundane choices you'd make in such volatile times. Your brain would have to continually identify threats, categorize them by priority and make rapid decisions about responding to them—any neuroscientist will tell you that is a tremendous cognitive load. Our brains may be incredibly fast processors, but they aren't biologically evolved for domination. When there are thousands of killers staring at you at all times, the chances are your species will never even discover its natural lifespan.

However, there is only so fast our brain can react to aid our chances of survival. When scrounging for food, it doesn't have the luxury of patiently examining all possibilities.

Deciding whether a bit of wood was actually a camouflaging predator would require snap judgement. We would need some mental shortcuts that provided us with an advantage over others. There's much more this piece of wood can tell us about ourselves, wait till the next section.

The brain's answer to this evolutionary challenge was heuristics, mental processes to cut through the noise to reach immediate conclusions. These are the subconscious tools our brain invented for practical purposes.

Psychologists Daniel Kahneman and Amos Tversky were amongst the first to hint at the existence of these tricks. Through a series of experiments over many decades, they discovered two kinds of systems that shape our behaviours. System 1, as they called it, is the fast, automatic, intuitive approach, while System 2 is 'the mind's slower, analytical mode, where reason dominates'.[3]

Heuristics are a feature of System 1 in our brain. They are the techniques that help us reach quick decisions. We may want to insist that System 2 is the 'real us', and our hasty judgements guided by System 1 do not really represent our inner selves because it indeed is pretty fallible (I didn't *mean* to shout at you). While the intuitive approach evolved to come to our rescue in urgent situations, we don't understand enough about it and end up employing it in places it wasn't meant for. Learning more about heuristics and cognitive

biases caused by them can help us make better decisions in
life and save ourselves from embarrassment (hopefully).

Soothsayers

Let's begin with that mysterious piece of wood we spoke
about in the last section. The chances are that our Palaeolithic
friend would have confused it for a lion and run for his life.
No, he isn't a special paranoid kind. Actually, the probability
of the rest of us making the same error is pretty high.

And that's because nature favoured the survival of those
who made quick judgements, even if some of them were
unnecessarily alarmist. Being diligent and taking fewer
decisions may result in a higher accuracy rate, but it wouldn't
matter if one was dead by then. You were guaranteed a
longer life if you chose to find another source of food at
being confronted with even the slightest sign of danger. We
became especially wary of living things since they happened
to provide the only plausible dangers that we were equipped
to avert. We could not predict a hurricane, hailstorm or
flood, nor do anything about it. But we did have a chance
against our wild competitors. This gave us our enthusiastic
tendency to apparently see or recognize patterns and images
in random shapes and lines, also called pareidolia.[4] (Yes, your
friend actually sees lions in floating vapours.)

Some people claim to have seen faces on Mars, the image
of a Ganpati on a potato, Jesus in a chapatti, the Virgin Mary
in a cheese toastie—all cases of pareidolia. Carl Sagan even
theorized this sensitivity for faces as an evolutionary need
shaped in babies millions of years ago; infants who could

recognize a face and smile back were likely to win the hearts of their parents and prosper, he wrote in his book *The Demon-Haunted World*.

In case you were wondering, the cheese toastie fetched over $28,000 in an eBay auction. It is a testament to our tendency to identify patterns where there are none, to assign meaning to random events and make faulty over-optimistic conclusions. It is about our habit of looking at the world through our prejudiced lenses, and not taking enough time to think above and beyond the little we know. It is about overconfidence in our limited mental horsepower in a world that is increasingly more complex than our individual intelligence can allow us to grasp.

The most popular error of this kind constitutes the 'Texas sharpshooter fallacy'. The story goes that once an ordinary Texan got overnight stardom for his ability to hit a bullseye every time he fired a bullet. If you looked at the bullet marks on the range, there's nothing you would conclude otherwise. What an extraordinary genius! Except that nobody saw him fire the shots! The legend would randomly shoot at clean wooden planks and paint the target around the bullet holes. His gullible neighbours were so impressed at what they saw that nobody bothered to ask for a live replay of his incredible artistry. Instead, they declared him the best shooter the state had ever seen.

If anything, the sharpshooter could honestly be lauded for perhaps only his neat painting skills. In cases like this, when the target follows the action instead of preceding it, the success of the actor is either just a favourable error or a lie. The Texas sharpshooter fallacy is the pareidolia of data and facts that are intentionally manufactured to manipulate people.

We find such charlatans around us all the time, who want us to look at results from tampered perspectives and give them the credit they don't deserve.

The announcement by Prime Minister Modi on 8 November 2016 about the ban on large currency notes mentioned attacking the black economy and breaking the backs of terrorists as the primary aim. That didn't seem to pan out, as hoarders of unaccounted money found ways to circumvent the system anyway. Mid-exercise, the government changed the narrative to promoting digital payments in the country. The original speech of 8 November had no mention of the words 'cashless' or 'digital', but by 27 November they were used thrice as much as 'black money'.

Either it was a very badly conceived move or the government had announced a currency-replacement scheme in the world's second-most-populous country with no objective assessment of the consequences and soon claimed the unintended consequences as the original intention for the sudden ban. They may have just fired in the wild and drawn the bullseye later.

A recognition of this fallacy can help us avoid becoming victims of populism and hero worship. Before garlanding the legends, we need to look closely at their claims with both telescopes and microscopes.

During the London bombing of World War II, some claimed that there was a very distinct pattern to the bombing raids, as they often missed certain neighbourhoods. The supremely confident ones even asserted that some buildings were untouched because German spies resided in them, coordinating the bombings.

They didn't.

However, the bullseye claim survived until almost a century later, when Kahneman and Tversky showed that the bomb-strike patterns were simply random. In short, even the Germans didn't know where they were dropping those bombs!

There is just no empirical way to predict the outcome of some events. However, since uncertainty has always been difficult to grasp for our imaginative minds, we start betting on our 'gut feeling'. Gambling is the epitome of this false art (hence the 'gambler's fallacy'). It convinces us that two events are interrelated, even though there is no real coherence between them. Your lucky number will not come again and your lucky horoscope isn't helping.

Those who make fortunes in stock market trading are in no better position to predict the value of their holdings in the next hour. Their bets on the future may be based on companies' financial positions, but they too cannot predict 'black swan events'. An educated guess is still a guess.

What about our psephologists who make predictions about the elections, and get it wrong so often? They aren't fighting the elections themselves; if they get their analyses wrong, they'll still be on the election talk shows the following year. Election commentators need to be increasingly careful in making forecasts about democracies. Their 'probable' suggestions become the propaganda weapons of trolls worldwide, triggering a cycle of self-fulfilling prophecies. Even if one outlandish opinion poll predicts the victory of an unlikely candidate, troll armies can multiply the likelihood thousandfold by selectively advertising that piece of news.

Is happiness spelt red?

We can fall in love with brands for as simple a reason as seeing them everywhere. From sleepy Himachali towns at cloud-floating altitudes to the thirsty arid villages of Rajasthan, it is likely that you will find more than one rolled-down shutter or a wall painted in Coca-Cola's trademark hues. Why would a soft-drink giant spend billions of dollars every year in only making itself more visible? Why is Coca-Cola so self-obsessed? It realized pretty early on how the image of the brand mattered more than the product itself. The ubiquitous placements brand Coke as the obvious love, making Coke the common-sense choice for soft-drinks.

Interestingly, the association between Coca-Cola and happiness isn't random. It has been engineered over several decades. The merry image of the pot-bellied grandpa draped in red was first created by the American illustrator Haddon Sundblom for Coca-Cola. Happiness is quite literally a Coca-Cola copyright.

Coca-Cola has managed to make itself the face of freedom and liberal democracy. Sheena Iyengar, the brilliant choice researcher, recalls her visit to Berlin in 1989, the month the Berlin War was torn down. Coca-Cola was at the forefront, distributing free Coke cans. The day that will be remembered in history as a 'triumph of freedom' had Sheena holding a piece of the wall in one hand and a Coke can in the other.

'Perhaps my own preference for Coke solidified right then, associated as it was with freedom and other American ideals,' she writes.[5]

And it has worked so well that we don't even need to taste a can of Coke to feel good about Coca-Cola any more. In 2004, researchers conducted a series of follow-up experiments of 'blind taste tests' in Houston. They asked participants to sip from a can of soda that may or may not be Coke. Even though it had nothing to do with the soda can, the candidates were shown an image of Coke before half the sips and a coloured light the rest of the times. A staggering 75 per cent of the people rated the soda sips preceded by the Coke photo higher, when in fact they had been sipping Coke in both cases! The fMRI (functional magnetic resonance imaging) monitoring revealed a higher brain activity in the hippocampus and dorsolateral prefrontal cortex, both of which utilize previous emotional experiences.

Unknown unknowns

You've probably heard of Bertrand Russell's famous dictum, 'The fundamental cause of trouble in the world today is that the stupid are cocksure while the intelligent are full of doubt.'[6] Russell wasn't being his usual cocky self but articulating a very real human problem—the delusion of competence, or the Dunning–Kruger effect. It is about the situations when we think we are capable of making the right choices but actually aren't, and our incompetence is precisely in not being able to know this fact. It is the academic explanation of knowing so little that we can't even pity our illiteracy.

It extends far beyond our ordinary overconfidence to include the pathological proclamation of expertise to cause big disasters in decision-making. If an investor is a new kid on the block, what makes him bad is not just his understandable naivety of choices but the self-perception that he indeed knows more about options than he really does. The blindness or delusion blocks any possibility of course-correction. Rather, individuals suffering from this bias turn into 'Smug Snakes', 'too arrogant to be rattled'. They think of themselves as a 'Magnificent Bastard'.[7]

Since Akshat began working in a start-up during his teenage years, he had the constant fear of saying stupid things and never being able to realize his stupidity on his own. Thanks to the Internet's immortal character, he had the privilege of watching himself grow on the blogs of giant media sites. He would be happy to pay to rewrite his own pieces. Hopefully, he wouldn't say the same about this book a few months later (interested in our buy-back programme already?).

It's a very crippling intellectual position. Once you acknowledge that you will humiliate yourself publically quite frequently, how do you get yourself to do things anyway? What helped him was a prearrangement of apologies whenever found guilty. Additionally, as a preventive measure, Akshat occasionally gets his friends to cut him to size. Akshay owns a minority stake in Akshat's company and provides the sole service of asking him to shut up and chill.

You see, all of us know that some things are better than others but still choose to ignore them. We know that being criticized is better for our projects and ideas, yet every time we are challenged, we instinctively turn vindictive. Even when we realize we are indulging in impulsive rationalizations for bad choices, the thoughtfulness of System 2 cannot save us. We can be indoctrinated with the hazards of smoking, unprotected sex, the high risks of cheating, and what not—yet it isn't this superior knowledge and understanding that dictates our actions.

The real emotional and physiological state at the time of being confronted by these perplexing scenarios are far more detrimental to how we react than all the previous resolutions. The term for this is 'empathy gap', coined by George Loewenstein, one of the fathers of behavioural economics. Also called the hot–cold gap, it occurs due to the absence of immediate feedback that some of our actions have. Having experienced a very gruelling debt trap last year, we can make a tight financial plan for ourselves the following year. But when the Satan of hunger craves a fine dinner, we may give in to the impulse because in that moment a little extra expenditure feels harmless. That's our hot state. It may destroy all our budget goals, but we will end up leaving a generous tip after the doomed dinner.

The ride-hailing app Ola's in-cab entertainment system, Ola Play tablets, commercializes the hot–cold gap quite well. It would let you stream content from top platforms for a part of your journey, and just when you begin to enjoy yourself a little—entering your hot state—it annoyingly stops! To continue listening, you must agree to add a charge to your total bill amount. Ola keeps tweaking the policy, though.

Deciding not to take a plastic straw, driving less, using less electricity and water are some Good Samaritan actions that don't usually have feedback. Good actions that prevent a negative event produce no evidence to encourage that behaviour further. You will feel gratification on smoking another packet even when you know it will impact your organs negatively, but restraining in that hot state will not teleport an oncologist to pat you on the back. Some of this is starting to change, with technology companies trying to provide real-time nudges against negative behaviour. Wearable devices allow technology to send effective notifications when it detects us defaulting on our personal goals. Smartwatches are already beginning to remind us of our 'true selves'.

In our hot state as unemployed, desperate citizens, we can vote in populists who promise to usher in an urgent economic boom. They will bring back jobs, transfer us direct cash, restart factories and drill more oil than ever. They will dismantle thoughtful environmental regulations, do away with the laws designed to protect workers and lower welfare spending to make up for the tax cuts. All of it certainly gives a quantum jump in the charts of money. But until catastrophes wreak havoc on our cities, you cannot convince climate-change deniers about the fatality of consequences. We are wired to ignore climate change.

The problem with resource abundance and the free economy is our skilful mental accounting. We treat money and resources, not for their absolute real value but their context. The money that one wins in a lottery and the money one receives by selling their kidney are essentially the same. But in our minds we create labels that permit being more reckless with windfall gains and practise unhealthy caution with hard-earned money. It might feel like if you won *Kaun Banega Crorepati*, you will multiply your money manifold and live happily ever after. For the actual winners, the quiz contest doesn't change many things.

Richard Thaler, the winner of the 2017 Nobel Memorial Prize in Economic Sciences, explains this as our different propensities to consume between current income and future income. We put lottery and other easy gains in the current-income bracket to go on guilt-free shopping sprees. Future income, on the other hand, is treated with far more deliberation. Credit cards leverage this by separating purchase from payment. For the mind, no actual deduction is taking place when you swipe your card. Paying by cash is a real-time removal of future income.

The rhetoric of us being responsible citizens who wouldn't waste free water and electricity is not scientifically founded. It is a better idea to make us pay a little for every unit or to promote limited consumption. Freebies have to be precisely at a bare minimum. Especially because welfare measures are directed at the poorest members of society and there is extensive research on decision fatigue caused by poverty.[8] Having too many decisions to make in a day reduces our cognitive resources to make any better ones.

Poverty is a vicious cycle because it disables a person from making superior choices that can lead to their emancipation. Ego depletion is not just a 'motivation' problem, it is a neurological design. When the urban elite blames the poor for their poverty for eating up their tax contributions, they fail to acknowledge that merit and talent are subject to circumstances. Being born poor and not dying as one requires miracle stories. It swimming against nature's tide.

When former British prime minister Margaret Thatcher said that poverty is a personality defect,[9] she wasn't using her System 2.

Labour of love

We often attach ourselves too strongly to our hypotheses and lose the objectivity to judge our ideas fairly. This error leads us to endowment bias—the feeling of something 'special' just because it is our own. Multiple experiments have demonstrated how when we come to identify ourselves with any object, we rate it as disproportionately valuable. We exaggerate and extol the virtues of everything belonging to us. May not be a few minutes that you became the owner of your dog, its 'real' price has already gone up several times.

The same is also true for our beliefs and passions. The company that most profitably took our endowment bias to its logical end is IKEA. The Swedish conglomerate known for its DIY furniture range opened its first store in India in 2018. What explains IKEA's success is not just their low pricing because of minimal manufacturing costs but the sweet psychological spot they managed to target.[10]

We love ourselves, and we love everything that involves us. When assembling IKEA pieces, we develop an association with the otherwise dead furniture. The rickety table that 'we' put together gives us more pleasure than a perfect pre-assembled table. Some researchers suggest that the IKEA effect is also due to the ego boost that we receive on the successful completion of tasks. It gives us a feeling of being competent and an opportunity to exhibit that competence in materials that stay in our homes for many years.

In fact, IKEA's get-the-customer-involved technique worked surprisingly well for food-mixture companies. The sale of ready-to-cook mixtures stayed flat for several years until the manufacturers understood the disconnect that homemakers felt with the packets. They decided to experiment by adding an extra step in the list, like breaking an egg into the mixture. And voila! Sales soared to an all-time high!

Turns out, the phrase 'labour of love' is more literal than we always assumed. It is easy to exploit our enthusiasm to participate in projects and be made into their salesmen or advocates. Politicians have used this cognitive bias very shrewdly during wartime. The 'our boys did not die in vain' syndrome is used to make those losing their sons and husbands feel like co-investors of a shared—even if failing or evil—endeavour.

We are exceptionally good at being reasonable when we don't have skin in the game. My favourite nasty illustration of both the IKEA effect and the sunk-cost fallacy is parental love: we find it easier to tell how horrible the children of others are, but never our own. No points for guessing who built (or assembled?) those kids. And while they may have turned out to be disastrous investments, we are never done with them.

But don't worry, there isn't anything particularly troubling with your rationality; resistance to conflicting truth and contradicting data has always been a part of our scientific and cultural evolution. It is not just the conservatives, we as a species have always avoided the new and unnerving. There's actually a name for it, the 'Semmelweis effect'. It comes from an 1846 story of a young Hungarian doctor named Ignaz Semmelweis. Appointed to the General Hospital in Vienna, Semmelweis was unsettled about the large number of deaths in maternity wards due to puerperal fever, also called childbed fever.

He found that between the two maternity wards, the one with all-male doctors and medical students had women dying five times more than the one staffed by female midwives, which meant that there were more chances of a woman dying after giving birth if attended to by a male doctor as compared to a midwife. There were several theories surrounding this, but none were able to prove this with data.

Semmelweis then had a breakthrough when one of his colleagues, a pathologist at the hospital, died of, guess what, childbed fever! This was startling since childbed fever wasn't what only birth-giving women could get. People got sick of it all the time and died. And the pathologists were frequently infected by it. While doing the autopsy of those dying of childbed fever, there was a high chance of contracting it yourself.

Semmelweis returned to his original question—why were more women dying in the ward handled by male doctors? Because, apart from the deliveries, the doctors also did the autopsies. The midwives didn't! He pinned the higher mortality rate on 'cadaverous particles', the invisible bits that stuck to the hands of students and doctors handling the childbed fever victims' dead bodies. During delivery, the same particles entered the wombs and infected the new mothers.

Cleaning hands with chemical disinfectants wasn't standard medical procedure at the time. It was then that he instructed washing hands with a chlorine solution, not just ordinary soaps. This one simple change dramatically decreased the deaths in maternity wards!

Not everyone was delighted, however. If childbed fever wasn't caused by anything external but a simple operating error, who was assigned the share of the guilt? The doctors. It was the doctors themselves who were the cause of deaths. Repulsion was but natural.

The story has an anticlimax. Semmelweis lost his job and became hated in the medical community. Persuading health professionals to change their soaps turned out to be a not-so-straightforward job. Raising hygiene standards even today remains a challenge for the community. Semmelweis, at forty-seven, was admitted to a mental asylum for having developed either syphilis or Alzheimer's. There the legendary doctor was beaten up and died of a blood infection, not very different from the one he had tried to save the women of the General Hospital from.

In Robert Anton Wilson's book *The Game of Life*, Timothy Leary provides a polemical definition of the Semmelweis reflex: 'Mob behaviour found among primates and larval hominids on undeveloped planets, in which a discovery of important scientific fact is punished.' Semmelweis's story is the perfect representation of our antipathy to facts that challenge our ossified ideas. To break out of groupthink requires both intellectual courage to defy common sense and mental grit to disregard the cost–benefit calculus. Sometimes brilliance may be caused precisely by the impulsiveness of

System 1 rather than the prudence of System 2. The myth of neurotic genius? Mostly not.

Are you paying attention?

Don't be surprised if after reading this you start to notice these heuristics and cognitive tricks all the time. It wouldn't just be a coincidence but another interesting documented phenomenon; the 'frequency illusion', or the Baader–Meinhof phenomenon. Baader–Meinhof isn't the name of a professor who discovered this illusion. In 1994, a commenter on the St Paul Pioneer Press online discussion board randomly heard mention of Baader–Meinhof, an ultra-left-wing West German terrorist organization active in the 1970s, twice in a span of twenty-four hours, and then suddenly started seeing references to them everywhere.

That's it fellas, grotesque origins without an epiphany.

If we ignore being a victim to the phenomenon ourselves, by noticing heuristics behind all biases—including this—we will see how there are two of them at play here. When we are exposed to something new, we start devoting an unusual pie of selective cognitive attention to it. The idea or the word isn't being a creep in chasing us, we ourselves are unconsciously on a constant lookout to locate it. The second is confirmation bias, when any random repetition feels like corroborating proof to our theory of its omnipresence. We find reasons to believe what we want to believe, and everything becomes an additional argument for our initial thoughts.

The danger of being stuck in our false beliefs is much more significant in times of personalized content feeds.

By listening to our banal conversations is how Facebook's algorithm changes and shows us more and more of what we are already talking about. Technology companies are thankfully careful in not being arbiters of truth yet, but their present business model is designed to exploit whatever we hold true to curate ads for us, thereby creating a self-reinforcing cycle. Facebook isn't just a social media company on a noble mission to connect the world; since its inception, it has also become the world's most powerful educator. We don't pay attention to the fact that there is no neutrality of randomness in consuming content on these sites.

There are many assumptions implicit in the 'recommending' or 'curating' algorithms. Should you see more of the friend who votes the same way as you and chats with you more often? Or should Facebook give greater preference to that old buddy you parted ways with? Which publication should be more prominent on your newsfeed, the one whose posts you like frequently or the one you don't agree with?

Let's not ignore the very labyrinthine position this puts companies in. If they begin holding our biases, dislikes and lies as sacred consumer preferences, then they are right in serving us what we like best. For anybody who tries to engineer a more objectively rational or liberal world (which is disputable), they run the risk of having their users switch to another platform.

The truth is nobody ever anticipated the utility reliance that billions of people would develop on their dorm room start-ups. Jack Dorsey, the CEO of Twitter, may have been trolled for confessing 'we have not figured this out',[11] when asked about efforts to curb fake news, but it's never going to be a bipartisan solution. It requires the evolution of a common census about who can have the power to influence our minds, what will be the rules of such an attempt and whether it would be optional for each user and every company or a universal agreement.

Knowing about these cognitive biases is no guarantee that we will make better decisions for ourselves. If some research in behavioural economics is to be believed, then we may end up making more errors than before.

This 'bias blind spot',[12] the bias to identify everybody's biases except our own, can make us pretty miserable. Feeling superior, we can end up being mindless enough to lose even our basic talent for self-diagnosis. And this unsurprisingly happens to be more common amongst intelligent, thoughtful and open-minded people. There are annoying folks we have known who are like this, but trust us we aren't amongst those delusional writers.

Not just a notification

Behavioural economics challenges the traditional assumption of the *Homo economicus*, or the economic man. By recognizing the larger developments of psychology, like heuristics, it tries to make economics more in sync with our irrationalities. Once we reconcile with the non-optimal decisions that consumers and citizens make, we start requiring an entirely different framework of choices.

If we are prone to so many biases and never really make the best decisions for ourselves, is it fair for governments and companies to make better choices on our behalf? In any democratic set-up, that is an atrocious idea by all measurements. Enlightenment's 'one man one vote' principle, or the free market economy's 'consumer is king' dictum is based on the fallible assumption of our rationality. And once that assumption breaks down, we'll find ourselves in an uncomfortable middle of nowhere.

Richard Thaler, along with scholars like Cass R. Sunstein, as a response, came up with the 'nudge' theory. These are positive tactics that work as 'indirect suggestions' to influence the behaviour of individuals and groups towards socially, medically and financially better decisions. Putting certain options as default, placing high-value items higher on the shelf with better lighting, playing soothing melodies in stores, using smaller plates to lower food intake, displaying social proofs of compliance (nine out of ten people file their income tax returns on time) are all examples of well-designed nudges to make us act in predetermined ways.

There are significant unresolved questions about nudge tactics that remain open to debate. While companies have understood our cognitive biases since much before and used them to influence us to buy more stuff, their motives can be far more than merely commercial. As we begin exhausting a large part of our attention on the Internet, it has never been easier to nudge our behaviour and opinions.

A simple notification nudge on Facebook[13] to vote can be used to boost the voter percentage of people with a particular political affiliation, thereby flipping elections. We can regulate Facebook if it tries to attempt such a subtle coup, but it can be extremely complicated if the very government expected to regulate Facebook also indulges in nudging people's behaviour in its favour.

As psychology unravels many more weaknesses and blind spots of our rational capacities, it is our urgent obligation to keep pace. The only antidote we as individuals have is to educate and upgrade ourselves more often. It may not be possible to identify and be immune to manipulating influences of all kinds, yet a consciousness of our thinking process and its fallibilities can leave us much better off. Heuristics is as essential as physics and civics, if not more.

8

Democracy: Why Don't We Teach Rhetoric School?

Google has done more for democratizing access to knowledge than any planned government policy could ever have. From us researching this book to the office boy who uses Google's voice search to find the nearest photocopy shop, we use the same gateways. When you google your next casual query, the link you click on will likely be among the first few search results. Only very rarely will you move beyond the first page of the search engine. The order in which the search results are ranked is detrimental to how useful it is to the user, and Google, like any other search engine, wants to be able to predict the most accurate web-page for your query.

But that's no easy feat, really. Ranking web pages is essentially ranking information or, in other words, the truth—the cause of most human bickering. There are almost always multiple claimants holding forth on what's really true and correct, and what's truer than the other is never objective. And after nearly two decades of living on the Internet, we know that Google isn't just helping us find the answers, it is also actively shaping the kind of questions we ask. By giving preference to one truth it might risk losing a few users who will be able to look through the game, but it will have largely changed the game for most of us.

This isn't just a Google problem. All human systems involving diversity need to figure out ways of organizing, inventing a system of meritocracy. After the collapse of the Soviet Union, democracy emerged as the best way to decide the most capable person to rule. Similarly, capitalism is the most successful mechanism in human history to determine the distribution of material goods. But in the end, these are all ways of ordering data, influence and wealth.

Each system involves a peculiar set of principles based on what's at stake. Democracy allows each person one vote irrespective of their expertise or skill set, while capitalism promotes the distribution of production based on skill set irrespective of numerical strength. Yanis Varoufakis, the former Greek finance minister who battled the debt crisis, has explained capitalism as a democracy but without the principles of one man, one vote. You vote for the products you like but how many votes you have is based on your purchasing power. For corporations wanting power in this democracy, the Below Poverty Line slum dwellers are not important till they can make money off of rich folks. Our political leaders though have to visit even the poorest neighbourhoods during the election cycle because all voters carry the same power.

Beyond the basic democratic ethos of allowing everyone to participate, how that participation is structured is not obvious either. A first-past-the-post system like India's doesn't technically give representation to everyone's vote. Only the ballots cast for the candidate with the highest cumulative votes are the ones that end up getting a seat in the Parliament. A marginal difference of a few hundred votes is enough to create a clear divide between victor and loser. A proportional-representation system like in Israel gives all votes a representation in the Parliament since the parties are allocated seats based on the total number of votes they receive in the country.

Neither of the two ways of allowing people to choose their rulers is intrinsically fair. Rather, it is a decision made by societies based on what they value more, crude equality or stability.

The US presidential elections are decided on the basis of electoral votes distributed across the fifty states. The number of electoral votes each state has is calculated by adding 2 to the number of congressional districts in the state, excluding some exceptions, like the District of Columbia. The congressional districts are similar to the Lok Sabha constituencies of any state. The number 2 represents the number of senators each state elects to the US's version of the Rajya Sabha, called the Senate, irrespective of its population. This helps provide smaller states representation in national politics. Except 2, all the states give all of their votes to the winner of the popular vote. So, for instance, if Uttar Pradesh has fifty electoral votes, it will not elect fifty different people from different parties; it will vote between the BJP and the Congress, and if the BJP gets more votes than the Congress, then all of UP's fifty electoral votes will be added to the BJP's kitty. The people who voted for the Congress will be ignored.

Democrats believe Republican Donald Trump carried the 2016 elections because all the electoral-college votes of every state get transferred to the winner instead of proportionally to the winner. Hilary Clinton got nearly 3 million more votes than Donald Trump. For the Republicans, the architecture of this system ensures that every state is treated equally and the federation is more democratic (event though candidate Trump himself didn't believe so before the elections). The Democrats disagree.

Selecting the dominant idea is never less than messy.

The Internet makes this problem even more real because, while it is a public good, it is designed by individuals and corporations. Companies are free to design ranking mechanisms as they like, but soon enough their private products come to impact public life in ways that warrant regulation. They have an incentive to be inclusive and have bipartisan systems to appeal to the largest user base. In fact, hate merchants and trolls are more active than you and us.

Google, the search engine that became the mammoth tech giant we now know, was born out of the PhD theses of two Stanford University students, Larry Page and Sergey Brin. While it took centuries of wars, stories and art for us to figure out our political and economic system, the challenge before the Stanford students needed an immediate answer. They had to determine which information or idea is better than the other in a way that did not reflect their own biases. Their challenge was to create a system of evaluating information on a metric that couldn't be easily manipulated. The system had to be difficult to game.

Their solution was the PageRank algorithm, named after Larry Page. According to Google, 'PageRank works by counting the number and quality of links to a page to determine a rough estimate of how important the website is. The underlying assumption is that more important websites are likely to receive more links from other websites.' These links are called backlinks and they are used to designate a score to every website.

The quality of the links is not based on Google's opinion on which views are worth it, rather on an objective mathematical quantification. If we create a page about Taj Mahal and include a hyperlink to the UNESCO website, it would imply that we think UNESCO is relevant to our theme. If there are too many pages that link to UNESCO, that should generally mean that a lot of people find UNESCO an important source. The other instance of when we would know if UNESCO is an authoritative source is if it was mentioned by a very credible and important site like that of the Government of India or the UN.

That is also how we judge the credibility of people we don't know much about. When interviewing someone for a job, it is more likely you will find a better candidate in someone who comes from a renowned institution that has a track record for successful alumni. The backlink of the candidate is their institution, and the backlink of the institution are the alumni. We decide whom to trust based on where they come from and how many people have trusted them before us. It can be difficult for new folks to establish their credibility, but this process works as a reliable guide of credibility.

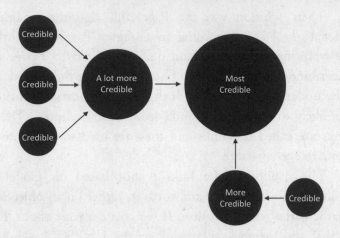

Before Google dominated the playground, several other search engines existed, and their failure can act as a cautionary tale. They used a text-based ranking system, which understood the relevance of a page by how many times the searched word occurred in a website. A search on the word 'Internet' famously returned a Chinese page[1] with frequent mention of the same but no useful information on it—like someone who throws around plenty of jargon but knows almost nothing about the theme.

The early search engines were so bad that in November 1997, when Sergey and Page put out their paper, only one of the top-four commercial search engines could find itself. Most couldn't even give their own link.[2] Google was unique in deciphering the authority of a page by links, making the result far more useful to the user.

Many other details of the evolution of the ranking process have been purposefully kept secret and changed many times over since their inception. Today, PageRank is one of the several algorithms used by Google. More details in the public domain would mean a greater risk of abuse.

It is a terrific achievement to have created a system of judging information and putting it in a hierarchy that is trusted by billions of people across the planet, across hugely diverse cultures and ideologies. Even the International Court of Justice doesn't enjoy this degree of public trust. Countries and communities within countries fight with each other all the time about who should be more prominent and favoured, but we have chosen Google over every other search engine because we find its algorithm fair enough to render the most relevant results. Sure, there are some of us who complain, and legitimately so, about the flaws in Google's algorithms, but almost an absolute majority of us believe in its impartiality more than our own governments. Googling stuff provides viable answers, because unlike individuals and institutions who can get their beliefs wrong, Google's algorithm is intelligent enough to downgrade facts and sources with doubtable veracity.

Ben Rattray, the founder of Change.org, brilliantly explains the idea on his blog:[3] 'The measure of how trusted a source is would not be based simply on their total number of followers but on the number and diversity of other highly trusted people who follow them, whose trustworthiness would be measured by the number and diversity of other highly trusted people who follow them, and so on.'

We are telling you this story because our crisis of democracy today is centred around finding out the truth. There are so many shades of grey such that it is increasingly difficult to agree on anything at all. Politifact.com, a site known for its gradations of facts, has interesting brackets of True, Mostly True, Half True, Mostly False, False and Pants on Fire.

However, this ability to have consensus on objective reality is the very starting line of crafting shared systems like democracies. When everyone can manufacture their own communities, media and expert authorities, nobody has an incentive to work towards reaching any meaningful compromise. Legend has it that an old priest was approached by a disgruntled couple. Listening to the husband rant about his wife's eccentricity, the priest said, 'You're right.' Then it was the wife's turn to rant about her neurotic husband who had problems with just about everything. 'You are right,' the old man announced once again. Seeing this arbitration going nowhere, the wife of the priest confronted him. How could both of them be right and still be fighting? The priest smiled once again, 'You are right too.'

Such polite answers hardly solve the conundrums society is faced with. Whoever is in power will bring along a new set of realities. Some institutions become more important than others. Some parts of history get amplified and others diminished. Some leaders get pursued for their petty crimes, while those aligned to the ones in power are forgiven for the time being. And if you think it is a problem of the right wing and the rise of populism, you couldn't be more wrong.

We have always ranked facts and truths.

If Google is representative of Western democracy's model of ranking information, the Russian search engine Yandex is another model of how things can work. With a 50 per cent plus market share in Russia and a strong presence in neighbouring countries including Turkey, Yandex is not a minor hobby of whiz-kids.

The largest Internet business of Russia has successfully managed to outsmart Google with tech that has its own defining features. It is a search engine that decided to switch on facial recognition with reverse image search, one of the hotly debated technologies in the liberal world.

Here's a fun game to play with your friend. Go to Yandex and upload your friend's portrait for a search. It should throw up similar faces from across the world. Take a screenshot and ask them to point at the commonality between them. It will creep them out.

Yandex places a much greater emphasis on regionalization or geo-targeting than Google. A connotation of this is the customization of search it can offer to authoritative regimes in parts of the world where Google is hesitant to enter.

Silicon Valley companies hold universalizing access to truth as central to their world emancipation agenda, the mission of Google is to organize the world's information. It is why Google drew strong protests against its Project Dragonfly, which was allegedly kneeling to the Chinese government's censorship demands. We need to be afraid of a world where if not Google, then another similarly capable company with less transparency or fewer principles will be able to provide less-than-democratic regimes the tool they need to exercise control.

The fall of democracy

The erosion of faith in democracy is one of the biggest challenges of the 21st century. We don't have to wait for the data revolution to make the authoritarian states more powerful and efficient. A lot of us are already getting convinced about the benefits of autocracies. Even the new crop of our democratic leaders is less gentle than the previous ones. We want strongmen who can get work done. Especially when it comes to very urgent problems like pollution and unemployment. We are getting impatient.

In our outrage, there are some fine details we miss about democracy, probably because we never take enough time to educate ourselves about it.

Authoritarian states do indeed respond better to their selfish interests, and if climate change happens to be one of them, they will not bat an eyelid before acting on it. But the main virtue of democracy never was the guarantee of the best rational outcome. Our affection for democracy is shaped by how the victors wrote the rules. We would have looked at democracy differently if the Soviet Union had been more than an Upper Volta (the Republic of Upper Volta, now Burkina Faso, a poor West African country) with rockets. The present geopolitics and technology favour democracy, but it might not forever.

We have confused the principle of human rationality given by the enlightenment revolution with the simultaneously occurring political revolution that gave people the right to vote. We never got the franchise because the decision output of groups is the best. In fact research tells us that whenever a lot of people are asked to make a decision, the quality of those decisions actually reduces.[4] H.L. Mencken quipped, 'Democracy is a pathetic belief in the collective wisdom of individual ignorance.'[5] Decisions made by people chosen by lottery, called sortition, are better than the ones made by elected representatives.

Democracy's biggest touted benefit isn't the brilliance of mobs, it is the protection against mobs and their decisions. The 'no-man-is-fit-to-rule-over-another-man' argument is not a sufficient one because people do indeed agree to be governed by rulers who get less than half the votes in an election. We are okay with systems that put people in power even without the consent of a majority.

Our personal favourite defence of democracy is that everybody should feel a little insecure.

Democracy is a system designed for the randomization of power. We don't look for one philosopher-king whom we can appoint for a lifetime. They may be excellent in their administrative competence and far kinder than our class of current politicians, but what history has told us loud and clear, many times over, is that people change. Power makes even the best of us do horrible things. The antidote to our fragile goodness, revolutionaries figured, was to make us insecure about our permanent positions. There should always be enough people ready to take your place if you don't do your job right. If you feel invincible, you have little incentive to rethink your decisions or strive for improvement.

Democracy trusts not in our ability to make good choices but in fact the opposite. We will vote unimpressive ignoramuses to power, our right to do that is sacred. But like any other choice in life, we should have a right to change our minds too. To assume static choices are in conflict with basic human nature to evolve with new experiences and data. The chaos of changing opinions is natural to both human beings and our power systems. Monopolies on power are worse than occasional errors of judgements. Expecting democracy to give us semantically varying leaders conforming to the same ideas is hardly a belief in democracy.

Not all democracies are equal

There is a difference between liberal democracy and democracy. Liberalism and democracy have been incompatible for most of history.[6] Greek democracy wasn't liberal; the French Revolution had liberals lamenting the unpreparedness of people to enjoy political rights; Napoleon's reign, which followed, was called 'democratic despotism', routinely verified with plebiscites. Winning elections by appealing to the basic instincts of hate and parochialism is historically easy, but to rouse the highest values during tough times, not so much.

The frustration with these early decades of the 21st century is evident. The political system that valued inclusivity, openness and civility in public discourse is throwing up leaders who believe they are 'correcting' historical biases and 'undoing' the wrongs against the majority.

Rousseau notoriously said, 'It is not enough to conquer, one must learn to seduce.' We can't blame the rise of populism without empathizing with the large percentage of the population that does not share our tongue. A friend used to say, the right relies on rhetoric, the left on poetry—except that not many people get the poetry.

Poetry, like graphs, has no stupid readers, only bad poems. Graphs that are supposed to make difficult information easier to understand cannot themselves be too difficult to read. The real burden of explaining policies and the logic of liberalism in relatable ways is on the politicians. Trump and Modi win in this modern-technology age because they can do something better than the liberals—they persuade us into liking them.

We have created a dichotomy of leaders who speak the banal truth and those who lie. However, it hasn't always been this way. Aristotle and other Greek philosophers had no doubt about human beings being irrational creatures (early behavioural economics). It is an important myth that runs our societies, but by denying it we abandon a race where someone will win anyway. Rhetoric is the art that lets us reconcile our cherished passions and the truth.

Subramanian Swamy, in an interview to a digital platform in 2018, quipped:[7] 'Elections are never won on economic performance. Narasimha Rao did not win on it, neither did Vajpayee or Morarji Desai. It is the emotions in the world that win you elections.' This part of the interview became a viral meme exposing BJP's strategy.

But there's no exposé here, really. Sure, Swamy has a reputation for being the human personification of clickbait, but it takes exactly this shamelessness to articulate a very prominent truth of politics. He is a member of the Rajya Sabha, 'a nominated member'.[8]

Rhetoric is not the art of manipulation or appealing to our mammalian instincts. The big red bus in the Brexit referendum bearing the message *'We send the EU £350 million each week—let's fund our NHS instead'* wasn't rhetoric, it was a wilful misrepresentation of statistics. In 2014, candidate Narendra Modi promising a transfer of Rs 15 lakh to citizens' bank accounts wasn't rhetoric either. *Make America Great Again* is rhetoric but the thousands of lies President Trump uttered since assuming the office are not.[9]

Aristotle gave three essential parts to a good persuasion—logic, credibility and passion. It is almost like he knew people without smartphones would be just as bored and impatient with sophisticated lengthy explanations. Saying vote for me because I will give you jobs is crude reasoning that doesn't make you any more attractive a candidate than before. Credibility for Aristotle means not Harvard or even Delhi University degrees but the shared empathy with the audience. It means affirming their values and validating their aspirations. Being original Hindu warriors is one kind of credibility, being anti-corruption crusaders another. Narendra Modi was a relatable tea-seller, Arvind Kejriwal is a prototype for a middle-class Indian with outsized clothes.

The last part is the emotional appeal. It is where you have to be charismatic in your speech, find what works with your audience, including knowledge of what they hate. The enemy doesn't have to be a political opponent or a fact, it can be values universally agreed upon as immoral. You frame your ideas into convenient moral positions, like being pro-life and not anti-abortionist, or being pro-choice and not anti-life. Nobody wants to destroy your forests or drown the tribal villages along the river, but who can disagree with the drive for development?

The United Progressive Alliance I & II, chaired by Sonia Gandhi with Dr Manmohan Singh as the prime minister, managed to keep power, but they were largely coalitions stitched together by political manoeuvring. It was more math than politics. Neither Gandhi nor Singh enjoyed the popularity that came anywhere close to Narendra Modi's experience in 2014. The Opposition is yet to find a liberal leader who can lock horns with BJP's rhetorical wit.

There's only one school in the UK that still teaches rhetoric, one that has also given Britain twenty prime ministers—Eton! Simon Lancaster is a popular speechwriter from the UK, credited with writing for various top politicians and corporate leaders, who believes we are missing the point of rhetoric—it is the basic entry point to being members of society. 'How could society be fair, unless everyone had equal ability to articulate and express themselves? Without it, your legal systems, your political systems, your financial systems are not fair.'[10]

Rhetoric can be learnt, like any other art form. But why aren't we teaching it? It is a major part of the divide between the elite educated liberal and the largely uneducated populace of India. Running a country is a complex job, which requires one to be smart and relatable to tens of millions of people.

Steve Jobs knew how to make us want Apple like we couldn't survive without it; he made consumers feel like missing out on the company's new offerings would be a terrible mistake. He invested real time in deliberating his speeches and planning a performance that awed people at every launch event.

The point of rhetoric is not only to sell us stuff or to get our votes but to get us to agree on things we previously didn't agree on. It is essential to change minds in these polarized times of short attention-spans and customizable content if we are to improve the world from the status quo. Unlike Google's ranking system, we as individuals and those around us don't rely on a fixed hierarchy of truths. We fervently disagree with their politics and their ways of working things out. We are right and they are wrong.

Rhetoric is the tool of making us talk to one another because getting angry seldom helps, and shouting angrily even less.

Jay Heinrichs in his brilliant book *Thanks for Arguing*[11] says the first step to persuading or using rhetoric is to make peace with what we truly want. If we want to get people to get things done, we will have to learn to lose small games of ego and pride. Nobody likes the badge of being a monster or a stupid learner. By assigning cruel nicknames to members of communities we disagree with, we are already blocking them from listening to our subsequent insults (if that's what we want).

Rhetoric IRL

We understand it can be difficult to remain calm when one feels violated and helpless. It is a cognitive privilege afforded to those at least-risk. It is frustrating to see the bad guys win. Yet, if we are to fix the poisonous divide between nationalists and anti-nationals, we will have to learn to talk better.

There are generally five broad moral foundations[12] that help us decide our positions on issues. The first one is care/harm, the feeling of kindness and pain. Compassion for the cow and for the victims of lynching for eating beef both come from this moral foundation. We are capable of selectively empathizing with the suffering of some but not others. You can care about both Kashmiri Pandits as well as pellet-gun survivors. Rhetoric is often used to prize one tragedy over another for political gains.

The second is fairness/cheating, relating to justice, equality and rights. Initially, this was also considered a strong liberal foundation until new data showed that conservatives were equally or more passionate about the proportionality of rewards and punishments. Arguments against or for reservation are mostly based on people feeling wronged over the allocation of jobs and college seats.

Loyalty/betrayal is the other foundation that underlies virtues of patriotism and self-sacrifice for the group. This is where nationalism, sedition, caste affinities or regional identities come from. Particularly in the last few years, with the rise of muscular nationalism, we have given too much importance to this foundation and begun seeking public evidence of our devotion to the country.

And the fourth is the foundation of authority and subversion, relating to the structures within which we engage with each other. How obedient or defiant we are, and how easily can we be paraded by a leader. Liberals are inclined towards challenging authority and hierarchies. The strict organizational discipline happens to be one of the reasons why a lot of people join the RSS. This was also how Prime Minister Modi escaped taking questions at his first-ever press conference as the PM: 'I am a disciplined soldier; the party president is everything for me.'[13]

The last is the most strongly conservative foundation of sacredness or degradation. Unfortunately, India still hasn't been able to get over its repugnant treatment of some communities because of its beliefs in purity and pollution. A leader can invoke both—the sacred value of truth or the decay of 'pure Aryan blood'—to build their politics.

In order to appeal to a wide base of supporters, one has to use the largest palette of moral foundations. Arguing for the safety of a minority because they are being hurt is one argument.

Greta Thunberg, a Swedish teenager, took the world by storm with her environmental activism in 2019. From being the lone protestor outside her nation's parliament to inspiring a march of millions, she's been a master rhetorician. She has managed to combine a powerful moral message with a rationale that is difficult to fight. Now that we've already talked about the not-too-inspiring uses of rhetoric in politics, Greta and her rhetoric is exactly the one we need to talk more about.

Look at this compelling bit from her viral speech at the UN Climate Action Summit in New York:[14]

> You have stolen my dreams and my childhood with your empty words. And yet I'm one of the lucky ones. People are suffering. People are dying. Entire ecosystems are collapsing. We are in the beginning of a mass extinction, and all you can talk about is money and fairy tales of eternal economic growth. How dare you!

Greta's anger is so personal it makes you look at climate change like an individual child's future is at peril. The delayed feedback on our actions and the multiplicity of causes makes climate change an abstract story for the human mind. But Greta instantly makes you feel guilty of being participants in such a sinister endeavour founded purely on our present greed. It also brands everybody not talking about climate change as incompetent and unable to define our priorities correctly.

She continues to recycle the phrase 'How dare you', a rhetorical repetition to reinforce a central point. The moral foundation of authority, fairness and loyalty are being used together in very subtle ways when questioning the rights of adults to destroy what isn't theirs.

She continued:

> For more than thirty years, science has been crystal clear, How dare you continue to look away and come here and say you're doing enough when politics and solutions needed are still nowhere in sight. You say you hear us and that you understand the urgency but no matter how sad and angry I am, I do not want to believe that, because if you really understood the situation and still kept on failing to act, then you would be evil and that I refuse to believe.

Greta believes in *you*. The differences between you and her aren't of scientific opinion, which she rightly assumes is settled, but that of knowledge. You would be forced to confess that maybe you didn't pay enough attention to the evidence because any other reason for not doing enough would make you evil. You are on the same page, she's telling you, just that one of you needs to read a little more.

You see, she doesn't want you to feel bad about yourself, for that would make you resentful against her and anything she has to say. This is the power of empathy in rhetoric, it includes you as part of a group.

There is also a slight assumption built in about your position being the same as hers. You agree on both the urgency and the numbers, what you wouldn't do is speak the truth. The trick is to turn the truth into an obvious consensus and put you in the unenviable position of making Sophie's choice.

> You are failing us. But the young people are starting to understand your betrayal. The eyes of all future generations are upon you. And if you choose to fail us, I say: We will never forgive you. We will not let you get away with this. Right here, right now is where we draw the line. The world is waking up. And change is coming, whether you like it or not.

There is a personal responsibility on her target audience. Her tone changes to assertive and threatening. In places where there is an explicit power imbalance, intimidation of a potential rebellion can be an effective tool to induce guilt and make people change their minds. Her monologue may not be enough to shift the complex technological and commercial barriers that make acting on climate change difficult, but if not anything, she is asking us to try harder and be more honest with ourselves.

Using rhetoric doesn't mean appealing to our worst parts. Right-wing populism managed to leverage the inclusivity and empathy offered by rhetoric in desperate times and geographies.

In 2016, when President Obama was witnessing the rise of Trumpian rhetoric, he clarified: 'That's nativism or xenophobia. Or worse. Or it's just cynicism.'[15] Obama claimed that he was the true populist.

And even if you disagree with Greta and Obama, that should be okay. Until our disagreements are so vigorous that we abhor each other's very existence, we would like to believe that all our differences are very trivial. And we've done that quite well for most of the history.

The upkeep of democracy in these new challenges needs appropriate public education. Our leaders need to get better at effectively using rhetoric to talk to those of us who feel betrayed or left behind. At the same time, we need to get smarter about differentiating healthy rhetoric from propaganda.

The challenge of not giving up on free expression while also not letting toxicity become normal is only going to get more real, but now that we're here, let's at least try?

9

Accountability: The Street Plays after Lynchings

Take 5 minutes to teach AI about emotions and help advance science. Tell us how you felt when writing your last three tweets.

That's the pitch made by MIT Media Lab's DeepMoji,[1] a scientific research project to understand (rather, to tag) human emotions and sarcasm. You can sign in with your Twitter account and make the AI smarter by choosing emojis that describe the sentiment of your words. While we can crudely categorize independent words, it is hardly of utility given the inherent genius of human beings. For instance, we can tell AI how love is a positive emotion and hurt is a negative one, but how in the world would something like this be classified: *You love hurting me, huh?*

It could be anger, a threat or an accusation, and would be impossible to decipher even for an outside person not part of the chat, let alone AI. This is why Instagram keeps getting op-eds written against it for creating an unhealthy digital space with no filters for bullying, violence and bigotry. This complex puzzle is nightmarish for all technologists, and they don't know what to do about it. The wealthiest corporations still need to hire humans for content moderation. They invest huge sums of money developing algorithms that can filter out violence and various forms of hatred and unscientific propaganda, but they haven't succeeded in winning both our trust and our forgiveness for when things go wrong. An algorithm failing to control violence is a more outrageous failure than human incapacity doing that at the same gig.

Tough problems do not mean nobody is accountable, especially if the companies involved have massive cash reserves that they don't know what to do with (Apple has almost a quarter of a trillion dollars in cash, more money than the yearly GDP outputs of most countries in the world).[2] Theirs is anything but a money problem. The pace of solving these technical challenges can easily be accelerated by putting more money behind the problems.

We need to look at Facebook and YouTube like we do at Coca-Cola or McDonald's. Technology and digital products can seem confusingly distinct from any other tangible good offering. It is a whole new range of services by multinational corporations, and their actions need to be scrutinized for how they impact our neighbourhoods. A messaging app with less than 100 employees is bought for more than 1,50,000 crore rupees because its lines of code can be exported to virtually any country in the world (we're speaking of the acquisition of WhatsApp by Facebook). No other product can be shipped so homogeneously for the world as technology. The cost of adding another user or distributing an additional unit of your digital product is almost zero. Facebook's gross margin is about 80 per cent!

This scalability and low variable cost are what make tech entrepreneurs billionaires before they can be emotionally mature. Or as the *Guardian* columnist Siva Vaidhyanathan wrote on the social media giant's naive understanding of freedom of speech: 'For his entire adult life, Facebook's CEO, Mark Zuckerberg, has been able to make up in hubris what he lacks in education.'[3]

None of this is natural and usual economics, the freedom of distributing digital products without the necessary auditing and study is a consequence of our legislators failing to keep up with their jobs. Customs officers tear books brought into a country sniffing for cocaine; if a product that makes more than half of the population addicted is brought in from another country, we expect our lawmakers to at least sniff it once. And we need a more nuanced approach than just banning TikTok. Not every nail needs a hammer.

The free rein given to tech companies gives them the power to design our world in ways in which the dangers are obvious only after the disasters occur. It is the nature of these products that makes them baffling, their utility changes with the number of users they have. If in a country of 10 million people, only 10 use Facebook, it means it is mostly a site listing privileged lonely folks. If 100 people join it, it becomes an exclusive community with esoteric interests. With 10,000 people, it begins to have commercial and social utility. You can ask for movie recommendations for the weekend or find potential buyers for your second-hand goods. At 10 million, it is a diversified platform with everyone running their fiefdom of friends. What you could do with 100 people versus 10 million is wildly different. Unlike Facebook, for a hot-dog company, 10 people eating the calorie monster would grow just as obese, even if 10,000 people began doing the same. We'd all be fatter together. The nutritional composition is an objective metric that doesn't change with user count and is thus simpler to judge. We can perform controlled trials and laboratory tests to know what level of risk it carries if consumed by masses. Food, a jacket or a car is meant for private consumption, whereas social media is consumed in the public eye; the potential of the latter to become venomous is endured by the whole society irrespective of who signed up for the service.

When it first arrived, we severely underestimated how a twenty-something's website could alter our social relationships, electoral democracies and conceptions of beauty, truth and goodness.

We've talked about algorithms in Chapter 2 (Automatic: The Human Algorithm), but the values behind the basic design of a network are important to evaluate. For a start, Silicon Valley companies love talking about eliminating the middleman, building direct and transparent systems with an assumption that all intermediaries are bad, that control by the government is evil and that the best way forward for the world is to make everything public for everyone to scrutinize. Facebook, for instance, is a champion of 'bringing the world closer together'—Zuckerberg can talk for days about building communities. End-to-end-encryption messaging services like Telegram are the real crusaders for private communication that nobody except the sender and the receiver can access.

YouTube is the noble company helping creators make money from their videos.

Though, if you look closely, there are huge assumptions embedded into all of these technologies. And like all assumptions, they take a very narrow view of what the right thing to do is. The degree of transparency, association and monetization valued by society are not universal to humans. They are very local and complex. Even if some values, like greater democracy, would be ideal for everybody to aspire for, how much a country is prepared to experiment with it depends on vastly varying factors like education, family values, the level of wealth, homogeneity of culture, individuality, corruption at the state level, dependence on welfare, and so on.

Democracy at gunpoint, as attempted by the United States in so many places throughout the world like Iraq, brings nothing but mayhem. Years after the downfall of the Saddam Hussein regime, the country is still in tatters. The *New York Times* thinks that it was being neutral when it broke the story of Hillary's emails, but reportage is never neutral; the timing and extent of the reportage matters. If Rahul Gandhi's private travels are made public right before the elections, one must not question the veracity of the claims (because they may as well be correct) but the veracity of the outlet that put it out when it did. The same goes for breaking the story about Modi's forgotten wife. The accountability of who is holding others accountable also matters, and we discuss more of these meta questions in Chapter 5 (Infinite Regress: Termites after Midnight).

Recall how WhatsApp and Facebook played their role in the lynchings and communal violence in north India in 2018. Toxic, hateful messages were circulated along with fake news to provoke mobilization against members of a particular minority. When faced with negative international press for its role, WhatsApp responded in the most histrionic manner possible—by organizing street plays to spread awareness.[4] Instead of amending the unfettered usage of its tools by technical internal interventions, the billion-dollar tech platform thought it would be able to help the polarized situation by getting a few college students, travelling around in the brand's signature light-green trucks in safe public places. Changing the structure and features of the application would not have made for good enough visuals for the news media. Performing on the streets is as serious as it gets.

Only much later did WhatsApp roll out the 'Forwarded' label on messages and limited the number of forwards and the size of the chat groups. Too little, too late.

By not fixing the tech or re-evaluating the choices of features, these companies are effectively practising victim blaming. Of course, India is a heterogeneous society brutally butchered along the lines of religion and caste, with low levels of education. And these aren't facts we are very proud of, but we didn't invite WhatsApp to provide a utility service we were urgently missing. It came here hunting for a market. If it failed to guard itself sufficiently well, our socio-political fault lines are not to be blamed.

And let us not delude ourselves into believing that any one of us has a solution to these complex challenges faced by these companies. Just as human beings find creative ways to protest against their all-powerful rulers, they also figure out methods of abusing tools previously considered benign. That's a natural part of any great tool's cycle. Gearwheels that brought us modern cars and electricity were first used by the state to execute people by tying their limbs across them.

The inventor of the famous AK-47 rifle, Mikhail Kalashnikov, was quite candid about the 'spiritual pain' of deaths that his invention had become the preferred tool for. He wrote in his letter to the Russian Orthodox Church, 'I keep having the same unsolved question: if my rifle claimed people's lives, then can it be that I . . . a Christian and an Orthodox believer, was to blame for their deaths?' He wondered why the Lord had allowed 'devilish desires of envy, greed and aggression'.[5]

Unlike Alfred Nobel, Mikhail didn't get rich of his design and lived on a pension from the government. His story starts with the good intention of creating an automatic weapon to match that of the Nazis. The Soviet Union was on the right side of history until it began to generously supply these arms to all the rebels it liked. The rifle created for the Soviet army now had a production scale large enough to become cheaper over the years. Oxford economist Phillip Killicoat in his 2006 paper 'Weaponomics: The Economics of Small Arms', says that out of 500 million firearms worldwide, 75 million are AK-47s alone.[6] Now that's a user base that most tech start-ups would kill for—metaphorically speaking.

AK-47s are a classic example of tools in history that get assigned a false absolute virtue. The lines between the good guys and the bad guys are brittle. Nobody starts a career wanting to hurt ordinary people. It is the promise of greater freedom, efficiency and happiness that turns rogue.

Encryption is a one-way street

At its core, encryption is a tool that prevents anyone other than the intended recipient from reading the contents of the message, including the company running the service. Encryption, or cryptography as it used to be called, was instrumental in the development of modern computing. Cryptography received mass adoption first in times of war, to encode and deliver messages to troops and allies without the enemies being able to decipher the secret messages. Cryptography's peak moment came during World War II, where encryption directly decided which side won. The Germans had developed the 'Enigma' machine, which let them quickly encrypt messages and send them across the globe. Alan Turing famously helped crack the Enigma encryption on a machine called the 'Bombe'. Mathematicians do have a sense of humour! The Bombe could be programmed every day according to the changing codes of the Enigma to figure out the key needed to decode the messages. This not only helped save numerous lives but was responsible for modern computer science. After his death, the mathematical concepts that he developed led to the creation of the world's first programmable computer.

Encryption[7] requires keys to encode and decode messages. One person uses the key, which is just a complex algorithm to transpose the normal readable data into essentially gibberish. The person on the other end of the line who also has the key can than inverse this operation to get plain data from the gibberish. This used to require a 'key' being shared offline in person between the parties, but some scientists figured out a way to send the key in encrypted form as well, so if someone did intercept the message they would not be able to obtain the key. This method is known as RSA, named after the three researchers who developed it in 1977—Ron Rivest, Adi Shamir and Leonard Adleman. In 2002, they won the Turing Award (named after Alan Turing), considered the Nobel Prize of the computer science world. RSA Security LLC, the company they started, is now responsible for making the RSA keys you must have seen an IT professional use to log in to their computers.

Jan Koum, one of the co-creators of WhatsApp, came to the United States from communist Ukraine at the age of sixteen with his mother. They could rarely afford to call family back home, where the tapping of phones was a common practice. Koum had all the good intentions of creating an encrypted messaging service that was priced at next to nothing, a single dollar per year for text and calls around the world. The idea behind encryption is to let only the sender and the receiver access the contents of a message.

The idea of private communication is essential to democracies. It is when people exchange ideas and information without a government or intelligence agency hearing them that they can truly exchange ideas that challenge the existing sense of values and morality in society. And without a healthy discourse about things that aren't currently acceptable, societies stagnate. Also, private communication allows mobilization—the thing that authoritarian governments fear the most. According to one report, the Chinese government's first item of censorship is not contrarian views but calls for people to assemble. It is more afraid of people getting together than talking against it. And this is exactly the kind of thing that an end-to-end encrypted service like WhatsApp can be useful for.

Let's come back to the lynchings. It begins with a communally charged message written by a man who will not be traced due to encryption and sent to hundreds of local WhatsApp groups managed by him. They mobilize, not to topple a dictator but to lynch a member of a vulnerable minority community in their neighbourhood. The lynching could have happened anyway, but the ease and security of the tool increased the odds exponentially. WhatsApp claims to be helpless in these situations, using encryption as an excuse.

The role of platforms in abetting violence is a serious global problem. Similar to WhatsApp, Telegram's encryption has received much flak for being the AK-47 of terrorist communication.

When done right, it is impossible to decipher today's encryption. Going a step further, Telegram uses distributed infrastructure to protect data that isn't covered by end-to-end encryption. It splits the decryption keys of your data into parts and stores them in multiple data centres across the globe. The keys and data are never kept in the same place and are thus under different jurisdictions. So you need to get official legal orders from not one but two or more governments to get Telegram to give up any data.

The genius of this game is Telegram's main appeal. Until there is a very serious moral consensus amongst several countries of the world, nobody gets to censor or monitor the flow of information via Telegram. The world can't yet agree

on climate change, the most important geopolitical issue of
our times, so what hope do local issues have?

Telegram doesn't think the problem is terrorists using
the platform for coordinating and propaganda; they, after all,
have 'a rich history of improvisation . . .'[8] Rather, Telegram
blamed the media for giving terrorists the unsubstantiated
coverage they are looking for. In terms of numbers, the
deaths due to terrorism in an entire year are far outweighed
by deaths caused by 'cancer, heart disease, road accidents, and
soap on the bathroom floor' in a day.[9] The media does this
to maximize its viewership excited by spectacular barbarity.
There's some truth to that argument, but it is not what we
should take from Telegram itself.

To be honest, it is a question of where to pick the
answers from. Having back doors to encryption will allow
security agencies to catch the originators of messages that
lead to lynchings and disinformation, but it will also give
your government the capacity to track you down if you do
not behave in ways it feels you should. Absolute anonymity
as promised by Telegram and its like shouldn't feel like an
obviously good idea. We signed up for this social contract
with our government because we wanted it to prevent
a few bad actors from making everyone's lives miserable.
We wanted it to have the power to stop the breakdown
of law and order even at the cost of some of our liberties.
But governments often flip that dynamic on its head, and
who do you trust when it's the government abetting the
lynchings? Think of it this way, would you be okay with
having Amit Shah listen to all your conversations in return
for him keeping you safe?

Can my prime minister block me?

Akshay owns a pair of Sony noise-cancelling headphones that are pretty nifty. Noise-cancelling headphones work by creating a reverse audio signal to the sounds within your vicinity and play that in almost real-time, which results in the unnecessary chatter getting cancelled out, enabling the user to focus on the task at hand. Now, social platforms that can often be much more overwhelming than a noisy cafe you are trying to write a book in offer similar tools. Twitter lets you ban people and bots alike, to help filter out the noise. Although this, on the surface, appears like an excellent solution to the problem, it has its own problems. Starting with how politicians should not be allowed to ban their constituents since they are accountable to them. Especially in a country like India, where the prime minister doesn't hold press conferences on account of being a 'disciplined party member'.[10] Donald Trump would often block people who criticized his policies. With the help of *Knight First Amendment Institute vs Trump*,[11] seven of these people went to court against Trump. The appeals court said that no elected official is allowed to ban people from an open online discussion taking place on an official social media account if they disagree with those people. In a similar case, the Internet's favourite senator Alexandria Ocasio-Cortez was also sued by two people whom she had blocked on Twitter.[12] Having an open channel for discussion whilst being able to block people you consider toxic on Twitter is an interesting new-world accountability problem.

During the first term of the Modi government, the late former external affairs minister Sushma Swaraj proactively used Twitter to provide respite to Indians stuck abroad and those with passport issues at home. It is a convenient way of reaching out to the government, but don't forget that Twitter is not an official grievance-redressal system. The rise of temporary technological solutions not fully owned or controlled by the government makes complaints conveniently optional to deal with. At the end of the day, the country's external minister is not really supposed to handle your visa woes, she should be engaged in diplomacy instead. Twitter is where she has access to your past political views, which could lead to her either helping you or blocking you. We need responsive and functional local public authorities that are accountable to the people at scale, not the news grabbing hack. That task is much harder.

Everyone loves to hate trolls, many of whom are just bots intended to amplify messages and make hate trend. India is the third-most-blocked country for bad bots, at 15.2 per cent.[13] It feels so natural to us that we don't even blame Twitter for this vicious muck. Yet, in California, where the company is headquartered, there is already a law that requires bots to disclose that they are not humans.[14] The law specifically targets these political and commercial Facebook and Twitter bot accounts, while excluding helpful chatbots on websites. Legislating this is one thing, implementation quite another.

If Twitter could handle and block these bot accounts, they already would have. In fact, from time to time, they do purge millions of such accounts from the system, but smarter bots find a way to reply with spam messages to a user's tweets. Elon Musk is especially attacked by such fake bots that show up in almost all of his tweets, purporting to be Musk himself claiming to give away free cryptocurrency—all a benign Musk follower needs to do to claim the free money is click on the spam link. These replies regularly rank high on Musk's tweets, buoyed by likes from other bots.

It is a tech problem that can only be solved within the offices of these companies. The problem is not a lack of legislation but rather a lack of intent. Their engineers are busy optimizing other metrics like screen time.

Most of us have had the experience of scrolling through endlessly on Twitter, almost in a trance, before suddenly being jerked back to the real world and realizing that hours have passed by. This is thanks to 'infinite scroll', a feature first put in use by Aza Raskin,[15] which was rapidly copied by all social media apps and media websites, to keep us mindlessly locked in and consumed in a sea of pixels. Raskin now feels guilty and has apologized for his invention. Leah Pearlman, the inventor of the Like button, conceded that she would often validate herself with the number of likes she received on a post. Only now are tech CEOs taking notice. Jack Dorsey acknowledged that having the follower count so prominent may have been the wrong incentive, and Instagram is experimenting with removing the number of likes a photo receives.

The fault in our computer code

Speaking of photos, in the 1940s, Kodak's cameras came with what was known as a Shirley card,[16] a template photo of a white woman used to adjust light and calibrate settings on the camera. The printers too were calibrated with that photo and the film's dynamic range favoured white tones as well. This resulted in photos of black people coming out bad for decades before Kodak realized this bias in the 1970s and worked to fix this. You would think we would learn something from Kodak's blunders, but we didn't.

Modern facial-recognition software often fails to work well with darker skin tones. An MIT scientist tested facial recognition software from the likes of IBM and Microsoft to see how well they could identify gender and found that it worked 99 per cent of the time if you were a white male.[17] The rates dropped sharply for dark-skinned people. For the darkest-skinned women of the group, the success rate was as low as 53 per cent. Do note that you would get a success rate of 50 per cent if you were tossing a coin with 'male' written on one side and 'female' on the other. This is happening because the data sets (aka the thousands of tagged pictures the AI looks at to learn how to identify faces) are mostly male and white.

An even bigger problem is human bias, because it is not easily quantifiable and tends to go unnoticed more easily. When an artist sets his brush to canvas, he paints from a certain experience, whether his or someone else's, as perceived by him. Even history, a field generally thought of as a string of plain facts, is very aware of its biases. An advanced study of the subject is incomplete without historiography, or the study of the writer's slant, i.e. whether the historian calls himself/herself a Marxist, nationalist or a subaltern scholar.

All algorithms are written by people too—people with biases and notions about a wide variety of things. So even if they actively try to avoid influencing their code with their feelings and beliefs, they will inadvertently build their biases into the algorithms they create. Often the data they use to train their AI will in itself have biases due to human error, judgement or otherwise. And as we see in Chapter 2 (Automatic: The Human Algorithm), often, how people interact with these AI systems will in turn bias these systems one way or another. It is impossible to build things without bias, but what we can do is acknowledge that there will be bias, so we are on the lookout to weed out the problems that will eventually arise and then go in and fix them quickly.

The fault in our human code

It is worth a mention that algorithms can at least be fixed once we know there's a problem. Some problems that seem to be solvable by technology on the surface might run a little deeper. Believers of blockchain and bitcoin technology, for simplicity, let's just call them 'bitcoin bros', believe that blockchain will relieve us of all our interpersonal trust issues. But the fact is that blockchain is just a database that is difficult to manipulate, not impossible. In a blockchain, the data, instead of being stored on a centralized server, is spread across nodes, so if you try to manipulate the data of one node, the system quickly checks the data across the other nodes and discards it. It's a majority-rules system.

This works as long as the nodes are really decentralized. As soon as someone has access to more than half the nodes in a blockchain, they can manipulate the data at will. Seems nonsensical right now, but given Russia and China's stance on censorship, and the fact that many public blockchain nodes are located in China and Russia, it's not overly paranoid to believe that this will be a problem in the near future. And even before the data enters any database, whether centralized or on a blockchain, there are a hundred other variables in all systems. If you input manipulated data in the first place, there is no need to take over or hack the blockchain.

Decentralization might not be an answer to our social media moderation problems either. A decentralized social network, an idea that has been supported by CEOs like Mark Zuckerberg and Jack Dorsey[18] at different times, only sounds like freedom in theory. What it will require is the painstaking management of content on a local level. While that might have worked for Wikipedia, it is unlikely to work for a social network at scale given the much larger amount of data produced on it. Governments can at least regulate centralized social media, something that might become impossible if we port the network from being a platform to a protocol like email. Jack Dorsey's dream might just remain that.

Akshay's dad, as part of his government job, was once put on election duty in a remote part of the country. As the day started to wear, goons of a particular party came with guns and swarmed the poll booth, asking to be allowed to cast multiple fake votes. They even had a list of voter IDs to boot. The police recommended that the duty officers let them have their way, that the election mattered less than their lives, and the goons had their way. An hour later, having caught the news, the opposing party sent in their goons as well, and they were allowed to cast the same number of fake votes! All men are equal, after all. Our technology isn't quite equipped to handle brute force attacks that happen in the real world.

Contrary to what it sells, the problem with blockchain is that it essentially envisions a future of a trustless, rather than trusting, society. It takes trust, the most intrinsic of human values on which the modern economy is built, and tries to detach and commodify it. It asks that we trust pieces of code rather than the person we transact with. We don't need better code for a database; we need a better code to treat each other better—in the real world and online. Some solutions can be designed around humans rather than tech. We discuss the design of elections in the Design chapter.

Winner takes a fall?

The biggest threat posed by tech to our democracy is that of monopolies. Unfortunately, for tech companies, monopoly is no longer a pejorative. Peter Thiel, one of the most successful Silicon Valley investors and the co-founder of PayPal, has said on record that he doesn't invest in companies that don't have a potential to become monopolies in their segment. He was one of the first investors in Facebook.

Tech monopolies, though, don't violate our current antitrust laws, or the rules that govern competition in the market. Even though Amazon is eating up its competition with its standard predatory behaviour, it is resulting in a net benefit for the consumer. When Amazon bought the Whole Foods retail chain, it ended up offering more discounts than ever and improving the overall customer experience. There's little anybody can call evil in such a situation. The benign behaviour of corporations today, while they are still in the process of killing all alternative service providers, is no guarantee against tomorrow's crippling exploitation.

The convenience may be fun today, but there is a good probability that no retail stores other than Amazon may be left to challenge its efficiency and quality. It might charge us higher in the future, but even if it doesn't, a single company does end up having too much control, not only over an industry but across industries, effects that we might yet not be able to foresee. Reliance's Jio brought all its competitors to its knees with its low prices, and after that led to market consolidation—there is no Jio Dhan Dhana Dhan offer anywhere to be found any more. The advent of AI will enable tech companies to be even more monopolistic, as we discuss in Chapter 2 (Automatic: The Human Algorithm).

We are entering into an era of an entirely different reality, where being monopolistic will help you earn more than just money. The next generation of intelligent products are distinguished by the quality of data they have access to. Companies that would promise to not use your personal data for creating virtual assistants like Google Home, Alexa or Siri will simply not exist because their products would be so bad that we'd never use them.

Facebook has this monopoly over social networking. No other social media platform allows one to talk with as many people. It's such a bad place to be in that to mobilize against Facebook, we need to use Facebook. When Elizabeth Warren, a Massachusetts senator and a presidential hopeful, announced her plans to break up big tech, speaking especially of Facebook, and ran advertisements on the platform, the company simply deleted them. It had to backtrack, though, after proving Warren's point even more strongly.

The US government's $5 billion fine on Facebook hardly affected the company. In fact, it made Mark Zuckerberg richer by $1 billion when the company's stock went up after the fine announcement. Traders found it lower than they had expected it to be. These slaps on the wrist become the routine cost of doing business, requiring almost zero change in how the company treats its users and their privacy. In his book *What Money Can't Buy*,[19] Michael Sandel describes an interesting study about when there's a price to doing evil, people begin doing more evil. In the study, a school put a fine on parents who were routinely late to pick up their kids, expecting a positive behaviour change. Instead, the cases of latecomers shot up, as the social guilt of making your kid wait was now replaced by just another payment for an error, making the act transactional in nature.

Regulatory agencies don't have to fear to sour a social relationship into a commercial one, but they can surely learn how a monetary fine barely achieves the objective of getting rich rogue actors to behave better. Penalizing corporations does not work, but we can penalize the executives who not only allow but order gross misconduct for fatter pay cheques. Take, for example, cab aggregators like Ola and Uber and how their business model optimizes for maximum profit with minimum liability. They classify their drivers as contractors instead of workers just because it helps reduce their liability.

There is a voluminous amount of literature on how technology companies end up damaging public systems. In the US, with its fairly-well-developed mass-transit system of rails and buses in major cities, the onslaught of Uber was expected to increase public-transportation usage by providing last-mile connectivity. But according to research[20] by a team from the University of Kentucky, each year, after Uber-like companies enter a market, heavy rail ridership can be expected to decrease by 1.3 per cent and bus ridership can be expected to decrease by 1.7 per cent. In Bengaluru, the total number of taxis doubled between 2015 and 2018, further congesting the absurdly narrow highways of the city.

Uber claimed it would declutter roads, thanks to carpooling, but studies showed that what ended up happening is that people previously using public means of transport switched to cars thanks to the added convenience and comparatively reasonable price.[21] The authors are personally guilty of the crime. Trying to mitigate the bad PR, Uber announced support for the Delhi Metro in its app, but the damage has been done. These conversations take much longer to hit public discourse than the technologies themselves. By the time we begin the discussion, our systems and societies have been irreparably damaged, while some other economy keeps getting rich.

Recall the 'Uber rape' case that was in the news a few years ago. It turned out that a high-ranking Uber official had illegally pulled up the victim's medical records to confirm whether she had made up the claims just to defame the company. Under pressure from the media and the investors that were pressured by the media, Uber replaced its founder CEO.

But a big reason why Uber was able to grow so rapidly is because of a culture of unethical 'growth hacks', which meant growth at any cost. This is a question of accountability and whether tech companies will own up responsibility, especially in locations where the state might not be up to the task.

From reining in Microsoft to the new privacy guidelines, the European Union has always led the way in holding tech companies accountable, but the rest of us have to rely on company founders upholding our rights on their own accord. Can we trust the humanity in the founders to lead them to do the right thing, or do we trust the media to hold them accountable when they don't?

And what happens when the same investors own both the media houses that report on tech and the tech companies they report on? Jeff Bezos already owns the *Washington Post* and India's new tech giant Jio's parent company controls Network18.

If the tech community won't self-correct, are the Indian courts and the Indian state at large prepared to make them pay? Maybe, as soon as the courts get a technology company to automate recruitments for their huge vacancies.

10

Viral Economics: Is Money Even Real?

A Stanford MBA named Roy Raymond wants to buy his wife some lingerie but he's too embarrassed to shop for it at a department store. He comes up with an idea for a high-end place that doesn't make you feel like a pervert. He gets a $40,000 bank loan, borrows another $40,000 from his in-laws, opens a store and calls it Victoria's Secret. Makes a half million dollars his first year. He starts a catalogue, opens three more stores and, after five years, he sells the company to Leslie Wexner and The Limited for 4 million dollars. Happy ending, right? Except, two years later, the company's worth 500 million dollars and Roy Raymond jumps off the Golden Gate Bridge. Poor guy just wanted to buy his wife a pair of thigh-highs.

—*The Social Network* (2010)

This is an irreverent monologue from the 2010 biopic about Mark Zuckerberg, *The Social Network*, and is a good, quick history of the famous lingerie maker. Victoria's Secret is one of those few brands that has single-handedly had more impact on women's diets and body image over the decades than any health advisory. The brand became a global behemoth famous for not just its padded bras but also its Angels (the spokesmodels in their annual fashion show). Their marketing head was once renowned for giving aspiring models their big breaks.

The name 'Victoria's Secret' has unashamed origins embodying Victorian-era aesthetics and notions of womanhood. The story was more about solving the problems of men than women, until its acquisition by L Brands in the 1980s. Though the brand's ideas of sexiness remained just as problematic, Victoria's Secret became a global brand with the highest lingerie-market share in the US.

It had a dramatic fall from grace during the #MeToo era as smaller brands with more body-positive and inclusive messaging began to challenge its dominance. A series of scandals rocked the company, including the CMO saying they didn't include transsexuals in the fashion shows since they were 'a fantasy.' He later apologized.[1]

After 2015, the revenues of the company stagnated. Investors had been pushing L Brands to get its house in order or spin off Victoria's Secret since it could no longer grow the struggling retail business. In 2019, an activist shareholder fund's CEO even accused the company of being 'tone deaf' in failing to respond to women's evolved fashion choices. When they ought to be making sports bras, Victoria's Secret was still busy stapling wings on to their Angels.[2]

This resulted in L Brands finally deciding to sell 55 per cent of Victoria's Secret and Pink (a subsidiary of

L Brands) for $525 million to a private equity firm, Sycamore Partners. The board approved the idea of L Brands in late February 2020. Sycamore had experience turning around retail businesses and L Brands could now focus on its more profitable Bath & Body Works brand. Both sides felt like they were the smarter party in the room.

At this time, President Trump was in New Delhi for his first state visit to the country. The hallmark trip comprised a stadium packed with a hundred thousand people. When asked a question about the virus outbreak in a little-known Chinese province, Trump responded that it would 'go away . . .'[3]

And of course, at least one problem did go away in 2020, but it wasn't the virus. In the coming weeks of March, Covid-19 would be declared a pandemic by the World Health Organization. The difference between an outbreak, an epidemic and a pandemic is of scale. When a disease suddenly spreads in a small but unusual scale it is called an outbreak. The cluster of pneumonia cases among the market goers in Wuhan made for a noticeable surge to classify it as an outbreak. An epidemic is the spread of disease over a larger geographical area but still contained within a region. A lot of people in China outside Wuhan testing positive for the virus turned it into an epidemic. And then, finally, when the emergency turns global, the world activates its highest response system by calling the disease a pandemic, which is what happened in March.[4]

What does this have to do with our lingerie company? Well, like most of the commercial establishments, Victoria's Secret was forced to close down more than a thousand US stores and furlough more than 80,000 workers. The pandemic is the worst disaster imaginable for all retail stores since there is no certain timeline on when it would safe for them to open back up or when people would feel safe enough to visit them. Remember how Victoria's Secret's original story was about giving people better in-store lingerie experience?[5]

The recent buyer of Victoria's Secret suddenly realized Covid-19 had turned the happy marriage into a suicide mission. Victoria's Secret was now worth much less than when the deal was originally conceived. On the day of deal's announcement, L Brands shares were valued at more than $23 a share. By late March they were trading for less than $10. And these grim new circumstances were indefinite. Whenever the pandemic subsides, the world would have changed in unimaginable ways. The traditional seduction of Victoria's Secret's retail network might have permanently died.

Sycamore Partners began trying to renegotiate the deal to suit the new reality. When that did not work out, they terminated the deal and filed a complaint, saying the actions of L Brands, like furloughing staff and rent defaults, had reduced the value of their prospective purchase. This is mostly true, and contract law does allow protection against such unexpected changes under force majeure, commonly called 'the act of god' clause. In India the often-ignored provision was made famous by Umesh Shukla's *Oh My God!* starring Paresh Rawal, in which the main character files a lawsuit against god for destroying his shop in an earthquake.

After the 2008 financial crash, Trump's lawyers had argued in court that even the crash was an act of god and that consequently the loan he had taken from Deutsche Bank AG should be voided. One of his lawyers pointed out that the former chairman of the Federal Reserve, Alan Greenspan, had called the crisis a 'credit tsunami', and a tsunami is an act of god. It might have explained the future—President Trump never accepting defeat in the 2020 presidential elections— since the virus too was an act of god.[6]

This would have been a plausible option for Sycamore, especially since a lot of other companies, including our own OYO, were also invoking it. The most interesting bit is that Sycamore's lawyers never used the clause in their filing because of how L Brands' lawyers had worded the contract. Mid-February, when even the President of the United States seemed dismissive of the virus becoming a major threat to the world economy, the law firm hired by L Brands—Davis Polk & Wardwell—to draft the contract had specifically excluded a global pandemic from the list of situations in which the 'material adverse event' clause could be used to justify termination. One doesn't usually find mentions of pandemics in mergers-and-acquisition contracts. It seems unfathomable now for anyone to have foreseen how the world economy would suddenly pause. Sycamore Partners and their lawyers would have laughed off such a minor detail.

A service worth the fee.

Sycamore Partners were arguing that though the pandemic cannot be a reason for termination, the decisions of L Brands' management after the signing of the deal was inconsistent with their past practices and hence they were in breach of the agreement. L Brands insisted on common sense—when in a pandemic you act like you are in a pandemic. They were trying to protect their workers and keep the company afloat.

Anyway, by May 2020, the equity fund and the company had decided to strike a deal to terminate the agreement and settle the pending lawsuits.

* * *

It is nearly the end of January 2021; we are a year into the pandemic and still almost every medical assumption and economic projection will seem ignorant even the following week (though we are emboldened by Slovenian philosopher Slavoj Žižek,[7] whose book on the virus was already out within a hundred days of the first acknowledged case in December 2019). But what wouldn't have changed is the historicity of the virus—it is already the worst debacle we are likely to witness during our lifetimes.

The problem faced by the most prosperous generation in the history of mankind is not of lack of money—it is plainly a technical problem. Our knowledge about any new pathogen and its prevention (vaccine!) expands under the limits of our broader scientific infrastructure. How long it takes for us to study the virus and create a vaccine is a process that cannot be accelerated in a few months of a global health crisis. And that speed of accumulating knowledge about the virus has to be faster than the spreading of the virus's mutation.

Covid-19[8] belongs to a family of coronaviruses that are also responsible for the common cold, the Middle East Respiratory Syndrome outbreak of 2012 and also the Severe Acute Respiratory Syndrome outbreak of 2002–04. All of the suspected places where the first person contracted Covid-19 have one thing in common—from the Wuhan wet market to minks reared for fur, they all involve humans going overboard with regard to animal farming. In fifteen months, the virus killed over 2.5 million people,[9] with millions more sick, but if we were to take the world's share of the virus and put it in one place, it would all fit in a single coke can.[10] And this is 200 quadrillion individual viruses.

The rapid rise in cases and deaths led to the pandemic being referred to as a 'black swan', an event that no country or corporation could have accounted for or included in its planning. This should have been the look-what-I-was-talking-about moment for the man who popularized the phrase, Nassim Nicholas Taleb, the Lebanese-American writer famous for his irreverent rants about economists, probability and randomness. Except that he was actually quite 'irritated' with the coronavirus being referred to as a black swan.

The phrase is not a 'cliché for any bad thing that surprises us',[11] Taleb said. And he's absolutely correct. We have been receiving warnings about contagions for a while, and we have also known that the last pandemic was only a century ago—a very short period in human history. While it is not possible to know the source of the upcoming outbreak, we already know it is a possibility. A pandemic is not act of god, it is a disaster caused by bad planning.

The world just went on like it was not a real risk we faced. In 2019, the world spent about $2 trillion on defence. That's almost $2 trillion a year to buy bombs[12] and yet every year more humans die of viral diseases than in wars. The entire WHO budget is about $2 billion per year.[13]

We were so unprepared there weren't enough masks nor the capacity to make them quickly enough. To stop people from buying the masks that the healthcare workers needed more, governments told people that masks could actually be unsafe, because people didn't know how to use them.[14] While that is in fact true, even an improperly fitted mask reduces the rate of infection. Later, all governments recommended home-made masks.

Doctors started using the infamous Crocs, the rubbery footwear that's more than a beach slipper but not quite a shoe as it is easily washable. And so Crocs decided to donate 10,000 pairs[15] a day to healthcare workers 'until stocks last'.

And apart from the government, there are the people. When they couldn't find toilet paper and masks, Americans went out and bought millions of guns, which were considered 'essential' items during the lockdown along with weed.[16]

Viral growth (how start-ups scale their R_0)

This crisis made us all armchair epidemiologists overnight, with terms like R_0 being used in everyday conversations. It essentially represents the spread factor of a virus. If an average person gives a virus to two people, the value is 2. If it takes two people to infect one person, the R_0 is 0.5. As soon as the R_0 gets below 1 the virus dies out in time.

When R_0 is 2 we get a diverging series:

R = 2 : 1K → 2K → 4K → 8K → 16K → ... → 1M → 2M → 4M → ... → ∞

When R_0 is 0.5 we get a converging series:
R = 2 : 1K → 500 → 250 → 125 → 62.5 → ... → 0

In the second case, where R_0 is less than 1, we get a finite total number (2000 in this case, if you recall your middle-school progressions). If it doesn't go down, the virus infects a majority of the population until there aren't as many people left to infect (hence decreasing the R_0). There are a lot of ways to decrease the R_0, the most popular of them being social distancing and handwashing. At this time an entire one-third of the world's population sits at home in partial or complete lockdown. If such a measure brings down the R_0 from 2 to, say, 1.1, the virus will still continue to spread, albeit at a slower pace, requiring people to stay home for longer. If it comes down to 0.9, we get rid of the virus.

This is weirdly similar to how companies grow—the network effect. Each time you used Zoom during the quarantine, you made your friends download the software as well. And after getting the app, they used it to zoom to their other friends. The virus doubled every few days—as did the number of Zoom users, from about 10 million to 300 million users in two months[17] (of course, they might drop just as quickly).

Oddly enough, though, the last major financial crash which happened in 2007–08 was also the period when major tech unicorns were born, including Airbnb and Uber (also Vox, Spotify, Dropbox, Evernote, Cloudflare and Github). These companies with positive network effects are also the ones reeling under the greatest pressure in a global lockdown.

Viral economics

In the decade before the pandemic, businesses took more and more risks in hopes of faster growth. They operated on thinner margins and faced high amounts of debt to finance growth. The problem with this much leverage is that it leaves little margin for error. The highly leveraged world that we live in can only function if everybody goes to work. If China shuts down, a coffee shop in New York will run out of coffee cups in a few months.

The primary driver for growth is productivity. We make things for each other and all our lives get better. Money is just a proxy to measure the value of products and services we make. The money we make can be used to either consume goods made by others or invest in a business, hence enabling the production of something others can buy. China is the world's largest manufacturing economy,[18] America the world's largest consumer.[19]

A key component that enables both the production and component halves of an economy to function smoothly is credit. It lets you borrow money against your own future productivity so that you can invest today for a bet on the future. When you take a car loan, you bet you will be able to pay it off from your future earnings. When a business takes credit, it's a bet on the future productivity of the business. So, essentially, access to credit is a key element in economic growth.

The more credit you take, the more leveraged your business becomes. The more leverage you have, the faster you can grow. You can also increase your leverage by optimizing operational processes. Manufacturing is the most operationally leveraged industry now. We have been afforded amazing efficiencies thanks to advances in supply-chain management.

A car manufacturer gets shipments of only the parts it is going to need in the next few weeks at most. These thousands of parts that arrive from different countries, owing to the complexity of cars, all have to arrive like clockwork. If even a single component is short, the entire production line goes out of whack. These efficiencies are what afford us cheaper cars and better phones, but when one country stops working, the entire world stops. Especially when the country in question is China, the parts supplier to the world.

Car ownership was too expensive so Uber leveraged taxi owners to provide everyone with a car only when they needed it. But this meant that when the government shut down taxis to avoid the spread of the virus, none of us had personal cars any more even to visit the hospital.

On the other hand, these leveraged business models are also what helped us glide through the pandemic. BigBasket was allowed to operate during the lockdown and delivered groceries for tens of lakhs of people every day, helping reduce human-to-human contact. And when Uber drivers were idle, they tied up with BigBasket to deliver for them, giving Uber drivers their monthly income and BigBasket the ability to deliver more orders. You could never mobilize such movements with the taxi operators of yore.

With countries shutting down their borders for six months and even cities sealing off their borders for a while, some reshoring is bound to happen.

A few months into the pandemic, tools that help us work from home have already seen an uptick. People are saving time spent on commuting and Netflix subscriptions are increasing. While students stay home, Akshat's learning company saw a predictable rise in the number of people wanting to learn new courses. A lot of these trends could go away when the pandemic ends—and entirely plausible is a scenario where we begin to realize what a scam expansive college campuses are!

Fifteen steps, then a sheer drop

The trouble with leverage is that you have no buffer. When the pandemic began, most retail brokers in the country let you buy stocks worth eight times the money you have if you sell them within the same day. This leverage enables you to make 8x profits—the problem being it also makes it very easy to make 8x losses, wiping out all your money in the process. The government regulated this down to 5x during the pandemic.

The pandemic has exposed the fault lines in companies that had been walking on a knife's edge, carefully managing growth via debt and lower margins. While that does not mean those companies were greedy—in fact, some businesses only work on razor-thin margins—it does propound the fact that these companies' models were not robust enough.

Like we said, debt can be good for business growth. You put your money in a bank, and the bank lends it to a business at a certain rate of interest. The bank gives you some of that interest in your account, pocketing the rest for profit. Wouldn't it be cool if you could make more money by lending the money directly to these businesses? You could be a legitimate loan-shark.

Well, that's what a debt-based mutual fund lets you do. The fund manager, of course, takes a fee but you can potentially earn a higher-percentage return on your money than if it is in a bank account. One such fund house, one of the largest in the country at the time of the pandemic, is Franklin Templeton. They were the first private debt fund in the country letting retail investors (normal folks like you and us) earn higher returns. They manage billions of dollars of retail investors' money in various debt instruments.

As the market crashed, people decided to take out money from the fund in case its value fell. The fund decided to pause any transactions in six schemes totalling $4.1 billion as they did not have enough money for people to be able to take money out. The money was given as loans via corporate bonds to companies that were riskier,[20] in hopes of higher returns for the investors. These turned out to be more susceptible to the increased stress of the pandemic. This unprecedented move locked people out of their own money at a time they might have needed it the most.

If some of these companies collapse, the investors' wealth will be wiped out, so there's no guarantee on any returns even after the lock-up period.

A company's valuation is one of the primary factors determining how much credit it can raise, as business owners can pledge their shares as a guarantee for the loan. But when a business's revenue shrinks and debt soars to compensate for the lower revenue, investors start valuing the company lower, wiping out vast percentages of a company's value over the span of a few days. Companies listed on the Indian stock market lost about two-thirds of their combined value during the 2008 crisis. When that happens, the pledged shares aren't worth what they were and can't be sold off by the lender to ensure returns. This is what famously happened to Big Bazaar during the pandemic. They couldn't furnish old loans and did not have new credit to buy more produce to sell to customers. This led to a rapid decline in their valuation, making it even harder for them to secure credit. The company ended up inking a deal that would give Reliance ownership at a discount compared to Big Bazaar's valuation a year ago.

Such market crashes can trigger a domino effect where all companies collapse one after the other and investors lose all their money. This is when a government has to step in to save the economy. The companies that took on debt have to be helped to survive or else they declare bankruptcy, leading to a loss of jobs and any hope of them returning the money they borrowed. The government now has to offer all public and private lenders money to cover their losses and keep the lights on. If it doesn't, the economy goes into a recession, i.e. negative growth.

During an economic recession, there is a fall in the aggregate demand in an economy. We buy fewer cars, ACs, vacations and smartphones. To deal with this, the manufacturers make fewer of these things and cut costs. But that means more people get laid off, and it is difficult to find a job since newer factories are not being opened. As a result, we bring home even less money to buy a new sofa or get the old one repaired. We start delaying our expenses and hold on to our money. The government collects less tax because you are not making money, and public utilities when you need them the most also deteriorate.

There is so little money to go around in the economy that everyone is worse off than yesterday. It turns into a gloomy, lifeless time, aka recession. The Great Depression that began in the United States in the 1930s is one of the worst economic recessions we've faced in history. In his inaugural address, President Franklin D. Roosevelt explained:

> Values have shrunken to fantastic levels; taxes have risen; our ability to pay has fallen; government of all kinds is faced by serious curtailment of income; the means of exchange are frozen in the currents of trade; the withered leaves of industrial enterprise lie on every side; farmers find no markets for their produce; the savings of many years in thousands of families are gone.
>
> More important, a host of unemployed citizens face the grim problem of existence, and an equally great number toil with little return. Only a foolish optimist can deny the dark realities of the moment.[21]

How do you think the government answers such a decline?

Those aligned with the British economist John Maynard Keynes argue that the government should increase its expenditure and generate demand in the economy in such a case. It should start building more bridges, airports and hospitals. These new public works were a part of the New Deal enacted by Roosevelt. It continues to inspire a new generation of climate activists and politicians like Alexandria Ocasio-Cortez and Bernie Sanders, who call for a Green New Deal to build infrastructure for a sustainable world at the scale of the Great Depression. Covid-19 and its destruction is that chance to build anew.

Others, more like the economist Milton Friedman, say the recession has a lot to do with how much money there is in the economy, hence the name—Monetarism. They agree, like Keynes, that the recession is caused by low demand but prefer it being dealt with managing the supply of money in circulation.

When the government realizes everyone is having a tough time, it can step in to provide the economy a booster. In a pandemic, it directly deposits money into your bank account, but in other times it will make you richer indirectly. The government does it by making it easier for your company to get a cheap loan from the bank. With low-interest loans, enterprises can expand production, take more risks and hire more people. The money trickles down to everyday consumers like you and us, and we start shopping more again.

But you see, this is an emergency step when things have gone wrong. It has to be carefully executed, because if you get too desperate to boost economic activity by pumping too much money into the economy, you can create hyperinflation. Hyperinflation is what happens when people have money to buy something that is simply not available in the stores. More money with the people should also mean more stores and factories. When many people line up outside the store to buy something that is likely to run out before everyone gets it, the shopkeeper decides to increase the price.

The virus is a nightmare for economists and policymakers because there is a risk of both recession and hyperinflation occurring together.

But here's the catch, inflation hasn't been behaving as predicted recently.

Some economists have been asking questions about inflation much before the pandemic, pointing out that low interest rates and government stimulus since the 2008 crash didn't lead to much inflation. In fact, the US has been struggling to meet its inflation targets despite high budget deficit and low interest rates for years now.

This super-interesting phenomenon spiked the popularity of the Modern Monetary Theory. Its champions argue for the idea of the government printing money to finance any ambitious programme it likes without worrying about stuff like who is going to pay for it. Let's say the government wants to build 3000 new hospitals tomorrow, and there are enough people without a job in the economy, then what's stopping the government from asking its central bank to create new currency and building socially useful infrastructure while also giving good jobs? If inflation starts to rise, the government can always increase the taxes and drain out some money. Utopia is only a printing press away.

The pandemic normalized the idea of the government handing out checks to people even when it has to borrow money itself. A version of basic income that would have been dismissed as a crazy leftist idea a few months earlier, because there would be no way for the government to pay for it. The other fear was that it would break the economy and people would carry bags of cash to buy toilet paper. That hasn't happened yet, and the government generously increasing its deficit is the only reason a lot more of us are still alive and okay. As some say, when your house is on fire, you don't worry about saving water.

There are far greater complexities at play here, but the core idea is that growth, inflation and debt are not correlated in the same ways for a country that they are for your personal income. It is a good habit to spend less money than what you make but when you own the printing press, you should worry about different things. Your extra shopping trip can pay for itself, if you use your credit card correctly. When governments are obsessed about staying in surplus, it is the private sector that gets into deficit. The governments which try only to balance their budgets forget that they created money to serve real people. If the people are destitute, unemployed and unhappy, it doesn't matter how clean your balance sheet is.

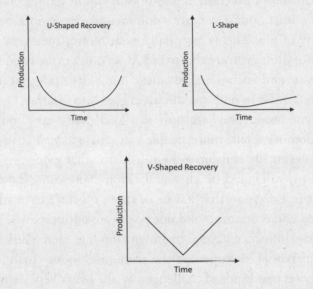

In a lockdown, the planet virtually stops producing much, leading to cascading effects of layoffs and bankruptcies. Businesses cannot meet their payrolls and pay their rents. Economists were first predicting a V-shaped recovery,[22] a sharp decline in production followed by an equally steep rise to nearly the same level of production before the pandemic. Then we realized that that might not be true, and the recovery might be slower than expected, taking up a few years. In truth, the U, V, W, X, Y, Z graphs are just ways to kill time until the vaccine becomes widely available. We cannot even predict the next week's developments; what we learn about the virus will change, and our response will change too. Only those who aren't friends with epidemiologists continue the illustration hobby.

Greater production of goods leads to more things for all of us which, unless you are a minimalist, results in a better quality of life. This is essentially what money measures: the kinds of things you are able to buy. If we don't make scientific, technical and operational advances, humanity's progress stalls and our quest to outgrow ourselves goes into disarray.

Our productions are now so siloed that even if only a few dominoes fall, more people can end up dead than the virus eventually ends up killing. It is true that reopening the economy will in fact be a braver decision than closing it down, but it is a decision that has to be taken together by medical experts and economists and not by private business owners.

The influence yielded by billionaires like Elon Musk and Sachin Bansal in reopening the economies sooner than later also poses new kinds of challenges. While Musk kept denying the severity of the virus and earned himself much hate, his electric automaker company Tesla also designed a ventilator out of car parts in two weeks to deal with an emergency situation. When the California county where Tesla's manufacturing plant is located refused to let them open up, Musk openly threatened to move out the plant elsewhere.

He further disobeyed the order and courted arrest for restarting production without clearance from the local administration.

Inventing a binary choice between employment and life because you have the financial power to do so is not a healthy pattern for democracies.

On the other side is a second billionaire—Bill Gates—who literally became the plan B of Americans baffled with their President. Gates has dedicated his life to eradicating disease and happens to be the second-largest contributor to the WHO after the United States of America. While it may sound alarming that a private individual is bested only by the biggest economy, the creation of non-governmental powerhouses has always been a feature of capitalism. If America does not fund vaccines, Bill Gates can.

While Mukesh Ambani can ready a Covid-19 hospital in a few days via his foundation, these uber-rich solutions to our structural problems are not alternatives to the government doing its job. It does take retirement for Musk to become Gates.

The day after coronavirus

This is the moment when we have an opportunity to reset, since a lot of our old systems and industries are being dragged back to the starting line anyway.

Even though the collapse of economic prosperity is terrifying, the mourning of its fall should not turn into an endorsement for its previous design. Our economic growth has been highly inequitable, especially so over the last few decades. When your income drops from INR 70,000 a month to INR 40,000, it pinches hard. But even before the crisis, the average monthly income in India was below INR 12,000.[23] We are still an extremely poor country, and we keep forgetting that fact until the next flood, drought or recession arrives.

Our public education hasn't prepared us to understand the urgency of a pandemic. What you've read in this book on data, complexity, economy and technology should be considered basic education. We were so busy bickering over Tipu Sultan's mention in our history textbooks[24] that we forgot to learn about the history of the Spanish flu and why there wasn't anything particularly Spanish about the 1918 influenza pandemic.

It is important to maintain civil order by converting a difficult fight against the virus into a temporary celebration of essential workers. But in a different world, our government would be able to explain to us a virus's non-linear growth graph, and we would pay our workers far better than we do. Making people bang pots and pans is okay only if we understand what we're dealing with and how long it's going to last. Otherwise, we are all at the mercy of our beloved leader and his wisdom.

With his utterances about injecting disinfectants and recommending unproven medical cures, Donald Trump may have made daily briefings look like a bad exercise in democracy. But they at least showed us how competent he was as a leader in handling emergencies, helping Americans divert him to other interesting things in the next election. To not show oneself at all during a moment of national crisis or conflict is a signature feature of tyrants. Stalin and Hitler were absent from public appearances for much of the war.[25]

A country of 1.3 billion people with very high linguistic diversity, no universal access to devices for listening to a live broadcast, an unstable electricity supply and a two-hour difference in mean solar times between its easternmost and westernmost points shouldn't be reliant on a charismatic head of state's address to the nation. No leader can appeal to the sensibilities and convenience of such a diverse population in an hour's time.

Our Internet penetration is at the highest-ever point in our history, our data rates are the cheapest[26] in the world and journalism is bleeding to death because of its open access—so why then were we still busy rioting as late as February 2020! Arundhati Roy called the madness of communal sickness our version of the coronavirus[27] before we officially got sick with Covid-19.

A pandemic lays bare our structural injustices. Just like with any other disease, the poor are at a disadvantage here too. Pre-existing medical conditions and weak immune systems both increase vulnerability and are, not so surprisingly, correlated in part to one's economic standing. Little access to nutrition, poor hygiene, few resources shared by more members in the family and safety hazards at repugnant jobs are all risks that Dalits and Muslims have faced for all of our developmental history.

When Ebola spread in a slum in Liberia, the area was sealed off[28] with the help of armed forces. At the rioting of residents, indiscriminate fire helped restore the desired calm. You never heard about this because it didn't happen in a gated community of rich citizens in a politically significant country.

The pandemic forces us to take very clear moral positions and own up to their consequences. The YouTube recommendation engine that we talk about in the book has also been put to the test. We have criticized the company for not taking a position, but the Covid-19 crisis forced it into action too. The platform's CEO, Susan Wojcicki, said in an interview to CNN that the company would ban 'anything that would go against World Health Organization recommendations . . . [It would be] a violation of our policy . . . So people are saying [things] like "take vitamin C, take turmeric, we'll cure you" . . . those are the examples of things that would be a violation of our policy . . .'[29]

'This is a complex position, least of all because half the Indian aunties will get banned for turmeric remedies, but mostly because our authority of information during the pandemic— the WHO—is already in a credibility crisis. The WHO is the most important international body where countries with all ranges of political systems, including authoritarian governments and democracies, come together to collaborate on matters of health and disease prevention. During the Covid-19 crisis, the WHO was accused of praising the Chinese response to the pandemic based on faulty data supplied by the regime. Now, the WHO is only as good as its member states, and its resources' dependence on them only make it harder for it to stand up to the member states' misbehaviour. If the American President announces they are going to limit their share of funds to the organization, it only makes the WHO more dependent on the next superpower, not less.

Coupled with this is the fact that the Covid-19 is a 'novel coronavirus', which means it was so new to us that our knowledge about it evolved with our response. The health guidelines were changing rapidly and the WHO would also change its recommendations based on what we currently knew about the symptoms, risks and its transmission. This is exactly the difference between science and dogma—one of them responds to evidence. It is both good and bad news that in a pandemic, science advances very quickly. The faster pace helps us learn more about the virus in time but it also makes it difficult for laypersons to take science as the gospel truth.

There is no bright side to a pandemic. In fact, ignorant optimism hurts more when the threat is a respiratory virus. Leaders who tell false stories to trick people into staying calm destroy public trust in leadership and create greater chaos. A pandemic is also the time when more and more of us grow comfortable with the idea of compromising our liberty to let the government act. Naomi Klein,[30] a strong advocate against neoliberalism's worst, has been warning for a decade that emergencies should not be allowed to worsen inequalities and decrease political transparency.

We cannot buy our way out of this virus, but as we wait for medical solutions to arrive we should remain vigilant about the ad hoc measures offered by our governments. A pandemic is the worst time to stop holding your government responsible. Edward Snowden, the exiled guest of Russia, doesn't have much choice to reject the pandemic's gift of CCTV cameras, facial recognition, data interlinkage and movement monitoring in Moscow.[31] We do.

11

Irrationality: Have Fun, while You're Here

The world is getting more complex, and we are not at the winning end of the fight against big data and AI. We can try to improve our decision-making and erect guards against manipulation by understanding how our subconscious parts are being tapped to sell us what we don't want and make us vote for leaders we don't like. But by now we also know how difficult it is to step out of ourselves and observe what we are a part of. No matter how powerful a telescope we can build to image other galaxies, picturing our own will require us to go a billion light-years away from earth and see it in full.

The common pattern in all our conversations in this book has been our attempt to enhance our rationality.

But actually, it is dishonest to not talk about what actually makes us human, our irrationality. The number of tasks that are distinct to human beings is shrinking rapidly. We already use neural nets to get work done while not knowing how it actually works. We are going to be participants of a world where only a small minority of us will have the sophistication to even partially know what's going on.

Is that terrifying? Well, actually, yes, it is.

This is also an opportunity to once again define what is most important for us as a species. How to make good decisions seems to be the focus of our education, even when there is little disagreement about the fact that making decisions is a fairly mechanical operation. Rationality is a reductionist algorithm. You need to collect data, clean it of prejudices and biases, divorce it from any useless influence, optimize for the right sample size and have a robust view of probabilities. Once you get these things right in a smart algorithm, even the smartest human will not be better at it.

It is tempting to believe that our rationality is what has helped us build the civilizations that we so cherish. At the heart of our progress is enlightenment, the Renaissance, the scientific revolution and the Industrial Revolution. Indeed, responding to new data and editing our world view is central to all the products of science that we enjoy, yet all of the human choices play out within a moral code.

Data can rob us

The old joke goes, an algorithm optimized to remove hunger from the world will figure out that the shortest and most everlasting way of doing the same is to eliminate the human race altogether, because the more mouths you feed, the more mouths you will have to feed thereafter. And in any scenario, there will be some who will go to bed without food. The best solution would be to not have any problems exist at all in the first place.

The complexity of human existence is not generated by the rational choices we make but the many irrational fates that we choose to embrace. We choose to endure suffering for the people we love and sacrifice our selfish interests for the stories we believe in. We value our wealth, happiness and survival but we also frequently settle for less when it affects those around us. This is not because letting others win small games is actually in our interest, but because we want to do the right things despite the calculus. That audacity to do stuff despite knowing you have a low probability of success and doing it anyway is what makes our future so much different from a deterministic simulation.

Researchers are constantly surprised by monkeys and chimpanzees behaving more rationally than us. In an experiment, Victoria Horner and Andrew Whiten set up a game where kids and young chimps could solve a puzzle by opening a box and taking out a prize.[1] In some cases, the box was transparent and covered with black tape in the others. It is rational to not waste time opening boxes that you can see have nothing in them. The chimps, with due credit to their smartness, skipped these unnecessary boxes and only did what made sense. The human kids, though, went about doing exactly as they were told, opening all boxes despite seeing that they were empty—80 per cent of the kids!

Our cousins clearly knew the most efficient and rational way to get the prize. But this 'mistake' of following instructions almost mindlessly is exactly what distinguishes us. It is harder for a chimp to trust you more than it can trust its own senses. Obeying the authority is often easy when you are at risk of being penalized, that's common sense for even a primate. Obeying and obliging when you don't have to, though, has fewer logical explanations.

A world guided by data certainly can improve our well-being and productivity. Those are important things without any doubt, and we need to do more to make our world work for everyone who is not included in the privileged class already.

Data tells us that good-looking people have a better chance in life[2] (the beauty bias!). They get shorter legal sentences, higher raises, ace their interviews and are generally treated better. We also know, because of evolutionary biology, what exactly makes us perceive some people as more attractive than others. Science presents clear evidence of bigger eyes, facial symmetry and healthy spotless skin, among other things, as being the objective criteria used by our subconscious to judge people. We may resent the facts, but we cannot deny them. And we read in Chapter 5 (Infinite Regress: Termites after Midnight) about our newly acquired powers to change some of these on a genetic level. The question is, should we?

It might take us a while to make up our minds about it. We don't want to rush in with our judgements. The stoic humility of accepting what you cannot change will be of little aid. The power to change what human beings don't like about themselves and the world has been central to our aggressive project. Philosophy is useful only in the intermediary phase of powerlessness.

It is only a matter of time before these technologies become accessible to everyone. And once the complaint against inequality is resolved, history tells us that not using the available means for improving our lives is not viewed kindly in retrospect. The farm-machine-destroying luddites of the industrial era are now a slur. We rarely reject available means to improve ourselves when everyone else is also doing so. It is game theory at play—if everyone cheats, not cheating puts us at a disadvantage. Morality evolves, like everything else.

Soylent and Huel (human + fuel) are great examples of such change. These companies bottle all the necessary nutrients for you in convenient packets with the desired flavours and without any of the disadvantages—you don't have to consume broccoli or pea for protein, it can all taste like your favourite coffee. We'd be healthier eating what we should and there'll be significantly less food wastage in the world—if you don't feel like eating it, just cap it for later. No time wasted in shopping for veggies, thinking about what to prepare, stirring it for minutes and still risking disappointment if the food doesn't taste good. Think of the productivity added to the global economy as billions of women across the world are recused of the chore. If they like, they could become food artists instead of being full-time family cooks.

The downside is that there's no art and romance to this food. It doesn't need your dead grandma's recipes, a family meal ritual or any candlelight handiwork. Though the cost of these meals is quite high right now, there are many reasons to believe the companies will figure out ways to make them cheaper. What then? Will it be the end of food as we know it, and should we be okay with it?

Almost 90 per cent of meal preparation is boring and mundane work. Will we agree to let go of the romantic food story?

Handicrafts are nearly the same story. There's a great generational transfer of learning and heritage required to produce the exquisite masterpieces by hand. Each unit of the embroidered cashmere shawl or intricately carved marble souvenirs takes arduous labour. To sustain their production without making the life of the artists hell, the products would have to be priced so high that these artists would ideally need to produce only one or a few copies. By economics, exotic items should be affordable only by the super-rich. If you and I can buy them in government-organized handicrafts fairs, then something is wrong. They deserve better.

The selection of material, the perfect execution of techniques, the distinctness of patterns, and so on, are things that technology does better than humans. If you want uniqueness, adjust for randomization; if you want a human-looking error, decrease the accuracy. The best handicrafts will be easily outsmarted by non-humans.

It is not the quality and art that we are saving. It is the story. And we are on your side, we want the tradition to be preserved, as their loss will be a terrible tragedy. But the cost of this preservation should be born absolutely voluntarily. The irrationality of missing the opportunity of income maximization for heritage is a gift that humans have. Whether the logic of stories should become a government policy, we are not so sure. Utilitarianism, or the maximum good of the maximum number, is, for the authors, the first religion of the developing countries. Statues after schools, please.

A similar debate is raging about the survival of languages. English has a monopolistic advantage over any other language in the world when it comes to knowledge and opportunity. There are incredible insights and great literature in thousands of other languages, of course. But if you want to get rich and smart in the world today, your best bet is not your vernacular. (And, no, WhatsApp users, Sanskrit is not the most scientific language in the world. There's nothing like a 'scientific language', there's only a language of science). It just happens that the speakers of this language came to dominate areas through often cruel expansion. They amassed wealth and that wealth led to greater knowledge-creation.

There's also a scientific argument for preserving as many languages as we can.[3] All languages have special cognitive insights, and understanding them unlocks unknown facets of human psychology. And there would be data we don't yet identify as data, so a loss of a historical–cultural product is not desirable.

A few years ago, the Government of India renewed its calls to have Hindi recognized as an official United Nations language, and even went as far as to tell the Lok Sabha that it would be willing to bear Rs 400 crore, if necessary, to lobby.[4] Except for a few island nations in the Indian Ocean and north India, Hindi isn't the lingua franca the world needs at all. Adding an official language would require all nations to pay for and endure our indulgence.

Right now also, if you make a speech in Hindi instead of English at the United Nations, you need to foot the bill of the translations. And real-time translations are choppy, even choppier than the English of speakers with a different first language. If you are talking about making yourself understood and not playing to your domestic audience, the best decision is to talk in the language that most of your audience and the global media understands. Politics and stupidity aren't the same as the irrationality of what it means to be human. Our affection for the language we spoke our first words in doesn't have to become a global annoyance agenda.

Machine learning has made real-time translations swift; Skype even allows patchy real-time translation on calls. These are terrific achievements in connecting us to each other. We hope they make us more thoughtful and not less.

What is a good metric anyway?

Greys are useful only in philosophy, and philosophy is useful only rarely in life—that is, until now. The biggest trouble in the age of big data is the difficulty to understand what's important. You measure what matters, but what matters is never an easy question. We have made those moral and social choices for all times in history, but never before have they been so consequential. A few engineers decide what we are going to optimize in life, and that changes the wiring of a generation.

The Joint Entrance Exam for the few thousand seats at the Indian Institutes of Technology and the National Institutes of Technology is a way to filter out kids. It is cruel, and we get it, Akshat wrote a damn book on it. But how do you allot seats to a million kids, more than half of whom you can safely assume are above a basic intelligence threshold? Even if arbitrary, there has to be some metric. Nobody is pretending that the metric is predictable of future success, which involves far too many variables.

Goodhart's law states that when a measure becomes a target, it ceases to be a good measure. We want smart, hard-working kids to get seats, but we don't want kids to spend their whole schooling trying to become test-ready. The Joint Entrance Examination system was designed as a metric of who deserved the seats, it ended up becoming the favourite cash-cow of a billion-dollar coaching industry.

If millions of kids are optimizing for the metric of these multiple-choice tests, shouldn't we spend more time thinking about what really matters? If we question YouTube engineers about their choice to optimize watch-time, or engagement, should we not take a few moments to re-evaluate the common sense of the education system we've built?

We are under no illusion that metrics cannot be gamed. They have been hacked and they will be hacked further. In American colleges, where metrics like extracurricular participation or essays are also important, there are scandals of a different variety. A United States' FBI affidavit highlighted[5] how parents paid proctors to get the answers of their kids changed on tests, faked learning disabilities and offered their kids up as probable candidates for sports they didn't ever try. Everybody wants to win, so everybody cheats, and we are willing to pay good money to whoever can help us cheat.

You need to be a giant corporation like Google with strong confidentiality measures to ensure your systems of ranking aren't gamed to inaccurately represent reality. But you can afford to be closed about your systems only if you are a private entity and not a public institution. Even then, there will be bad days when outcomes aren't as expected——so just keep iterating.

Different from the search-engine business, the architecture of YouTube is more open since it is centred around creators. The result has been not so delightful. YouTube ended up incentivizing the mimicking of the Colosseum and has been gamed to optimize for audience engagement. YouTubers have some of the largest data sets on human psychology. After you've uploaded a few videos, you begin to understand the curve of what your audience likes. Their hypothesis is testable with every upload and the data points produced by it. You don't have to rely on the love of your people to tell you the truth, they will throw it in your face.

Are informed creators better off?

Artists for centuries have tried to understand the world in its fine print. Only when you master the rules of social behaviour can you create art that aspires to break them. The plot of the Ayushmann Khurrana–starrer *Andhadhun* revolved around an artist trying to play blind to understand how the lack of sight impacts a person. Eventually, he ends up being involved in a crime scene and it gets complicated. Even so much trouble isn't necessary any more. If you have to collect data to learn more about humans, you can hire a bunch of them on Amazon's Mechanical Turk, which functions like any 'labour chowk' in India. They can fill your obnoxious personal surveys or be the paid subjects of your experiments.

When feedback data about art gets more precise, the incentive of the artist to violate the beliefs and primitive biology of the people declines. And this warrants a real conversation.

Akshat's first attempt at creating something was a content company called StoryAlert, then India's No.1 life-zine for teenagers. If you are wondering what a life-zine is, don't worry, it's just a blogging company that keeps redefining itself until it has created an entirely new category. Then it is the only one there and hence the best one. This was 2012, the golden age of ScoopWhoop and WittyFeed. It seemed anybody with a listicle and a funny feature image could become a millionaire. The initial few days of growing a community around content are largely experimental. You don't know what works, so you try a bit of everything. You try clickbait, you try original rebellious ideas, you try Open Letters to Open Letters and the traits of millennials with different zodiac signs.

StoryAlert grew to around 50,000 followers and several hundred thousand views a month. We knew what was working. For a few dollars in ads, we could buy very targeted data about our audience from Facebook. We weren't trying to create content worthy of your attention, we were trying to optimize our content to whatever got us ad money. Like so many publications similar to ours, having real insight into the minds of our users was good for the business.

Akshat couldn't make it work. The trade-off was one he was unwilling to make and thus had to sell off the site. It died a year later.

What does it all mean?

It can quickly start to feel overwhelming. There is the determinism of data and algorithms with accurate predictions about our lives. Universal basic income might be here very soon. Whether it is pitched like pocket money for health and education, or like the dividend of our collective progress, is the only question left. All of us might be staying home playing video games, with a more vibrant virtual life than physical life. Our worst fears of meaninglessness and the end of free will are knocking on the door.

Kathleen Vohs, then at the University of Utah, and Jonathan Schooler, of the University of Pittsburgh,[6] speculated on what it would be like if we lost the belief in our agency to choose. In 2002, they decided to run an experiment on two groups of people to find out the answer. The participants of the first cohort were instructed to go through a passage about the illusion of free will. The other group read an essay on a neutral topic. Following this, both groups were tested for a range of impulses to record their responses.

Surprisingly, the belief in free will, or the lack of it, influenced people's moral behaviour more than anyone could have anticipated. Those who had recently read that they had little control over their lives happened to cheat and steal more. The two psychologists concluded that people were more likely to behave immorally when they did not subscribe to the idea of free will, implying that they weren't in charge.

We stop feeling the blame for our actions on surrendering our agency and thus begin responding to our primitive urges. The same is true even if you don't participate in the experiment.

The book of reality has only two routes—determinism and randomness. The debate of consciousness is basically the debate of free will, the ability of a few ounces of chemicals to come together momentarily in defiance of entropy to determine their own future. Some of the biochemists argue for this exact reason that the ideas and opinions we form are really random neurons interacting amongst themselves. We don't really choose to have the kind of ideas we do, it is just a matter of fact that we happen to own them.

We can predict so little about the outcome of our own actions, let alone how that outcome is going to change the lives of others. This is actually a great problem in science. Scientists have to be lost gypsies for a long time before they find something they didn't originally set out to discover. Einstein said that if you know the outcome, it is engineering, not science. But that luxury to float towards the shore without drowning is quite expensive. If you have already won a Nobel Prize, securing a grant for your exploratory research can be easy with a vague hypothesis, but without a track record of changing the world, you will never get those million dollars to prove that you also can change the world.

The legend goes that at the commissioning of the Mount Palomar telescope, a reporter asked Dr Edwin Hubble what he intended to observe with this costly adventure. After pausing for a while, Dr Hubble replied, 'We hope to find something we hadn't expected.'[7] Neither did the scientists at CERN working to understand the nature of the universe know that they would create the first website in the world and the World Wide Web.

Do it anyway

Only a few of us are ever fortunate (or unfortunate) enough to have one singular passion and find it early on in life.

Though most of us do have a long list of deep interests, we don't select these randomly over a weekend. They are something we have cared about and cultivated for many years. So a good way to find out what to do is to do something that combines your interests. The best things happen from the intersection of two or more specializations. A lawyer with a technical background is at an advantage of building a tech product for the law industry as opposed to an outsider. So having a few deep interests helps.

Akshay, with a technology and engineering story, chose to learn more about public policy and the human side of things. Akshat, with his greater liberal arts disposition, understood the new challenges of an artificially manipulated world. They brought together their insights in the book that you are currently reading. Alone and in their narrow holes, both would have remained less educated than they presently are.

The correct way of honing in on your specializations is, we recommend, supposed to be preceded by learning broadly before you go deep. And that is why we wrote this book. Pick a few interests that will be relevant in the future and then go deep. Casey Neistat says he's not the best cameraman and neither is he the best guy to ride an electric skateboard, but he is the best at vlogging on an electric skateboard.[8] And that's how Casey became the best vlogger on the Internet. He is considered a pioneer in the field and had his own HBO show in 2004 in the format of a vlog, which predated YouTube.

Being in the 0.1 percentile of excellence at a singular traditional craft like a John Mayer or a Taylor Swift is hard, but being in the 30th percentile at two or three crafts is very doable. And by being that, you become the 0.1 percentile at the intersection of these crafts. Naval Ravikant, founder of AngelList, says, 'You want to be number one. And you want to keep changing what you do until you're number one. You can't just pick something arbitrary. You can't say, "I'm going to be the fastest runner in the world," and now you have to beat Usain Bolt. That's too hard of a problem. Keep changing your objective until it arrives at your specific knowledge, skill sets, position, capabilities, location and interests. Your objective and skills should converge to make you number one.'[9]

So pick and choose. And then iterate towards something people need.

When Akshay's first business had stagnated, he went to an adviser. He recommended that the author take a hard look at the opportunity cost. The idea was to see if the business model was viable or not. As co-founders, you compute your combined potential salaries if you took jobs and extrapolate your revenues to see if you would be able to at least match that. If not, you would be better off with a job. Even though this is a good metric to have at the back of your mind before starting your own business, sometimes it can be counterintuitive and make starting out seem daunting. You might not necessarily have the path to large revenues when you start out, and you will likely pivot your business model several times anyway.

Establishing a start-up is like setting sail on a fog-covered ocean. You only have 10 metres of visibility and can't really see how far the ocean stretches, but you set sail anyway because you've heard tales of others having made it to the promised land. And as you go deeper into the ocean, your visibility starts to improve. It is okay not to have all the answers.

As long as you are making something a few people will pay for, you should be just fine. The rest can be iterated upon later. Connect the dots looking backwards, said Steve Jobs.

It is not about blind bets but calculated risks. Optimize for both opportunity cost and passion. Life is often about managing more than two variables and choosing the best path you can come up with at the moment, rather than making an absolute correct decision. For example, here's what an opportunity cost or profit vs passion decision will look like.

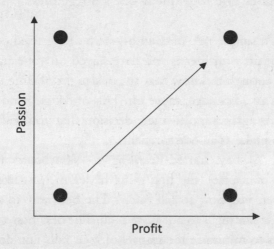

Assuming everything that you can do is a point on this graph, you should aim to be in the orange curve.

Carveth Read, an English philosopher, is rumoured to have said, 'I would prefer being vaguely right than exactly wrong.'[10] The general idea with decision-making is to make more decisions that are somewhat correct and let them have a compound effect on your life, rather than a few perfect ones. And one good way to compound more is to make more decisions. Time is the greatest leverage you will ever have.

'How do you know when to call it quits,' an entrepreneur friend asked Akshay once. 'Well, when you start asking such questions, it might be a good time,' the author joked.

Perseverance is obviously one of the most useful traits to have, not just in a start-up but whilst taking on any project. The Airbnb guys slogged for a long while before they found their mojo. And so did a hundred other billionaires.

How does one find out if one's doggedness is smart or stupid?

Here's a simple rule of thumb—if you have tried out all options within your means and have stayed on your current path long enough to know that the onslaught of time is not giving you an advantage, move on. This of course is no hard science. It is again a multivariate decision that you will have to learn to make as an entrepreneur.

When Akshay started learning to skateboard (from YouTube, of course), the first thing he learnt, just like any other skater, was how to fall safely. The best way to avoid falling while skating is to not skate at all. The next best way to handle it is to minimize the impact of your fall. You do that by reducing the momentum of the fall by gently pulling your body towards the ground and then rolling over your back. You don't quite land well the first time, but after a few falls, you get the hang of it and get to a point where you can land painlessly. Well, almost painlessly.

As must be apparent, the above was a metaphor for life as well as for any projects or paths you might be pursuing.

Just like skateboarding, life is about learning to fall safely after the action, rather than failing to take action.

Like Albert Camus said, life may be absurd; nonetheless, let us imagine Sisyphus happy.

Acknowledgements

We had great fun writing this book. Thanks to our editor at Penguin, Manasi Subramaniam, we were able to refine and rethink it as an optimistic fun guide for the future. Despite us missing the first deadline by several months, she showed unwavering patience. We wouldn't ourselves have been so generous to others, we think.

Aparna Kumar and Rachita Raj at Penguin provided many substantive suggestions to improve the initial drafts. They were very kind in putting up with our behavioural economics experiments to get ourselves to finish the book on time. In the end, we confidently conclude that the Nobel Prize–winning Nudge theory has quite a few practical limitations.

Thanks to Siddharth Singh, the foremost policy expert on climate in the country, for giving very actionable feedback. The world would be a lot nicer, albeit just as polluted, if more people were as generous with their time and aid as he is.

Book writing was the only time Akshay found Shahbaaz Mhaisale's alliance with Apple holy. His insights from working on Siri and AI helped us empathize with a perspective that came from the belly of the beast. It was useful in breaking down the jargon to only the real bits.

Prince Verma would be far more content with his Alexa saying thanks than us. Making his American dream work with two jobs, one as a pricing analyst at a tech company, the other as Bezos's unrequited lover (he is always paying for their escapades), he still found time for several rounds of feedback.

Anirudh Shukla was a reliable case study for many of Akshat's ideas about the impact of technology on young people. Thanks for making sure not every absurd-sounding theory made its way into the book, and for everything else.

Akshat is also very grateful to Silicon Valley–based Asha Jadeja Motwani and the Motwani Jadeja Family Foundation who provided massive support during his time writing this book. The resources allowed him the latitude to let go of the first marshmallow and think with an abundance mindset. They have done tremendous work in South Asia and the United States to support young people like him.

We wrote this book while working out of a co-working start-up, WeWork, where we commuted by Uber-ing on most days and eating food ordered on Swiggy and Zomato. We used Notion as our writing pad while listening to our weekly discover playlist of Spotify and coordinating on Slack. These great start-ups built by earnest founders enabled greater productivity and fluidity for us, and they deserve thanks too.

All images are owned by the authors or are available for open use under a Creative Commons licence. All the graphs have been prepared by the authors as well.

Countless many who read parts of the book for A/B testing of the jokes and analogies must be acknowledged for their unpaid suffering. We are keeping them nameless for safety reasons.

Notes

Chapter 1: Non-Linearity: Sorry, No Easy Answers

1. Chris McCoy, 'The inevitability of tokenized data', TechCrunch, 16 March 2019, https://techcrunch.com/2019/03/15/the-inevitability-of-tokenized-data/

2. 'Bill Gates speaks at the Economic Club of Washington, DC – 06/24/2019', YouTube video, 1:27:48, posted by CNBC Television, streamed live on 24 Jun 2019, https://www.youtube.com/watch?v=v7mLfQTqTZE.

3. Neil Padukone, 'The Unique Genius of Hong Kong's Public Transportation System,' Atlantic, 10 September 2013, https://www.theatlantic.com/china/archive/2013/09/the-unique-genius-of-hong-kongs-public-transportation-system/279528/.

4. Lincoln Leong (the CEO of MTR Corporation), 'The "Rail plus Property" Model: Hong Kong's Successful Self-Financing Formula,' McKinsey & Company, https://www.mckinsey.com/industries/capital-projects-and-infrastructure/our-insights/the-rail-plus-property-model.

5. Shirin Ghaffary, 'America has a terrible digital divide. Elizabeth Warren has a plan for that too', Vox, 7 August 2019, https://

www.vox.com/recode/2019/8/7/20757705/elizabeth-warren-broadband-digital-divide-broadband-access.

6. Sounak Mitra and Surajeet Das Gupta, 'Caller tunes earn Rs 8,185 cr for telcos in 3 years', *Business Standard*, 5 April 2013, https://business-standard.com/article-amp/companies/caller-tunes-earn-rs-8-185-cr-for-telcos-in-3-years-113040400380_1.html.

7. Sanjana Varghese, 'The spectre of Theranos looms large over the diagnostic world', *Wired*, 13 February 2019, https://www.wired.co.uk/article/blood-startups-theranos-diagnostics.

8. Ha-Joon Chang, *23 Things They Don't Tell You about Capitalism* (London: Bloomsbury, 2013).

9. Lant Pritchett, 'Where Has All the Education Gone?' *World Bank Economic Review*, vol. 15, no. 3 (2001): pp. 367–91, https://www.jstor.org/stable/3990107.

10. Paul Glewwe et al., 'A Better Vision for Development: Eyeglasses and Academic Performance in Rural Primary Schools in China', *Journal of Development Economics*, vol. 122 (2016): pp. 170–82, doi:10.1016/j.jdeveco.2016.05.007.

11. 'Roti Served With Salt As Mid-Day Meal For Primary School Students In UP', *Outlook*, 23 August 2019, https://www.outlookindia.com/website/story/india-news-roti-served-with-salt-as-mid-day-meal-for-primary-school-students-in-up/336911.

12. 'Growing at a Slower Pace, World Population Is Expected to Reach 9.7 Billion in 2050 and Could Peak at Nearly 11 Billion around 2100', Department of Economic and Social Affairs, United Nations, https://www.un.org/development/desa/en/news/population/world-population-prospects-2019.html.

13. Linda Pressly, 'How India makes Parsi babies', BBC News, Mumbai, 15 July 2015, https://www.bbc.com/news/magazine-33519145.

14. Amartya Sen, *Poverty and Famines: an Essay on Entitlement and Deprivation* (Oxford: Oxford University Press, 2013).

15. Krishna Bahadur K.C., Goretty M. Dias, Anastasia Veeramani, et al., 'When too much isn't enough: Does current food production meet global nutritional needs?', *PLoS ONE* 13(10): e0205683 (2018), https://doi.org/10.1371/journal.pone.0205683.

16. Elon Musk, Twitter post, 26 November 2018, https://twitter.com/elonmusk/status/1066955853985570817?lang=en.

17. 'Does the Amazon Provide 20% of Our Oxygen?' *Yadvinder Malhi* (blog), 24 August 2019, https://www.yadvindermalhi.org/blog/does-the-amazon-provide-20-of-our-oxygen.

18. Scott Denning, 'Amazon Fires Are Destructive, but They Aren't Depleting Earth's Oxygen Supply', TheConversation, 30 August 2019, theconversation.com/amazon-fires-are-destructive-but-they-arent-depleting-earths-oxygen-supply-122369.

19. Amy Iggulden, 'The Churchill you didn't know', *Guardian*, 28 November 2002, https://www.theguardian.com/theguardian/2002/nov/28/features11.g21.

20. Chris Welch, 'Google reportedly paid Andy Rubin $90 million after he allegedly coerced sex from employee', The Verge, 25 October 2018, https://www.theverge.com/2018/10/25/18023364/google-andy-rubin-payoff-90-million-sexual-misconduct-harassment

21. Brittany Spanos, 'Timeline of Chris Brown's History of Violence Towards Women', *Rolling Stone*, 1 September 2016, https://www.rollingstone.com/music/music-lists/timeline-of-chris-browns-history-of-violence-towards-women-103402/.

22. S. Matthew Liao, 'Opinion | Do You Have a Moral Duty to Leave Facebook?', *New York Times*, 24 November 2018, https://www.nytimes.com/2018/11/24/opinion/sunday/facebook-immoral.html.

23. Chris Welch, 'Google reportedly paid Andy Rubin $90 million after he allegedly coerced sex from employee', The Verge, 25 October 2018, https://www.theverge.com/2018/10/25/18023364/google-andy-rubin-payoff-90-million-sexual-misconduct-harassment

Chapter 2: Automatic: The Human Algorithm

1. John West, 'Microsoft's Disastrous Tay Experiment Shows the Hidden Dangers of AI', Quartz, 2 April 2016, qz.com/653084/microsofts-disastrous-tay-experiment-shows-the-hidden-dangers-of-ai/.

2. Chloe Rose Stuart-Ulin, 'Microsoft's Politically Correct Chatbot Is Even Worse than Its Racist One', Quartz, 30 July 2018, qz.com/1340990/microsofts-politically-correct-chat-bot-is-even-worse-than-its-racist-one/.

3. Maureen Dowd, 'Elon Musk's billion-dollar crusade to stop the A.I. apocalypse', Vanity Fair, April 2017, https://www.vanityfair.com/news/2017/03/elon-musk-billion-dollar-crusade-to-stop-ai-space-x

4. 'Democratizing the study and production of artificial intelligence', https://turingbox.mit.edu/.

5. The World's First Robot Lawyer', https://donotpay.com/.

6. 'Better Language Models and Their Implications', OpenAI, https://openai.com/blog/better-language-models/.

7. 'Talk to Transformer', https://talktotransformer.com/.

8. David Cole, 'The Chinese Room Argument', Stanford Encyclopedia of Philosophy (Spring 2020 Edition), https://plato.stanford.edu/archives/spr2020/entries/chinese-room/.

9. 'Elon Musk and Y Combinator President on Thinking for the Future - FULL CONVERSATION', YouTube video, 47:53, posted by Vanity Fair, 8 October 2015, https://www.youtube.com/watch?v=SqEo107j-uw&t=2244.

10. Ja-Young Sung, Lan Guo et al., '"My Roomba is Rambo": Intimate Home Appliances', Ubiquitous Computing, vol. 4717 (2007), https://doi.org/10.1007/978-3-540-74853-3_9.

11. Renee DiResta, 'How Amazon's Algorithms Curated a Dystopian Bookstore.' Wired, 7 March 2019, https://www.wired.com/story/amazon-and-the-spread-of-health-misinformation/.

12. Joan E. Solsman, 'Ever Get Caught in an Unexpected Hourlong YouTube Binge? Thank YouTube AI for That', CNET, 10 January 2018, https://www.cnet.com/news/youtube-ces-2018-neal-mohan/.

13. Guillaume Chaslot, 'The Toxic Potential of YouTube's Feedback Loop', Wired, 11 July 2019, https://www.wired.com/story/the-toxic-potential-of-youtubes-feedback-loop/.

14. 'YouTube Now: Why We Focus on Watch Time', YouTube Creator Blog, 10 August 2012, https://www.youtube-creators.

googleblog.com/2012/08/youtube-now-why-we-focus-on-watch-time.html.

15. Guillaume Chaslot, 'How Algorithms Can Learn to Discredit the Media', Medium, 21 February 2018, medium.com/@guillaumechaslot/how-algorithms-can-learn-to-discredit-the-media-d1360157c4fa.

16. Joseph Bernstein, 'How PragerU Is Winning The Right Wing Culture War Without Donald Trump', BuzzFeed News, 10 November 2018, https://www.buzzfeednews.com/article/josephbernstein/prager-university.

17. James Bridle, 'Something is wrong with the internet', Medium, 6 November 2017, https://medium.com/@jamesbridle/something-is-wrong-on-the-internet-c39c471271d2.

18. Mark Ledwich, 'Algorithmic Radicalization — The Making of a *New York Times* Myth', Medium, 28 December 2019, https://medium.com/@markoledwich/youtube-radicalization-an-authoritative-saucy-story-28f73953ed17.

19. 'India: Distribution of the Workforce across Economic Sectors 2018.' Statista, https://www.statista.com/statistics/271320/distribution-of-the-workforce-across-economic-sectors-in-india/.

20. Rachel Gordon, 'Robot hand is soft and strong', *MIT News*, 15 March 2019, https://news.mit.edu/2019/new-robot-hand-gripper-soft-and-strong-0315.

21. Tasha Keeney, 'On the Road to Full Autonomy with Elon Musk', Ark Invest, 19 February 2019, https://ark-invest.com/research/podcast/elon-musk-podcast.

22. David Graeber, 'On the Phenomenon of Bullshit Jobs: A Work Rant', *Strike!*, August 2013, https://www.strike.coop/bullshit-jobs/.

23. Supriya Sharma, 'Your car has been built on an assembly line of broken fingers', Scroll, 1 December 2014, https://scroll.in/article/692477/your-car-has-been-built-on-an-assembly-line-of-broken-fingers.

24. Zach Weinersmith, 'Why Humanity Is Doomed', *Saturday Morning Breakfast Cereal* (online comic), July 2016, https://smbc-comics.com/comic/doom.

25. Bill Gates, 'Not enough people are paying attention to this economic trend', Gates Notes, 14 August 2018, https://www.gatesnotes.com/Books/Capitalism-Without-Capital.
26. Venkat Subramaniam, Twitter post, 30 January 2015, https://twitter.com/venkat_s/status/561046784186015744.
27. 'Physicians (per 1000 people): India', World Health Organization's Global Health Workforce Statistics, OECD, supplemented by country data, World Bank, https://data.worldbank.org/indicator/SH.MED.PHYS.ZS?locations=IN.
28. Kevin J. Delaney, 'The Robot That Takes Your Job Should Pay Taxes, Says Bill Gates', Quartz, 23 August 2018, qz.com/911968/bill-gates-the-robot-that-takes-your-job-should-pay-taxes/.
29. Abhijit V. Banerjee and Esther Duflo, *Good Economics for Hard Times* (New Delhi: Juggernaut Books, 2019).
30. Robyn Sundlee, 'Alaska's Universal Basic Income Problem.' Vox, 5 September 2019, https://www.vox.com/future-perfect/2019/9/5/20849020/alaska-permanent-fund-universal-basic-income.
31. 'FY19 Unaudited Fund Value of $66.3 Billion and a Performance Return of 6.32%', Alaska Permanent Fund Corporation, 5 August 2019, apfc.org/fund-news/fy19-unaudited-fund-value-of-66-3-billion-and-a-performance-return-of-6-32/.
32. 'We will wipe out poverty': Rahul Gandhi announces minimum income guarantee scheme', Scroll, 25 March 2019, https://scroll.in/latest/917806/it-will-bring-justice-to-the-poor-rahul-gandhi-announces-minimum-income-guarantee-scheme.
33. 'India Labor Force Participation Rate: 2005–2018 Data | 2019–2020 Forecast', Trading Economics, https://tradingeconomics.com/india/labor-force-participation-rate.
34. A.H. Maslow, 'A Theory of Human Motivation', *Psychological Review* 50 (1943): pp. 370–96, https://psychclassics.yorku.ca/Maslow/motivation.htm.
35. 'Won't Allow Driverless Cars in India: Gadkari', *Economic Times*, 24 September 2019, economictimes.indiatimes.com/industry/

auto/auto-news/wont-allow-driverless-cars-in-india-gadkari/
articleshow/71282488.cms.

36. Mark Tracy and Kevin Draper, 'Vox Media to Cut 200
Freelancers, Citing California Gig-Worker Law', *New York Times*,
16 December 2019, https://www.nytimes.com/2019/12/16/
business/media/vox-media-california-job-cuts.html

37. Athena Lam, 'The Countries with the Longest and Shortest
Commutes', Dalia Research, 2 October 2019, daliaresearch.
com/the-countries-with-the-longest-and-shortest-commutes/.

38. 'People in richer countries work less', OurWorldInData.org
https://ourworldindata.org/working-hours#people-in-richer-
countries-work-less.

39. 'Beyoncé: Ghost', YouTube video, 2:31, posted by
Beyoncé, 24 November 2014, https://www.youtube.com/
watch?v=aY9vZv7HCvo.

Chapter 3: Data: Why I Don't Have Aadhaar

1. 'Ninth Report on Notice of question of privilege dated 24
March, 28 March and 10 April, 2017', Committee of Privileges
(Sixteenth Lok Sabha), 3 January 2018, https://164.100.47.193/
lsscommittee/Privileges/16_Privileges_9.pdf.

2. Ibid.

3. 'Clarification, apology regarding an infographic about
Lok Sabha MPs' attendance published in HT's March 23
edition', Twitter post, 24 March 2017, twitter.com/httweets/
status/845306863344279556.

4. 'Ninth Report on Notice of question of privilege dated 24
March, 28 March and 10 April, 2017', Committee of Privileges
(Sixteenth Lok Sabha), 3 January 2018, https://164.100.47.193/
lsscommittee/Privileges/16_Privileges_9.pdf.

5. 'Here's A Look At The MPs Who Are Most Regular And
Most Absent In Parliament', ScoopWhoop, 24 March 2017,
https://www.scoopwhoop.com/after-modi-heres-a-look-at-
the-mps/.

6. Arnav Das Sharma, 'Diminishing Returns: ScoopWhoop's unending list of troubles', *Caravan*, 1 December 2017, https://caravanmagazine. in/reportage/scoopwhoop-unending-list-of-troubles.

7. 'Each Minute of Running Parliament in Sessions Costs Rs 2.5 Lakh: Govt.', NDTV, 7 September 2012, https://www.ndtv. com/india-news/each-minute-of-running-parliament-in-sessions-costs-rs-2-5-lakh-govt-498784.

8. Akshay Deshmane, 'Documents Show How Modi, Jaitley Gamed World Bank's Doing Business Rankings', HuffingtonPostIndia.in, 20 November 2018, https://www.huffingtonpost.in/2018/11/20/ how-modi-and-jaitley-gamed-the-world-banks-doing-business-rankings_a_23594375/.

9. 'Here's A Look At The MPs Who Are Most Regular And Most Absent In Parliament', ScoopWhoop, 24 March 2017, https:// www.scoopwhoop.com/after-modi-heres-a-look-at-the-mps/.

10. Simon Rogers, 'Bobby Kennedy on GDP: 'measures everything except that which is worthwhile', *Guardian*, 24 May 2012, https://www.theguardian.com/news/datablog/2012/may/24/ robert-kennedy-gdp.

11. Akshat Tyagi, 'The HRD'S NIRF Ranking of Colleges Is Laughable & Ridiculous', Quint, 7 April 2018, https://www. thequint.com/news/education/opinion-education-india-college-ranking-system-a-critique-teaching-learning.

12. Gyan Varma and Pretika Khanna, 'Census 2011 Shows Islam Is the Fastest Growing Religion in India', LiveMint, 25 August 2015, https://www.livemint.com/Politics/ XkVYBX2IaBk5Sqf8yr2XMM/Hindu-population-declined-Muslims-increased-2011-census.html.

13. Sagnik Chowdhury, 'Census 2011: Hindus Dip to below 80 per Cent of Population; Muslim Share up, Slows Down', *Indian Express*, 27 August 2015, indianexpress.com/article/india/ india-others/indias-population-121-09-crores-hindus-79-8-pc-muslims-14-2-pc-census/.

14. 'Minority Report: Muslim Families Shrinking Fastest among Indian Communities', *Hindustan Times*, 20 May 2016, https://

www.hindustantimes.com/india/minority-report-muslim-families-shrinking-fastest-among-indian-communities/story-hkO5699sGJUFEcYGBEmmrM.html.

15. Daniel Levitin, *A Field Guide to Lies and Statistics: A Neuroscientist on How to Make Sense of a Complex World* (New York: Penguin Random House, 2017).

16. David Heath, 'The Lie of Low-Tar Cigarettes', *Atlantic*, 5 May 2016, https://www.theatlantic.com/politics/archive/2016/05/low-tar-cigarettes/481116/.

17. 'Apple Watch Saves Man's Life after Warning Him of Heart Problems', *Telegraph*, 16 July 2019, https://www.telegraph.co.uk/news/2019/07/16/apple-watch-saves-mans-life-warning-heart-problems/.

18. Ewen Macaskill and Gabriel Dance, 'NSA Files: Decoded', *Guardian*, 1 November 2013, https://www.theguardian.com/world/interactive/2013/nov/01/snowden-nsa-files-surveillance-revelations-decoded#section/1.

19. Jitendra Bahadur Singh, 'Modi Govt Allows Those Staying in India on Long Term Visa to Open Bank Accounts, Purchase Property', *India Today*, 20 August 2016, https://www.indiatoday.in/india/story/long-term-visa-modi-government-refugee-minority-communities-336314-2016-08-20.

20. Vaidyanathan and Deepshikha Ghosh, 'Aadhaar Data Safe Behind 5 Feet Thick Walls: Centre to Supreme Court', NDTV, 21 March 2018, https://www.ndtv.com/india-news/aadhaar-data-safe-behind-5-inch-thick-15-feet-high-walls-centre-to-supreme-court-1826931.

21. Vidyut, '#AadhaarLeaks: A Continuously Updated List of All Aadhaar Data Leaks', Medianama, 4 May 2018, https://www.medianama.com/2018/05/223-aadhaar-leaks-list/.

22. Zoe Kleinman, 'Politician's Fingerprint "Cloned from Photos" by Hacker', BBC News, 29 December 2014, https://www.bbc.com/news/technology-30623611.

23. Devjyot Ghoshal, 'Nandan Nilekani: Aadhaar is being demonised because it's so transparent', Quartz, 13 April 2017, https://qz.com/

india/957607/nandan-nilekani-aadhaar-is-being-demonised-because-its-so-transparent/.

24. 'Aadhaar verification to cost Rs 20', *Economic Times*, 8 March 2019, https://tech.economictimes.indiatimes.com/news/internet/fee-for-aadhaar-transactions-for-commercial-entities/68310655.

25. 'Of 42 "Hunger-Related" Deaths Since 2017, 25 "Linked to Aadhaar Issues"', Wire, 21 September 2018, thewire.in/rights/of-42-hunger-related-deaths-since-2017-25-linked-to-aadhaar-issues.

26. 'Delhi School Becomes First Ever to Provide Live CCTV Video Feed to Parents: CM Arvind Kejriwal', *India Today*, 8 July 2019, https://www.indiatoday.in/education-today/news/story/delhi-school-becomes-first-to-provide-live-cctv-video-feed-to-parents-cm-arvind-kejriwal-1564401-2019-07-08.

27. Desmond Ng, 'From Dispensing Toilet Paper to Shaming Jaywalkers, China Powers up on Facial Recognition', CNA, 7 February 2019, https://www.channelnewsasia.com/news/cnainsider/shaming-jaywalkers-china-facial-recognition-technology-privacy-11196684.

28. 'Facial recognition system helps trace 3,000 missing children in 4 days', *Economic Times*, 22 April 2018, https://economictimes.indiatimes.com/news/politics-and-nation/facial-recognition-system-helps-trace-3000-missing-children-in-4-days/articleshow/63870277.cms.

29. Saurabh Trivedi, 'Delhi Police using facial recognition system to identify protesters', *The Hindu*, 31 December 2019, https://www.thehindu.com/news/cities/Delhi/police-using-facial-recognition-system-to-identify-protesters/article30437756.ece.

30. 'India will be data rich before being economically rich: Nandan Nilekani', *Economic Times*, 20 April 2017, https://economictimes.indiatimes.com/et-now/experts/india-will-be-data-rich-before-being-economically-rich-nandan-nilekani/videoshow/58281393.cms.

31. Varun Singh, 'Govt Selling Vehicle and DL Data of Indians for Rs 3 Crore, 87 Private Companies Already Bought It', *India Today*,

10 July 2019, https://www.indiatoday.in/auto/latest-auto-news/story/govt-selling-vehicle-and-dl-data-of-indians-for-rs-3-crore-87-private-companies-already-bought-it-1565901-2019-07-10.

32. 'How Do I Unlist My Phone Number?' Truecaller, https://support.truecaller.com/hc/en-us/articles/212063089-How-do-I-unlist-my-phone-number-.

33. 'Passport, Aadhaar, all in one: Amit Shah moots idea of multipurpose card', *Indian Express*, 23 September 2019, https://indianexpress.com/article/india/passport-aadhaar-all-in-one-amit-shah-moots-idea-of-multipurpose-card-6019814/](https://indianexpress.com/article/india/passport-aadhaar-all-in-one-amit-shah-moots-idea-of-multipurpose-card-6019814/.

34. Rama Lakshmi, 'After Aadhaar, NRC, Amit Shah proposes a new agni parkisha for Indians', ThePrint, 26 September 2019, https://theprint.in/opinion/after-aadhaar-nrc-amit-shah-proposes-a-new-agni-parkisha-for-indians/296819/](https://theprint.in/opinion/after-aadhaar-nrc-amit-shah-proposes-a-new-agni-parkisha-for-indians/296819/.

35. Noah Robischon, 'If Privacy Is the New Celebrity, Then Ashton Kutcher Needs a New Career', Fast Company, 3 April 2014, https://www.fastcompany.com/1639832/if-privacy-new-celebrity-then-ashton-kutcher-needs-new-career.

Chapter 4: Design: Iterate Everything

1. William Willard Howard, 'The Rush to Oklahoma', *Harper's Weekly* 33 (18 May 1889): pp. 391–94, https://urbanplanning.library.cornell.edu/DOCS/landrush.htm.

2. Delaney Hall, 'The Worst Way to Start a City', 99% Invisible, 1 January 1970, 99percentinvisible.org/episode/the-worst-way-to-start-a-city/.

3. 'Grid Plan', Wikipedia, Wikimedia Foundation, 1 October 2019, en.wikipedia.org/wiki/Grid_plan.

4. Dan Kedmey, 'Skyscrapers—but No Sewage System. Meet a City Run by Private Industry', Ideas.ted.com, 20 June 2017, ideas.

ted.com/skyscrapers-but-no-sewage-system-meet-a-city-run-by-
private-industry/.

5. Gautam Datt, 'Indian Air Force lost half of MiG fighter jets
    in deadly crashes', *India Today*, 3 May 2012, https://www.
    indiatoday.in/india/north/story/iaf-lost-half-of-mig-fighter-jets-
    in-deadly-crashes-100926-2012-05-03.

6. Ron Elving, 'The Florida Recount Of 2000: A Nightmare That
    Goes On Haunting', NPR, 12 November 2018, https://www.
    npr.org/2018/11/12/666812854/the-florida-recount-of-2000-a-
    nightmare-that-goes-on-haunting.

7. Dana Canedy, 'Florida Democrats Say Ballot's Design Hurt
    Gore', *New York Times*, 9 November 2000, https://www.nytimes.
    com/2000/11/09/us/2000-elections-palm-beach-ballot-florida-
    democrats-say-ballot-s-design-hurt-gore.html.

8. 'The Gerrymandering Project', FiveThirtyEight, https://
    fivethirtyeight.com/tag/the-gerrymandering-project/;   and
    'Wisconsin: The Atlas Of Redistricting', FiveThirtyEight,
    25 January 2018, projects.fivethirtyeight.com/redistricting-
    maps/wisconsin/.

9. 'Manual on Electronic Voting Machine and VVPAT', Election
    Commission of India, 26 August 2019, https://eci.gov.in/files/
    file/9230-manual-on-electronic-voting-machine-and-vvpat/.

10. 'VVPAT Verification: Supreme Court Orders Counting of
    Paper Slips of Five EVMs in Every Constituency', Scroll, 8 April
    2019, https://scroll.in/latest/919313/vvpat-verification-supreme-
    court-orders-counting-of-paper-slips-of-five-evms-in-every-
    constituency.

11. Shweta Jadhav, 'As EVMs are debated, this is how the ballot
    box was made for India's first 1952 election', ThePrint, 27
    January 2019, https://theprint.in/opinion/as-evms-are-debated-
    this-is-how-the-ballot-box-was-made-for-indias-first-1952-
    election/183790/.

12. Diana Budds, 'The Brilliance of Alexandria Ocasio-Cortez's
    Bold Campaign Design', Vox, 2 July 2018, https://www.vox.
    com/policy-and-politics/2018/7/2/17519414/ocasio-cortez-
    campaign-design-campaign-posters-tandem-branding.

13. Aileen Kwun, 'How the Alexandria Ocasio-Cortez Campaign Got Its Powerful Design', Fast Company, 9 July 2018, https://www.fastcompany.com/90180561/how-the-alexandria-ocasio-cortez-campaign-got-its-powerful-design.

14. Rachel Lears, *Knock Down the House*, Netflix, 2019, https://www.netflix.com/watch/81080637.

15. Zaid Jilani, How a Ragtag Group of Socialist Filmmakers Produced One of the Most Viral Campaign Ads of 2018', The Intercept, 5 June 2018, https://theintercept.com/2018/06/05/ocasio-cortez-new-york-14th-district-democratic-primary-campaign-video/.

16. Donald A. Norman, *The Design of Everyday Things* (Massachusetts: MIT Press, 2013).

17. Vidyadhar Date, 'HDFC spikes: Mumbai's tony Pali Hill also uses hostile design to deter workers, hawkers from sitting', Scroll, 1 April 2018, https://scroll.in/article/873947/hdfc-spikes-mumbais-tony-pali-hill-also-uses-hostile-design-to-deter-workers-hawkers-from-sitting.

18. Byung-Chul Han, 'Why, in China and Japan, a Copy Is Just as Good as an Original', Aeon, 2 October 2019, https://aeon.co/essays/why-in-china-and-japan-a-copy-is-just-as-good-as-an-original.

19. Rachel Nuwer, 'This Japanese Shrine Has Been Torn Down And Rebuilt Every 20 Years for the Past Millennium', SmithsonianMag.com, 4 October 2013, https://www.smithsonianmag.com/smart-news/this-japanese-shrine-has-been-torn-down-and-rebuilt-every-20-years-for-the-past-millennium-575558/?fbclid=IwAR3y89Dl4Bne8mZY8qiQlwVb2G73OzAe10GnX-JGf1D1jVZM3_ys__IICkU.

20. Kim Kardashian West, Instagram post, 8 February 2019, https://www.instagram.com/p/Btn7Tm6nEof/.

21. Ashley Carman, 'Kim Kardashian West Wins $2.8 Million from Company That Kept Tagging Her in Instagram Posts', The Verge, 3 July 2019, https://www.theverge.com/2019/7/3/20681128/missguided-kim-kardashian-west-lawsuit-instagram-tag-fashion.

22. An example: 'I Fall Apart [Post Malone Cover]', YouTube video, 4:05, posted by YONAKA Music, 17 November 2017, https://www.youtube.com/watch?v=5OW4Zj5pP9w.

23. Zack O'Malley Greenburg, 'Kanye's Second Coming: Inside The Billion-Dollar Yeezy Empire', *Forbes*, 19 September 2019, https:// www.forbes.com/sites/zackomalleygreenburg/2019/07/09/kanyes-second-coming-inside-the-billion-dollar-yeezy-empire/.

24. 'Dark Patterns', Dark Patterns, https://www.darkpatterns.org/.

25. 'Dua Lipa - Don't Start Now (Official Music Video)', YouTube video, 3:01, posted by Dua Lipa, 1 November 2019, https:// www.youtube.com/watch?v=oygrmJFKYZY.

26. Mike Isaac, 'Uber's C.E.O. Plays With Fire', *New York Times*, 23 April 2017, https: https://www.nytimes.com/2017/04/23/technology/travis-kalanick-pushes-uber-and-himself-to-the-precipice.html.

27. Iman Zambasri, 'The Nudge – How IKEA's Store Layout Design Influences Your Spending', Thoughts on Wayfinding, 19 November 2017, https://wp.nyu.edu/thoughtsonwayfinding/2017/11/19/the-nudge-how-ikeas-store-layout-design-influences-your-spending/.

28. 'TCS Reimagines Passport Services Across India', Tata Consultancy Services, https://www.tcs.com/e-governance-passport-transform-indian-passport-office.

29. Kieren McCarthy, 'Two Years Ago, 123-Reg and NamesCo Decided to Register Millions of .Uk Domains for Customers without Asking Them. They Just Got the Renewal Reminders . . .', The Register, 17 September 2019, https://www.theregister. co.uk/2019/09/16/123reg_namesco_uk_domains/.

30. 'List of Apollo Astronauts', Wikipedia, Wikimedia Foundation, 13 September 2019, https://en.wikipedia.org/wiki/List_of_Apollo_astronauts.

31. Veritasium, 'Why Machines That Bend Are Better', YouTube video, 12:51, posted by Veritasium, 12 March 2019, https:// www.youtube.com/watch?v=97t7Xj_iBv0.

32. Kurt Kohlstedt, 'Beyond Biohazard: Why Danger Symbols Can't Last Forever', 99% Invisible, 1 January 1970, https://99percentinvisible.org/article/beyond-biohazard-danger-symbols-cant-last-forever/.

33. 'Human Interference Task Force', Wikipedia, Wikimedia Foundation, 24 August 2019, https://en.wikipedia.org/wiki/Human_Interference_Task_Force#Thomas_Sebeok.

34. 'A Portable, Life-Saving Defibrillator', IDEO, https://www.ideo.com/case-study/a-portable-life-saving-defibrillator.

35. 'Cardiac arrest and automated external defibrillators (AEDs)', U.S. Department of Labor Occupational Safety and Health Administration,OSHA Publication No. TIB 01-12-17, https://www.osha.gov/dts/tib/tib_data/tib20011217.html.

36. Isaac Asimov, *I, Robot* (New York: Penguin Random House, 2008).

37. E. Awad, S. Dsouza et al., 'The Moral Machine experiment', *Nature* 563 (2018): pp. 59–64, DOI: 10.1038/s41586-018-0637-6, https://www.media.mit.edu/publications/the-moral-machine-experiment/.

38. Peter Dizikes, 'How Should Autonomous Vehicles Be Programmed?' MIT News, 24 October 2018, https://news.mit.edu/2018/how-autonomous-vehicles-programmed-1024.

Chapter 5: Infinite Regress: Termites after Midnight

1. A.K. Ramanujan, 'Three hundred Rāmāyaṇas: Five Examples and Three Thoughts on Translation', in *The Collected Essays of A.K. Ramanujan*, ed. Vinay Dharwadker (New Delhi: Oxford Universty Press, 2004), https://www.sacw.net/IMG/pdf/AKRamanujan_ThreeHundredRamayanas.pdf.

2. 'Ravi Shankar Prasad: The wily counsel of 'Ram Lalla' and Modi's Digital India minder', *Economic Times*, 30 May 2019, https://economictimes.indiatimes.com/news/politics-and-nation/ravi-shankar-prasad-the-wily-counsel-of-ram-lalla-and-modis-digital-india-minder/articleshow/69584754.cms?from=mdr.

3. Krishna N. Das, 'Factbox: India's Ayodhya temple dispute', Reuters, 22 November 2018, https://www.reuters.com/article/us-india-election-religion-factbox/factbox-indias-ayodhya-temple-dispute-idUSKCN1NR03O.

4. *M Siddiq (D) Thr Lrs vs Mahant Suresh Das & Ors*, Civil Appeal
    Nos 10866-10867 of 2010 in Supreme Court Of India, https://
    indiankanoon.org/doc/107745042/.

5. Scott Lucas, 'Cities Don't Have Souls. Why Do We Battle For
    Them?', City Lab, 17 April 2019, https://www.citylab.com/
    life/2019/04/soul-of-the-city-san-francisco-gentrification-urban-
    planning/587173/.

6. 'Bandeh | Lyrical Video | Indian Ocean | Black Friday', YouTube
    video, 8:14, posted by Times Music, 28 March 2019, https://
    www.youtube.com/watch?v=R5LNFXeceIo.

7. 'I Agree with Subramanian Swamy', YouTube video, 21:42, posted
    by Newslaundry, 16 June 2012, https://youtu.be/Wz5AJpG-cXI.

8. *Pani Haq Samiti & Ors. vs Briham Mumbai Municipal Corporation
    & Ors.*, Public Interest Litigation No. 10 of 2012 in High Court
    of Judicature at Bombay, https://www.ielrc.org/content/e1407.
    pdf.

9. 'A Narrowing Space: Violence and discrimination against India's
    religious minorities', Center for Study of Society and Secularism
    & Minority Rights Group International, June 2017, https://
    minorityrights.org/wp-content/uploads/2017/06/MRG_Rep_
    India_final.pdf.

10. 'What is Tejo Mahalaya controversy?', *Indian Express*, 18 October
    2017, https://indianexpress.com/article/what-is/what-is-tejo-
    mahalaya-controversy-taj-mahal-vinay-katiyar-bjp-4896716/.

11. Nikita Doval, 'Babri Masjid demolition: The key political players
    and their roles', LiveMint, 6 December 2017, https://www.
    livemint.com/Politics/JhG2CWUn0ULrcw5Ue6wJgO/Babri-
    Masjid-demolition-The-key-political-players-and-their.html.

12. Andrew Prokop, 'Where does the term gerrymandering
    come from?', Vox, 14 November 2018, https://www.vox.
    com/2014/8/5/17991968/gerrymandering-name-elbridge-gerry

13. Michael Livermore and Dan Rockmore, 'France Kicks Data
    Scientists Out of Its Courts', *Slate*, 21 June 2019, https://slate.
    com/technology/2019/06/france-has-banned-judicial-analytics-
    to-analyze-the-courts.html.

14. Benjamin L. Liebman, Margaret Roberts et al., 'Mass Digitization of Chinese Court Decisions: How to Use Text as Data in the Field of Chinese Law', 21st Century China Center Research Paper No. 2017–01; Columbia Public Law Research Paper No. 14–551 (October 1, 2019), https://dx.doi.org/10.2139/ssrn.2985861.

15. Robert M. Sapolsky, *Behave: The Biology of Humans at Our Best and Worst* (New York: Penguin Random House, 2018).

16. Maria Popova, 'Charles Bukowski, Arthur C. Clarke, Annie Dillard, John Cage, and Others on the Meaning of Life', BrainPickings.org, https://www.brainpickings.org/2012/09/17/the-meaning-of-life/.

17. Grognor, '[Transcript] Richard Feynman on Why Questions', LessWrong, 9 January 2012, https://www.lesswrong.com/posts/W9rJv26sxs4g2B9bL/transcript-richard-feynman-on-why-questions.

18. Ibid.

Chapter 6: Sustainability: Don't Break the Planet

1. Roland Geyer, Jenna R. Jambeck and Kara Lavender Law, 'Production, use, and fate of all plastics ever made', *Science Advances*, vol. 3, no. 7, e1700782 (19 July 2017), DOI: 10.1126/sciadv.1700782.

2. Chris Edwards and Jonna Meyhoff Fry, 'Life cycle assessment of supermarket carrier bags: a review of the bags available in 2006', *Evidence*, Environment Agency, Bristol, February 2011, https://assets.publishing.service.gov.uk/government/uploads/system/uploads/attachment_data/file/291023/scho0711buan-e-e.pdf.

3. Anisha Bhatia, 'Plastic Ban: What India Can Learn from Other Countries', Swachh India NDTV, 30 June 2017, https://swachhindia.ndtv.com/plastic-ban-india-can-learn-countries-6161/.

4. Jennifer Clapp and Linda Swanston, 'Doing away with plastic shopping bags: international patterns of norm emergence and policy implementation', Environmental Politics 18, no. 3 (2009): pp. 315–32, DOI: 10.1080/09644010902823717.

5. 'Five things to know about plastic waste and recycling in India',
    Phys.org, 2 October 2019, https://phys.org/news/2019-10-
    plastic-recycling-india.html.
6. Rajanya Bose and Anirban Bhattacharya, 'Why Ragpickers,
    Unrecognised and Unpaid, Are Critical for Waste Management
    In India', India Spend, 12 May 2017, https://archive.indiaspend.
    com/cover-story/why-ragpickers-unrecognised-and-unpaid-are-
    critical-for-waste-management-in-india-43164.
7. Marc Bain, 'Adidas is learning it's not easy to make 100%
    recyclable sneakers', Quartz, 14 November 2019, https://qz.com/
    quartzy/1747230/adidas-says-it-successfully-recycled-its-first-
    batch-of-futurecraft-loop-sneakers/.
8. James Temple, 'Sorry—organic farming is actually worse for
    climate change', *MIT Technology Review*, 22 October 2019,
    https://www.technologyreview.com/s/614605/sorryorganic-
    farming-is-actually-worse-for-climate-change/.
9. Lauren Singer's YouTube channel, Trash is for Tossers: https://
    www.youtube.com/channel/UCgjw6tZNyjR_8zIFDsIPpww.
10. Jordan Crook, 'Package Free picks up $4.5 million to scale
    sustainable CPG products', TechCrunch, 26 September 2019,
    https://techcrunch.com/2019/09/26/package-free-picks-up-4-5-
    million-to-scale-sustainable-cpg-products/.
11. '9.16 cr toilets built, 5.5 lakh villages declared ODF since
    2014: Govt', *Economic Times*, 7 February 2019, https://
    economictimes.indiatimes.com/news/politics-and-nation/9-16-
    cr-toilets-built-5-5-lakh-villages-declared-odf-since-2014-govt/
    articleshow/67886006.cms.
12. 'Combating Plastic Pollution', SC Johnson, https://www.
    scjohnson.com/Our%20Purpose/Environmental%20
    Responsibility%20News/Ocean%20Plastic.
13. 'Electric power consumption (kWh per capita) - United States',
    World Bank, https://data.worldbank.org/indicator/EG.USE.
    ELEC.KH.PC?locations=US.
14. Muhammad Tabish Parray and Rahul Tongia, 'Understanding
    India's Power Capacity: Surplus or not, and for how long?',

Brookings India Research Paper No. 082019, August 2019, https://www.brookings.edu/research/understanding-indias-power-capacity-surplus-or-not-and-for-how-long.

15. 'Global Emissions', C2ES: the Center for Climate and Energy Solutions, Energy/Emissions Data, https://www.c2es.org/content/international-emissions/.

16. Website for the Global Cooling Prize: https://globalcoolingprize.org/.

17. 'BEE Notifies New Energy Performance Standards for Air Conditioners: All Room Air Conditioners to have Default Temperature Setting of 24 Degrees Celsius from Jan 1, 2020', Ministry of Power, PIB Delhi, 6 January 2020, https://pib.gov.in/PressReleasePage.aspx?PRID=1598508.

18. 'Life-cycle greenhouse-gas emissions of energy sources', Wikipedia, Wikimedia Foundation, 11 April 2020, https://en.wikipedia.org/wiki/Life-cycle_greenhouse-gas_emissions_of_energy_sources.

19. Hannah Ritchie, 'What Was the Death Toll from Chernobyl and Fukushima?' Our World in Data, 24 July 2017, https://ourworldindata.org/what-was-the-death-toll-from-chernobyl-and-fukushima.

20. Hannah Ritchie, 'What are the safest and cleanest sources of energy?', OurWorldinData.org, 10 February 2020, https://ourworldindata.org/safest-sources-of-energy.

21. Hari Kumar, 'India Struggles to Save 15 Trapped Coal Miners', New York Times, 27 December 2018, https://www.nytimes.com/2018/12/27/world/asia/india-trapped-coal-miners.html.

22. Mara Hvistendahl, 'Coal Ash Is More Radioactive Than Nuclear Waste', ScientificAmerican.com, 13 December 2007, https://www.scientificamerican.com/article/coal-ash-is-more-radioactive-than-nuclear-waste/.

23. Sudarshan Varadhan, 'Coal-fired plants around New Delhi running despite missing emissions deadline', Reuters, 1 January 2020, https://in.reuters.com/article/us-india-pollution-coal-idINKBN1Z01VD.

24. 'Ather Energy gets FAME II nod for electric scooter Ather 450', Economic Times, 8 May 2019, https://energy.economictimes.

indiatimes.com/news/power/ather-energy-gets-fame-ii-nod-for-electric-scooter-ather-450/69237107.

25. 'Breakthrough Energy Ventures Board and Investors', Breakthrough Energy, https://www.b-t.energy/ventures/board-investors/.

26. Abhinav Soman, Karthik Ganesan and Harsimran Kaur, 'India's Electric Vehicle Transition: Impact on Auto Industry and Building the EV Ecosystem', Council on Energy, Environment and Water, New Delhi, 2019, https://www.ceew.in/publications/india%E2%80%99s-electric-vehicle-transition.

27. American Chemical Society, 'Motorcycles Emit "Disproportionately High" Amounts Of Air Pollutants', ScienceDaily, 1 January 2006, https://www.sciencedaily.com/releases/2006/01/060101155000.htm.

28. 'Ather Energy gets FAME II nod for electric scooter Ather 450', Economic Times, 8 May 2019, https://energy.economictimes.indiatimes.com/news/power/ather-energy-gets-fame-ii-nod-for-electric-scooter-ather-450/69237107.

29. Matthew Zampa, 'How Many Animals Are Killed for Food Every Day?', Sentient Media, https://sentientmedia.org/how-many-animals-are-killed-for-food-every-day/.

30. Alex Thornton, 'This is how many animals we eat each year', We Forum, 8 February 2019, https://www.weforum.org/agenda/2019/02/chart-of-the-day-this-is-how-many-animals-we-eat-each-year/.

31. 'Tracking Clean Energy Progress', International Energy Agency, https://www.iea.org/tcep/#.

32. 'Transcript: Greta Thunberg's Speech at the U.N. Climate Action Summit', National Public Radio, 23 September 2019, https://www.npr.org/2019/09/23/763452863/transcript-greta-thunbergs-speech-at-the-u-n-climate-action-summit.

Chapter 7: Behavioural Economics: Coca-Cola Is a Happy Colour

1. Emma Graham-Harrison and Carole Cadwalladr, 'Revealed: 50 Million Facebook Profiles Harvested for Cambridge Analytica

in Major Data Breach', *Guardian*, 17 March 2018, https://
www.theguardian.com/news/2018/mar/17/cambridge-analytica-
facebook-influence-us-election?fbclid=IwAR1FEATjZ0ZJ68uNG0
hpeWJozr3f8fynCvgvtXSPQvF6uFYy3lGh378oiCE.

2. 'Alexander Nix: From Mad Men to Math Men | OMR Festival
    2017 - Hamburg, Germany | #OMR17', YouTube video, 30:17,
    posted by Online Marketing Rockstars, 10 March 2017, https://
    www.youtube.com/watch?v=6bG5ps5KdDo.

3. Colleen Walsh, 'Layers of choice', *Harvard Gazette*, 5 February
    2014, https://news.harvard.edu/gazette/story/2014/02/layers-of-
    choice/.

4. Rebecca J. Rosen, 'Pareidolia: A Bizarre Bug of the Human
    Mind Emerges in Computers', *Atlantic*, 7 August 2012,
    https://www.theatlantic.com/technology/archive/2012/08/
    pareidolia-a-bizarre-bug-of-the-human-mind-emerges-in-
    computers/260760/.

5. Sheena Iyengar, *The Art of Choosing: The Decisions We Make
    Every Day of our Lives, What They Say About Us and How We Can
    Improve Them* (New Delhi: Abacus Books, 2012).

6. Bertrand Russell, 'The Triumph of Stupidity', in *Mortals and
    Others: Bertrand Russell's American Essays, 1931–1935*, v.2,
    p. 28, https://russell-j.com/0583TS.HTM.

7. 'Smug Snake', TV Tropes, https://tvtropes.org/pmwiki/pmwiki.
    php/Main/SmugSnake.

8. Sendhil Mullainathan and Eldar Shafir, *Scarcity: The True Cost
    of Not Having Enough* (New York: Penguin Random House,
    2015).

9. Richard Dowden, 'The Thatcher Philosophy', *Catholic Herald*,
    22 December 1978, https://www.margaretthatcher.org/
    document/103793.

10. Michael I. Norton and Dan Ariely, 'The "IKEA Effect": Why
    Labor Leads to Love', PsycEXTRA Dataset, 2005, doi:10.1037/
    e640112011-015.

11. Brian Heater, 'Jack Dorsey Admits Twitter Hasn't "Figured out"
    Approach to Fake News', TechCrunch, 19 August 2018, https://

techcrunch.com/2018/08/19/jack-dorsey-admits-twitter-hasnt-figured-out-approach-to-fake-news/.

12. Richard F. West, et al., 'Cognitive Sophistication Does Not Attenuate the Bias Blind Spot', *Journal of Personality and Social Psychology*, vol. 103, no. 3 (2012): pp. 506–19, doi:10.1037/a0028857.

13. Hannes Grassegger, 'Facebook Says Its "Voter Button" Is Good for Turnout. But Should the Tech Giant Be Nudging Us at All?', Guardian, 15 April 2018, https://www.theguardian.com/technology/2018/apr/15/facebook-says-it-voter-button-is-good-for-turn-but-should-the-tech-giant-be-nudging-us-at-all.

Chapter 8: Democracy: Why Don't We Teach Rhetoric at School?

1. Raluca Tanase and Remus Radu, 'Lecture #3, PageRank Algorithm—The Mathematics of Google Search', The Mathematics of Web Search, Department of Mathematics, Cornell University, New York, https://pi.math.cornell.edu/~mec/Winter2009/RalucaRemus/Lecture3/lecture3.html.

2. Sergey Brin and Lawrence Page, 'The Anatomy of a Large-Scale Hypertextual Web Search Engine', Computer Science Department, Stanford University, California,https://infolab.stanford.edu/~backrub/google.html.

3. Ben Rattray, 'How Tech Can Help Save Democracy', Medium, 4 December 2016, https://medium.com/@benrattray/how-technology-can-improve-democracy-c089fc8f9463#.nf8cochk1.

4. Tim Dunlop, 'Voting Undermines the Will of the People – It's Time to Replace It with Sortition', *Guardian*, 14 October 2018, https://www.theguardian.com/australia-news/2018/oct/14/voting-undermines-the-will-of-the-people-its-time-to-replace-it-with-sortition.

5. H.L. Mencken, *Notes on Democracy* (New York: Knopf Doubleday Publishing Group, 1926).

6. Ibid.

7. 'Swamy to PM Modi: 'Elections Are Not Won on Economic Performance', Quint, 20 June 2018, https://www.thequint.com/

videos/news-videos/swamy-to-pm-modi-elections-not-won-on-economic-performance.

8. Suhasini Krishnan, 'Subramanian Swamy and His Long, Long List of Enemies', Bloomberg Quint, 22 June 2016, https://https://www.bloombergquint.com/politics/subramanian-swamy-and-his-long-list-of-enemies-rss-raghuram-rajan.

9. Glenn Kessler, Salvador Rizzo and Meg Kelly, 'President Trump made 16,241 false or misleading claims in his first three years', *Washington Post*, 20 January 2020, https://www.washingtonpost.com/politics/2020/01/20/president-trump-made-16241-false-or-misleading-claims-his-first-three-years/.

10. Simon Lancaster, 'Tap into the Power to Persuade by Using These 6 Techniques of Clear and Compelling Speech', 'How to Be a Better Human' series, TED, 10 September 2019, https://ideas.ted.com/tap-into-the-power-to-persuade-by-using-these-6-techniques-of-clear-and-compelling-speech/.

11. Ibid.

12. Moral Foundations Theory, Moral Foundations, https://moralfoundations.org/.

13. 'Narendra Modi 'Attends' First-Ever Press Conference as PM, but Takes No Questions', the Wire, 17 May 2019, https://thewire.in/politics/narendra-modi-amit-shah-press-conference-questions.

14. Mahita Gajanan, '"You Have Stolen My Dreams and My Childhood": Greta Thunberg Gives Powerful Speech at UN Climate Summit', *Time*, 23 September 2019, https://time.com/5684216/greta-thunberg-un-climate-action-summit-climate-speech/.

15. M.D., 'Is Donald Trump a populist?', The Economist Explains, *The Economist*, 4 July 2016, https://www.economist.com/the-economist-explains/2016/07/04/is-donald-trump-a-populist.

Chapter 9: Accountability: The Street Plays after Lynchings

1. DeepMoji, MIT Media Lab. MIT, https://deepmoji.mit.edu/.

2. Annie Palmer, 'Apple now has $210.6 billion in cash on hand', CNBC, 30 July 2019, https://www.cnbc.com/2019/07/30/apple-now-has-210point6-billion-in-cash-on-hand.html.

3. Siva Vaidhyanathan, 'Mark Zuckerberg doesn't understand free speech in the 21st century', *Guardian*, 18 October 2019, https://www.theguardian.com/commentisfree/2019/oct/18/mark-zuckerberg-free-speech-21st-century.

4. 'WhatsApp Leans on Street Theater to Spread Awareness about Lynching, Fake News', Firstpost, 12 October 2018, https://www.firstpost.com/tech/news-analysis/whatsapp-leans-on-street-theater-to-spread-awareness-about-lynching-fake-news-5367531.html.

5. Scott Neuman, 'Letter: Kalashnikov Suffered Remorse Over Rifle He Invented', NPR, 13 January 2014, https://www.npr.org/blogs/thetwo-way/2014/01/13/262096410/letter-kalashnikov-suffered-remorse-over-rifle-he-invented.

6. Phillip Killicoat, *Weaponomics: The Economics of Small Arms* (MA thesis), 2006, Department of Economics, Oxford University, UK, https://www.prio.org/Projects/Project/?x=1363.

7. Simon Singh, *The Code Book: The Science of Secrecy from Ancient Egypt to Quantum Cryptography* (New York: Anchor Books, 2000).

8. Markus Ra, 'Don't Shoot the Messenger', *Telegraph*, 25 January 2018, https://telegra.ph/Dont-Shoot-the-Messenger.

9. Ibid.

10. Pratul Sharma, '"Disciplined party worker" Modi lets Amit Shah do the talking', *Week*, 17 May 2019, https://www.theweek.in/news/india/2019/05/17/Disciplined-party-worker-Modi-lets-Amit-Shah-do-the-talking.html?fbclid=IwAR3HnnWTuF0qLfhp17-ebKm7NnrlaOvMaBhwElF_86fwkN2SfYmZZrhmGGo.

11. *Knight First Amendment Institute at Columbia University vs Donald J. Trump, President of the United States*, Case 18-1691, Document 25, 08/07/2018, 2362018, SCU Mabie Law Library, Santa Clara Law Digital Commons, https://digitalcommons.law.scu.edu/cgi/viewcontent.cgi?article=2780&context=historical.

12. Sasha Ingber, 'Alexandria Ocasio-Cortez Is Sued Over Blocking Twitter Followers', NPR, 12 July 2019, https://www.npr.org/2019/07/12/741038121/alexandria-ocasio-cortez-is-sued-over-blocking-twitter-followers.

13. Leslie D'Monte, 'Bad Bots Originating from India See Increase, Says Study', LiveMint, 18 April 2019, https://www.livemint. com/technology/tech-news/bad-bots-originating-from-india-see-increase-says-study-1555580306934.html.

14. Gail J. Kamal, 'California's BOT Disclosure Law, SB 1001, Now In Effect', National Law Review, 15 July 2019, https://www. natlawreview.com/article/california-s-bot-disclosure-law-sb-1001-now-effect.

15. Hilary Andersson, 'Social Media Apps Are "Deliberately" Addictive to Users', BBC, 3 July 2018, https://www.bbc.com/news/amp/technology-44640959.

16. Mandalit del Barco, 'How Kodak's Shirley Cards Set Photography's Skin-Tone Standard', NPR, 13 November 2014, https://www.npr. org/2014/11/13/363517842/for-decades-kodak-s-shirley-cards-set-photography-s-skin-tone-standard.

17. 'Study Finds Gender and Skin-Type Bias in Commercial Artificial-Intelligence Systems', ScienceDaily, 12 February 2018, https://www.sciencedaily.com/releases/2018/02/180212121231.htm.

18. Jack Dorsey, Twitter post, 11 December 2019, https://twitter.com/jack/status/1204766078468911106.

19. Michael J. Sandel, *What Money Can't Buy: The Moral Limits of Markets* (New York: Penguin Books, 2013).

20. Gregory D. Erhardt, Sneha Roy, et al., 'Do transportation network companies decrease or increase congestion?', *Science Advances*, vol. 5, no. 5 (8 May 2019): eaau2670, DOI: 10.1126/sciadv.aau2670.

21. Harini Nagendra, 'Have Ola and Uber eased India's traffic problems or made them much, much worse?', Opinion, Scroll, 5 September 2018, https://scroll.in/magazine/891171/have-ola-and-uber-eased-indias-traffic-problems-or-made-them-much-much-worse.

Chapter 10: Viral Economics: Is Money Even Real?

1. 'Victoria's Secret "sorry" for transgender model comments', BBC. com, 10 November 2018, https://www.bbc.com/news/world-us-canada-46163922.

2. Mary Hanbury, 'An activist shareholder is urging Victoria's Secret parent to update 'tone-deaf' brand image to boost sales', BusinessInsider.in, 6 March 2019, https://www.businessinsider. in/retail/an-activist-shareholder-is-urging-victorias-secret-parent-to-update-tone-deaf-brand-image-to-boost-sales/ articleshow/68278186.cms.

3. Aaron Rupar, 'Trump still thinks schools should reopen because Covid-19 "will go away." Really', Vox.com, 5 August 2020, https://www.vox.com/2020/8/5/21355413/trump-fox-and-friends-coronavirus-school-reopening-mail-in-voting.

4. Rebecca S.B. Fischer, 'What's the difference between pandemic, epidemic and outbreak?', TheConversation.com, 9 March 2020, https://theconversation.com/whats-the-difference-between-pandemic-epidemic-and-outbreak-133048.

5. Jordyn Holman and Kim Bhasin, 'Victoria's Secret Has Limited Options in Sycamore Battle', BloombergQuint.com, 23 April 2020, https://www.bloombergquint.com/business/victoria-s-secret-has-few-options-with-sycamore-deal-in-peril.

6. Joe Nocera, 'Get Ready for a Tsunami of Pandemic Lawsuits Over Broken Deals', Bloomberg.com, 4 May 2020, https://www. bloomberg.com/news/articles/2020-05-04/pandemic-lawsuits-will-ask-is-the-coronavirus-an-act-of-god.

7. Slavoj Zizek, *Pandemic!*, https://www.orbooks.com/catalog/ pandemic/.

8. 'COVID-19, MERS & SARS', National Institute of Allergy and Infectious Diseases, Maryland, United States, 18 August 2020, https://www.niaid.nih.gov/diseases-conditions/covid-19.

9. 'WHO Coronavirus Disease (COVID-19) Dashboard', World Health Organization, https://covid19.who.int/.

10. Tom Levitt, 'Covid and farm animals: nine pandemics that changed the world', *Guardian*, 15 September 2020, https://www. theguardian.com/environment/ng-interactive/2020/sep/15/covid-farm-animals-and-pandemics-diseases-that-changed-the-world.

11. Bernard Avishai, 'The Pandemic Isn't a Black Swan But a Portent of a More Fragile Global System', *New Yorker*, 21 April

2020, https://www.newyorker.com/news/daily-comment/the-pandemic-isnt-a-black-swan-but-a-portent-of-a-more-fragile-global-system.

12. 'Global military expenditure sees largest annual increase in a decade—says SIPRI—reaching $1917 billion in 2019', Stockholm International Peace Research Institute (SIPRI), 27 April 2020, https://www.sipri.org/media/press-release/2020/global-military-expenditure-sees-largest-annual-increase-decade-says-sipri-reaching-1917-billion#:~:text=for%20the%20media-,Global%20military%20expenditure%20sees%20largest%20annual%20increase%20in%20a%20decade,reaching%20%241917%20billion%20in%20 2019&text=(Stockholm%2C%2027%20April%202020),Peace%20Research%20Institute%20(SIPRI).

13. 'The U.S. Government and the World Health Organization', KFF, 25 January 2021, https://www.kff.org/global-health-policy/fact-sheet/the-u-s-government-and-the-world-health-organization/.

14. 'Clip of health officials on federal response to coronavirus outbreak: User Clip: Fauci asked about masks: 3 March 2020', C-SPAN, 11 April 2020, https://www.c-span.org/video/?c4867816/user-clip-fauci-asked-masks.

15. Mary Hanbury, 'Crocs is Donating 10,000 Pairs of Free Shoes to US Healthcare Workers Every Day Until Stock Lasts', *Business Insider*, 26 March 2020, https://www.businessinsider.in/retail/news/crocs-is-donating-10000-pairs-of-free-shoes-to-us-healthcare-workers-every-day-until-stocks-last/articleshow/74834823.cms.

16. Lois Beckett, 'Americans have bought record 17m guns in year of unrest, analysis finds', *Guardian*, 30 October 2020, https://www.theguardian.com/us-news/2020/oct/29/coronavirus-pandemic-americans-gun-sales.

17. Nicro Grant, 'Zoom Daily Users Surge to 300 Million Despite Privacy Woes', Bloomberg.com, 23 April 2020, https://www.bloomberg.com/news/articles/2020-04-22/zoom-daily-users-surge-to-300-million-despite-privacy-woes.

18. Felix Richter, 'These Are The Top 10 Manufacturing Countries in the World', WeForum.org, 25 February 2020, https://www.weforum.org/agenda/2020/02/countries-manufacturing-trade-exports-economics/.

19. 'Households and NPISHs Final consumption expenditure (current US$)', World Bank national accounts data, and OECD National Accounts data files, World Bank, https://data.worldbank.org/indicator/NE.CON.PRVT.CD?most_recent_value_desc=true&year_high_desc=true.

20. Anurag Joshi, Nupur Acharya and Ravil Shirodkar, 'Franklin Templeton's $4.1 billion fund freeze shows lingering credit pain', Economic Times, 24 April 2020, https://economictimes.indiatimes.com/mf/analysis/franklins-4-1-billion-fund-freeze-shows-lingering-credit-pain/articleshow/75343936.cms.

21. 'President Roosevelt's Inaugural Address: 4 March 1933', PBS.org, https://www.pbs.org/newshour/spc/character/links/roosevelt_speech.html.

22. Simon Kennedy, Michelle Jamrisko, 'V, L Or "Nike Swoosh" Economists Debate Shape of Global Recovery', Bloomberg.com, 02 April 2020.

23. 'India's Per-Capita Income Rises 6/8% to Rs 11,254 a month in FY20', Business Today, 7 January 2020, https://www.businesstoday.in/current/economy-politics/india-per-capita-income-rises-68-to-rs-11254-a-month-in-fy20/story/393333.html.

24. 'Tipu Sultan to Be Removed From History Textbooks? Education Minister Seeks Report', India Today, 29 October 2019, https://www.indiatoday.in/education-today/news/story/tipu-sultan-to-be-removed-from-history-textbooks-education-minister-seeks-report-1613649-2019-10-29.

25. Adam Gopnik, 'The Field Guide to Tyranny', New Yorker, 16 December 2019, https://www.newyorker.com/magazine/2019/12/23/the-field-guide-to-tyranny.

26. Niall McCarthy, 'The Cost of Mobile Internet Around the World', Forbes, 5 March 2019, https://www.forbes.com/sites/

niallmccarthy/2019/03/05/the-cost-of-mobile-internet-around-the-world-infographic/.

27. Arundhati Roy, 'Arundhati Roy on Delhi Violence: "This is Our Version of the Coronavirus. We Are Sick"', Scroll, 1 March 2020, https://scroll.in/article/954805/arundhati-roy-on-delhi-violence-this-is-our-version-of-the-coronavirus-we-are-sick.

28. Jonathan Paye-Layleh, Wade Williams, 'Clashes in Liberian Slum Sealed Off to Halt Spread of Ebola Virus', washingtonpost.com, 20 August 2014.

29. 'Coronavirus: YouTube bans "medically unsubstantiated" content', BBC.com, 22 April 2020, https://www.bbc.com/news/technology-52388586.

30. Naomi Klein, *The Shock Doctrine* (Ontario: Penguin Random House Canada, 2007).

31. Andrew Roth, '"Cybergulag": Russia Looks to Surveillance Technology to Enforce Lockdown', *Guardian*, 2 April 2020, https://www.theguardian.com/world/2020/apr/02/cybergulag-russia-looks-to-surveillance-technology-to-enforce-lockdown.

Chapter 11: Irrationality: Have Fun, while You're Here

1. Victoria Horner and Andrew Whiten, 'Causal knowledge and imitation/emulation switching in chimpanzees (*Pan troglodytes*) and children (Homo sapiens)', *Animal Cognition* 8 (2005): pp. 164–81, https://risweb.st-andrews.ac.uk/portal/en/researchoutput/causal-knowledge-and-imitationemulation-switching-in-chimpanzees-pan-troglodytes-and-children-homo-sapiens(444c4895-d484-4e80-97c9-13f229586e4e)/export.html.

2. Deborah L. Rhode, *The Beauty Bias: The Injustice of Appearance in Life and Law* (Oxford: Oxford University Press, 2011).

3. Rebecca Roache, 'Should Endangered Languages Be Preserved, and at What Cost?', Aeon, 3 October 2019, https://aeon.co/essays/should-endangered-languages-be-preserved-and-at-what-cost.

4. '"India Ready To Spend Up To 400 Crore To Make Hindi An Official Language Of UN": Sushma Swaraj', NDTV,

3 January 2018, https://www.ndtv.com/india-news/india-ready-to-spend-up-to-400-crore-to-make-hindi-an-official-language-of-un-sushma-swaraj-1795348.

5. Complaint.pdf, United States Department of Justice, https://www.justice.gov/file/1142876/downloa.

6. Azim F. Shariff, Jonathan Schooler and Kathleen D. Vohs, 'The Hazards of Claiming to Have Solved the Hard Problem of Free Will', in *Are We Free?: Psychology and Free Will*, ed. John Baer, James C. Kaufman, and Roy F. Baumeister (Oxford Scholarship Online: May 2008), pp. 181–204, doi:10.1093/acprof:oso/9780195189636.003.0009.

7. 'Two Hubbles Achieve Great Heights', NASA's John F. Kennedy Space Center and Goddard Space Flight Center, 22 January 2004, https://www.nasa.gov/missions/deepspace/f_two-hubbles.html.

8. Casey Neistat's YouTube channel: https://www.youtube.com/channel/UCtinbF-Q-fVthA0qrFQTgXQ.

9. 'Keep Redefining What You Do', Naval, 13 May 2019, https://nav.al/redefining.

10. Susan Ratcliffe, *Oxford Essential Quotations* (Oxford University Press, 2017), https://www.oxfordreference.com/view/10.1093/acref/9780191843730.001.0001/q-oro-ed5-00016758.

Bibliography

1. The Art of Choosing—*Sheena Iyengar*
2. *What Money Can't Buy: The Moral Limits of Markets*—Michael J. Sandel
3. *Behave: The Biology of Humans at Our Best and Worst*—Robert Sapolsky
4. *23 Things They Don't Tell You About Capitalism*—Ha-Joon Chang
5. *The Design of Everyday Things*—Don Norman
6. *Good Economics for Hard Times*—Abhijit V. Banerjee and Esther Duflo
7. *Nudge: Improving Decisions about Health, Wealth, and Happiness*—Richard H. Thaler
8. *Thinking, Fast and Slow*—Daniel Kahneman
9. *Do Androids Dream of Electric Sheep?*—Philip K. Dick
10. *The Beauty Bias: The Injustice of Appearance in Life and Law*—Deborah L. Rhode
11. *Homo Deus: A Brief History of Tomorrow*—Yuval Noah Harari
12. *I, Robot*—Isaac Asimov
13. *Think Like a Freak*—Stephen J. Dubner and Steven Levitt

14. *The Code Book: The Science of Secrecy from Ancient Egypt to Quantum Cryptography*—Simon Singh
15. *Notes on Democracy*—H.L. Mencken